THE PRAIRIE WINNOWS OUT ITS OWN

Paula M. Nelson

THE PRAIRIE

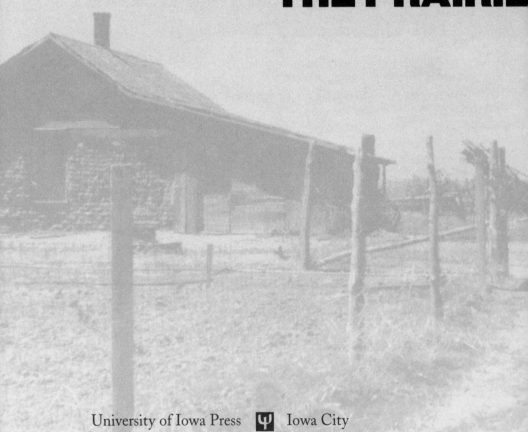

University of Iowa Press Iowa City

WINNOWS OUT ITS OWN

The
West River
Country
of South
Dakota
in the
Years of
Depression
and Dust

University of Iowa Press,
Iowa City 52242
Copyright © 1996 by the
University of Iowa Press
All rights reserved
Printed in the United States
of America
Design by Richard Hendel
No part of this book may be
reproduced or used in any form
or by any means, electronic or
mechanical, including photocopying
and recording, without permission
in writing from the publisher.
Printed on acid-free paper

Except as noted, all photographs
are reproduced courtesy of the South
Dakota Archives, South Dakota State
Historical Society.

Library of Congress
Cataloging-in-Publication Data
Nelson, Paula
    The Prairie winnows out its own: the
west river country of South Dakota in the
years of depression and dust / by Paula M.
Nelson.
        p.   cm.
    Includes bibliographical references
(p.   ) and index.
    ISBN 0-87745-525-2
    1. South Dakota—History.   2. South
Dakota—Economic conditions.
3. Agriculture—South Dakota—
History—20th century.   I. Title.
F656.N455   1995
978.3′032—dc20   95-24904
                                      CIP

01 00 99 98 97 96 c 5 4 3 2 1

Close are the meshes, as bleak years have shown

By which the prairie winnows out its own

—Eva K. Anglesberg, "The Mills of Destiny," 1938

Contents

Preface

BETWEEN 1900 and 1942, in just two generations of settlement, the west river plains of South Dakota went from promised land to hinterland.[1] My first book, *After the West Was Won: Homesteaders and Town-Builders in Western South Dakota, 1900–1917*, tells the story of the frontier years and the first great crisis of settlement. It is the story of the last great land rush on the Northern Plains, when more than 100,000 homesteaders flooded into the west river country of South Dakota, a land noted for its aridity and unpredictable weather, its treelessness and endless sky. The settlers of the "last great frontier" weathered their first great crisis in the severe drought of 1910–1911, which winnowed out many of the speculators and faint of heart; those who remained in the region abandoned their founding hopes of quick success and substituted a new ethos of "next year country"—while this year was hard, next year would be better, an ironic outlook at once optimistic and fatalistic.

This book picks up the story at the end of World War I, with the next great crisis of west river life, the crash of the agricultural economy in the early twenties. It was here that west river residents learned that "next year" was rarely better. The collapse of the agricultural economy in the immediate aftermath of the boom years of World War I initiated a trend of regional decline amidst national prosperity and cultural change. The rise of radio and mass culture during this period increased rural folks' awareness of national trends and tastes, a development

which paradoxically increased their sense of remoteness and isolation.
The failure of the farm economy to recover to any substantial degree in
the twenties caused a less dramatic, but cumulatively greater impact
on the west river country's population and prospects than had the
drought of 1910–1911.

The Great Depression and dust bowl years of the thirties were the
greatest test of the west river people. The drought of 1910–1911, hereto-
fore seen as the benchmark of bad times, faded even in the remem-
brances of the original pioneers in the face of the thirties' relentless
drought, grasshoppers, and blowing dust, and the accompanying starvation, struggle, and despair. Government-proposed solutions to the
problems of the thirties challenged their most dearly held ideas and
their very history. The Depression in the west river country was a blast
furnace from which a diminished population emerged, hardened yet
still hopeful, scathed but undefeated.

Many people have helped me in the years it took to research and
write this book. I would like to thank the American Historical Association for the Beveridge grant I received in 1987. That money purchased
many reels of newspapers on microfilm and made my work much easier. I would also like to thank the personnel at the University of Iowa's
Main Library for allowing me to borrow books and to order microfilm
from the Center for Research Libraries during the years I lived in
Dubuque, Iowa. The access to research materials that they provided
helped make this book possible. I would also like to thank the personnel at the Carnegie-Stout Public Library in Dubuque for the haven
they offered during the year I was without a paid teaching position. I
appeared there daily as the doors opened to use their microfilm readers;
their warmth and interest in my project speeded my work and eased
some of the isolation associated with the writer's craft. Since I joined
the history department at the University of Wisconsin-Platteville in
1988, the staff at the Karrmann Library has assisted me in many ways,
and I am grateful for their help.

I owe special thanks to several people at the South Dakota State
Historical Society in Pierre. My dear friend Nancy Tystad Koupal, Director of Publications, is a constant source of encouragement and good
cheer. LaVera Rose located many of the photographs found in this
book; Ann Jenks, the librarian at the State Archives, responded to my

many requests with enthusiasm and dispatch. Linda Sommer, State Archivist, allowed me access to the federal relief records that were new to the collection at the time. Cindy Glum took on the tedious task of copying the hundreds of pages of relief records for me.

The staff at the University of Iowa Press has also been a joy to work with. Holly Carver's patient encouragement and good humor have sustained me. Bob Burchfield capably copyedited the manuscript and did some important photo research on the side. The Press treats its authors with respect and care, which are reciprocated.

Many people helped me type the manuscript, and I want to acknowledge their invaluable service. Mary Strottman took the virtually illegible first draft and converted it into a manuscript. Sheri Lindquist helped type early revisions. Kathy Faull, the history department secretary, typed the later revisions, providing service well beyond the call of duty.

Other friends contributed so much. Sheri Lindquist, besides typing, made copies from microfilm, took occasional notes from newspapers, and babysat our cats while I was away on research trips. Holly Kamm has provided inspiration and a long view at critical times. My dear friend Emma Shellenberg moved into a nursing home in January 1995, in her ninety-seventh year. Although her knees no longer work, her mind remains as sharp as ever. Her love of the farming life is a constant inspiration to me.

My greatest thanks go to my husband, Steve Krumpe, for many hours discussing my work and historical issues, editing my prose, untangling footnotes, and traveling to research sites. This is his book as much as it is mine.

Introduction: After the West Was Won

A sod house built by a west river pioneer in 1900, Pennington County.
Photograph taken in 1936. Library of Congress, courtesy of the South Dakota Archives.

We have ample faith in any community such as this that is pervaded by
the spirit of willingness to do in the hope that Next year's success will make
up for This year's failure. Just keep your eye on western South Dakota for it
is the greatest "next year" country in existence.
— *Kadoka Press*, April 24, 1927

ON THANKSGIVING DAY 1924, the residents of the west river town
of Kadoka, South Dakota were interrupted in their celebrations by
tragedy. Otto Sharon, the fifty-two-year-old local postmaster, had
hanged himself in the stockyards at Wentworth, South Dakota, two
hundred miles to the east. Two days before, he had asked a friend to
drive him to a nearby town where he planned to take a rest. From there,
apparently unobserved by family and friends, he rode the rails away to
his death. A train crew traveling through the Wentworth switchyard
found the body "stiff and cold," hanging from the rafter of a feed rack.
Sharon had arrived in Wentworth on Wednesday, taken a room at the
Commercial Hotel, eaten supper, walked to the stockyards, and hanged
himself. He left notes to the local sheriff and his wife in his overcoat
pockets.

The town of Kadoka "experienced a severe shock" when the telegram
arrived announcing the discovery of Sharon's body. Rumors flew, but
the *Kadoka Press* discounted all but two reasons for Sharon's drastic act:
first, he had never recovered from the blow of his first wife's death four
years before, although he had remarried, and, second, "the recent depression in the economic world." Sharon had been a key stockholder in
both Kadoka banks and had lost heavily when they had failed in the
spring. His suitcase at the hotel in Wentworth contained what was left
of his resources: "$205 in gold and $101.33 in currency," all of which was
to be shipped to his wife.

Sharon had been an important presence in Kadoka since its beginning. He and his first wife were pioneers; they had come to the area in
1906 to homestead. After they proved up and won the title to their
claim, the family moved to Kadoka to open a confectionery store.[1]
Sharon quickly became a pillar of the community. He served as an officer of the Commercial Club, was on the town board for several years,
was elected county auditor for three terms, and at the time of his death
was the Kadoka postmaster. Sharon's name appeared frequently in *Press*

accounts of civic projects as well as in the lists of lodge officers; he belonged to at least seven fraternal organizations. His lonely death on a cold November night so far from home was symbolic of much that had gone wrong in west river life following World War I.[2]

Otto Sharon, like thousands of others, had been propelled to the west river country in a final homesteading rush, a third Dakota boom that settled the plains west of the Missouri River after 1900.[3] The country that they came to was high, dry, and rich with a romantic and tragic history. This land had been the home of the Lakota Sioux. The discovery of gold in the Black Hills, the presence of the U.S. Army, and the resulting interest in the region by non-Indian settlers forced some of the tribe onto its first reservation, the Great Sioux Reservation, defined by the Fort Laramie treaty in 1868. According to the treaty, the United States recognized all of present-day South Dakota west of the Missouri, including the Black Hills, as belonging to the Sioux. When George Armstrong Custer's exploratory expedition to the Hills in 1874 confirmed the presence of gold, the rush to claim it began. The Lakota were pushed aside in the clamor for riches; their anger led to the Sioux War of 1876. Custer played a pivotal role here as well. When a combined army of Sioux and Cheyenne wiped out him and his command at Little Bighorn, Congress voted to withhold all appropriations to the Lakota until they signed over the Black Hills. They had no choice but to do so or starve. In October 1876 the approximately 16,000 Lakota received a new, smaller, and more tightly managed reservation west of the Missouri River. They gave up the Hills and acknowledged the 103d meridian as the new western boundary of the reservation, except for the territory between the two branches of the Cheyenne River, which they also ceded to the government. As miners and merchants altered the face of the Black Hills forever, the Lakota began their long and painful adjustment to reservation life.[4]

Once again in 1889 the government pressured the Lakota to surrender more of their territory. Ranchers large and small had scattered their spreads across government lands in the west river country. The Black Hills boomed with mines and towns but seemed isolated from the growing agricultural settlement east of the Missouri River. Dakota promoters wanted to bridge the gap that Sioux reservation lands created in their soon-to-be state. Boosters dreamed of farms and towns by the

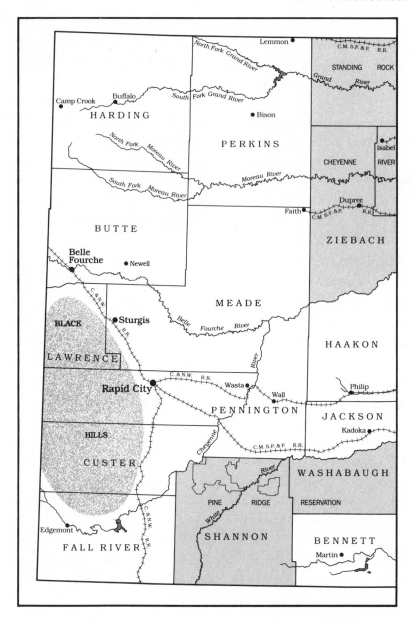

dozen springing up on the dry western plains. To build the state, they argued, the land had to be available to people who would use it properly and develop it into homes and farms and villages.

The Dakota boomers' pressure on the federal government to reduce Lakota territory coincided with a new idea in Washington, the assimi-

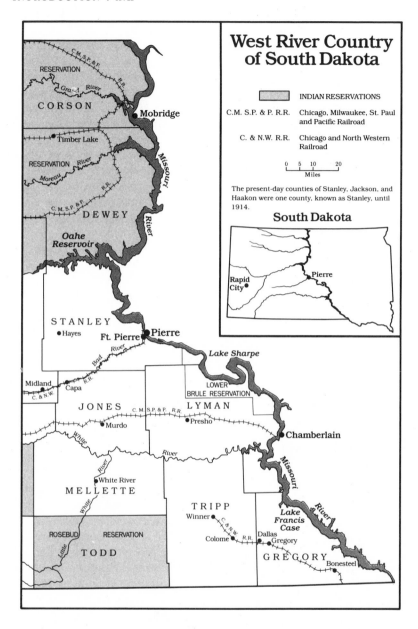

West River Country of South Dakota

▨ INDIAN RESERVATIONS

C.M. S.P. & P. R.R. Chicago, Milwaukee, St. Paul and Pacific Railroad

C. & N.W. R.R. Chicago and North Western Railroad

0 5 10   20
Miles

The present-day counties of Stanley, Jackson, and Haakon were one county, known as Stanley, until 1914.

South Dakota

lation of Indian peoples into American life through individual land ownership. The so-called allotment process would provide Indian peoples, including the Lakota, with enough land for farms for all. The remainder would revert back to the government for sale or distribution to non-Indian peoples for their own farms or villages. In 1889 the government overcame Lakota resistance to the idea of further reductions in the reservations; the Lakota signed over nine million acres for settlement under the Homestead Act. It was not snapped up by homesteaders immediately; drought and depression held the pioneers back. After 1900, however, many thousands of eager settlers, the Otto Sharon family among them, made their way to the west river country and began to build their dreams.[5]

The west river homesteading frontier would see its own era of triumph and tragedy, heroism and mere survival. The people who pioneered west of the Missouri River believed that they could conquer nature, that they had both the technological tools and the will to do the job. The nature that they confronted was a stronger foe than most imagined.

THE WEST RIVER COUNTRY is part of the Great Plains of North America, a physiographic province noted for its dry and often unpredictable weather, its treelessness, and its endless sky. Most of the west river country lies west of the 100th meridian. Famed explorer John Wesley Powell believed that the land and climate west of that line were fundamentally different; he urged the federal government to allot settlers west of the 100th meridian 2,500 acres of land, compared to the 160 acres available generally under the Homestead Act, and encouraged settlers to live in central villages to help eliminate isolation.[6]

There was little public concern about these vital boundaries at the time of the west river homestead rush. The 160-acre homestead was government policy, adequate if the land taken up was located in humid regions. The Enlarged Homestead Act of 1909 provided 320 acres per claim, but the states had to acknowledge that they were "dry" before the federal government extended this policy to them. South Dakota promoters feared such an acknowledgment might keep settlers away; not until 1915 did they agree to a "dry" designation and therefore allow settlers to claim more than 160 acres. Local promoters hoped to encourage as many homesteaders and town builders as possible to come and fill the empty spaces of the west. Talk of caution and "go slow" often met with opprobrium. The *Dakota Farmer*, an important farm journal based in Aberdeen, South Dakota, urged new settlers to keep their eyes open and to experiment with crops suited for the surroundings. West river boosters wrote angry letters to protest the perceived snub of their region. For the latter-day homesteaders, it was full speed ahead to the next Garden of Eden.[7]

They would have been wise to be cautious. As the *Dakota Farmer* put it, "A country where cactus is perfectly at home cannot be farmed the same as where clover grows." Cactus did grow in parts of the west river country. Its presence indicates a fundamental fact about the region—it was semiarid and became drier and drier as one headed west from the Missouri River. In Gregory County, on the Missouri, the average annual precipitation was 21.16 inches. In Harding County, on the western border, the annual average was 13.66 inches. But averages were deceiving. In parts of the west river country precipitation was below average 40 percent of the time; in the far west it was below average 60 percent of the time. Successful grain production required at least 15 inches of precipitation; if less than 10 fell there would be no crop at all. In between those numbers, the smallest variation could have tremendous impact. Twelve inches of rain might produce a thin crop but 14, only 2 inches more, might double the yield.[8]

Other factors helped create the semiaridity of the region. High temperatures are common in the summer in central South Dakota; the average maximum temperature is 105 degrees. Low humidities make people more comfortable but bring late frosts in spring and early frost in fall; the scorching of crops in summer also can result. Wind speeds are relatively high year round. When combined with high temperatures, the winds cause rapid evaporation. Entire fields can wither or die within hours or days.[9]

So homesteaders confronted the problem of limited rainfall, compounded by other climatic factors such as temperature, humidity, and wind. Taken together with the general unpredictability of the weather, the lighter, less fertile nature of the soil in much of the area, and the rougher, more broken topography, uncertainty and risk became major components in the daily lives of the settlers.

But they came anyway, by the tens of thousands, either unaware of the enormous challenge ahead or unafraid of it. Between 1900 and 1910, more than 100,000 homesteaders and town builders took advantage of the Homestead Act or participated in government lotteries to get themselves claims in the west river country of South Dakota. The expansion of two key railroads—the Milwaukee Road from Chamberlain to Rapid City and from Mobridge to Faith, and the Chicago Northwestern from Ft. Pierre to Rapid City—helped fuel the boom. Small towns proliferated along the rail lines and far from the rail lines in places where enterprising entrepreneurs hoped to build cities that the railroads could not afford to bypass.[10]

Many settlers came to the west river country between 1900 and 1910 imbued with the ethos of frontier conquest and empire. They had hoped to participate in the successful settlement of the last agricultural frontier and build for themselves farms, homes, and businesses that would reflect their accomplishments and prosperity. Others came for mere speculation, to share in a final frontier adventure but with no real long-term commitment to the land or the developing society. These people planned to stay only until they held title to their homestead claim. After their departure they would depend on luck, and the hard work of their former neighbors, to boost the value of their deserted farms. Then they could sell the land at a big profit or borrow money against their land.[11]

To achieve their dreams the settlers had to build everything from the ground up. The government required each homesteader to build a house of at least 10 by 12 feet, find a water source, and break a few acres of the native sod. Those who intended to stay and develop a true farm did much more than the minimum as quickly as they could afford to do so. All homesteaders confronted a series of problems created by the environment. For example, water was difficult to find. The west river country does not have an abundance of streams, and many of those that do meander through the region dry up in midsummer. Wells had to be deep and were expensive, and they did not always tap into a dependable water source. Homesteaders improvised; they built dams on the low spots of their claims to catch the rainwater and runoff. Such dams were often not convenient to the house, and the water was none too clean, but they served their purpose reasonably well. Water hauling became a major preoccupation for the settlers—one more task among the many necessary on a pioneer farm.[12]

The extremes of weather posed another challenge. West river winters could be fierce with severe cold, strong winds, and blowing snow. Homesteaders weathered them the best they could in their small, drafty shacks. They banked their homes with sod or used animal bedding from the barn, kept their fires going all night, and adopted the techniques used on the earlier plains frontier to insure safety. Ropes strung between house and barn allowed those doing chores to find their way between buildings without becoming lost in the blinding blizzards.

Summer, too, required vigilance. The treeless plains were extremely hot; the small claim shacks — often sided as they were with black tar paper — heated up like ovens. The winds did keep the air moving, but sometimes too fast for real comfort. With limited means to refrigerate water or foods, it was difficult to cool down. Fortunately, nights were considerably cooler than the blistering days, which allowed a modicum of relief and refreshing sleep. Migrants from the humid Midwest, where hot, sticky days came accompanied by hot, sticky nights, appreciated the contrast.

The omnipresent wind also required adjustments. One homesteader reported in a letter home that people in her new neighborhood talked very loudly. She discovered that the constant wind forced conversation into high volume. The wind blew dirt and sand about; clothing on the line or water pails kept outdoors might be truly gone with the wind if settlers were not careful. The winds helped create one of the most dreaded elements of plains life, the prairie fire. A careless match, a spark from a passing train, or a bolt of lightning might start a fire. The wind carried it at amazing speeds across miles and miles of grasslands, farms, and fields. Families could lose everything, including their lives, if they did not follow the age-old rule: everyone must plow a wide firebreak around their homes and buildings, and everyone must help fight fires when they occurred.[13]

The town builders who came to the west river country also faced unique and challenging circumstances. They, too, built what they had from the ground up but in an economy where the rules were changing quickly. The merchants wanted to be in on the ground floor of economic, social, and political development in a new land. Yet they often had to buy town lots platted by the railroad, one of the largest, richest corporate entities in the United States and a symbol of the centralizing, industrializing society located so far in space and in development from the small west river towns. They depended on the railroad to bring their goods in and take produce out; the railroad was the link that allowed them to grow and prosper. Towns without railroads schemed to attract a line. If they did not get one, they knew their ability to attract farm families in to trade would be limited, as would the town's viability. So town builders came to the west river country with individualistic, entrepreneurial motives but often had to play the game by rules made elsewhere. In spite of this, they enjoyed the opportunities to shape their businesses and their towns as much as the impinging corporate world allowed.[14]

People on the claims and in the towns worked as well to create a viable social world — a community — for themselves. Social institutions and informal social networks also had to be built from the ground up. Farm families quickly organized local school districts, Sunday schools, and churches. Schools and churches became gathering points for these neighborhoods; literary societies, fund-raising dinners, and socials flourished, as farm families willingly traveled miles to mingle with friends and neighbors. Town dwellers had the advantage of a centrally located population. In both the rural neighborhood and the small town, the voluntary assistance of neighbor to neighbor meant much. Although towns were likely to have more formal services, such as doctors or funeral directors, the help of family, friends, and community members was as essential to the fabric of life in the towns as in the countryside.[15]

For a few years, hard work and hope appeared to be enough to build an empire. Homes sprang up on nearly every quarter section of available land, while small towns grew up every few miles along the railroads and were scattered around "inland" areas without rail lines as well. Dozens of local post offices dotted the landscape to serve patrons farther from the towns. More than 100,000 homesteaders and town builders came to build new homes for themselves. Calamity struck in 1910 and 1911. Severe drought, one of the fiercest enemies of an agricultural society, stalked the land; crops withered and died, and the prospects of the region dried up along with the grass, corn, and wheat.

Water became scarce. Families with stock tried to find green pastures elsewhere for the animals and rationed their own water supplies even more stringently than before. Even food became scarce. With no crops and no gardens there was no produce; some had little cash to buy necessary supplies. Real suffering resulted.

The drought led to a mass exodus. Some counties lost as little as 10 percent of their populations; others, harder hit, lost a fourth, a third, or even half. Meade County, for example, went from a population of 12,640 in 1910 to a population of 8,724 five years later. Perkins County population figures in 1910 were 11,348; in 1915 only 7,641 people lived in that county. Old Stanley County in 1910 was home to 14,975 people. By 1915 it had been divided into three counties—Jackson, Haakon, and Stanley—with a total population of 7,881. Those who stayed in the region struggled to organize relief for drought sufferers; they failed. There were no federal or state institutions equipped to offer much aid during this period, and the ideology of self-reliance and independence militated against effective innovation. Settlers who stayed in the west river country had to find solutions on their own.[16]

The drought of 1910–1911 became a defining event in west river life. The years after the drought were a time of readjustment and redefinition for the west river pioneers. They had come to the west river country as confident empire builders, ready to write the final chapter in their nation's grand frontier history. They had failed. They had not conquered nature; it had conquered them. Homesteads and farms stood empty; towns struggled to survive. Where had they gone wrong?

Over time they found the answers. They had come into the country with the wrong ideas about its development, but they could learn the right ways to handle the land if they were willing to experiment. Such experimentation would take time and commitment and hard work. Settlers, in the meantime, would have to do without many of the material comforts of life, but they would be compensated by the rewards of the struggle. For those who were faithful to the land and the dream of empire, success would surely come—if not now, then next year.[17]

When the United States entered World War I in 1917 the frontier era in the west river country came to an end. The focus became the war; the west river country sent its sons to distant lands, wound bandages and knitted sweaters and stockings for the Red Cross, and bought Liberty Bonds with cash that otherwise might have gone to the school box social or in the church collection plate. Prices for farm goods went up; the demand for cattle and horses, important products of the west river country, soared. The struggle to tame the land and build a new society, however, was not over; it was merely subsumed into something larger.

For Otto Sharon and his family and all of the others who had come to stay even in the face of severe adversity, the initial challenge had been met and, if not overcome, at least had been accommodated. In the hopeful years during and immediately after World War I, they could not have imagined the even more fearful trials that lay ahead.[18]

THE PRAIRIE WINNOWS OUT ITS OWN

1

Room at the Bottom

The Eugene Miner Young farm, Corson County, circa 1920.

Forlorn, Dejected and Mortgaged to beat hell

— Reliance-area auction bill, *Kadoka Press*, October 13, 1922

THE FIRST great crisis of west river life, the drought of 1910–1911, had taught the west river pioneers hard lessons. They learned that booms could quickly bust, bringing down all that had been so hopefully built up. They learned that workable solutions to complicated problems took time and sustained effort. They learned that people engaged in a good work could fail.[1]

In spite of the hard lessons, the west river pioneers maintained staunch hopes. While they knew that this year might be hard, they had faith that next year would be better. They believed that rewards would come to them for maintaining their commitment to building up the region. In light of this ethos, then, it seemed logical to them that the high prices of the World War I era might be the long-sought solution to the problems indigenous to the region. If farm families could rely on steady returns in the marketplace, it would pay for them to take the risks that west river life required. New settlers would come to the region and develop farms from the ever present rangeland. Towns would grow and flourish as a result of the increased rural population and the trade it would bring. Nationally, strong markets and high prices promised to move farm families up the ladder of material progress into solid middle-class status. In the west river region, the pioneers hoped high prices could overcome some of the uncertainties and drawbacks intrinsic to the place. As events would demonstrate, there was no solution to be found in outside economic forces. Instead, such forces would bring about the second great crisis of west river life.

Certainly, the prices of the war years and immediately after were beneficial in the short run. Although economic conditions were unsettled when the war ended and necessary goods were occasionally scarce and high priced, the sense was that economic stability would quickly return and that higher prices and prosperity would remain. In January 1919 the *Timber Lake Topic* prominently displayed a reassuring Dun and Bradstreet report that promised continued high agricultural prices due to strong demand. By April, Timber Lake in Dewey County began to boom. The editor reported a building spurt, which included a Catholic school and dormitory, a garage for auto repair, a new store, an

International Order of Odd Fellows lodge hall, a large modern house reportedly costing $5,000, and ten other homes. In August the *Topic*'s editor commented on the large number of autos on the street on a Saturday; although there were only an ordinary number of people in town, 67 autos were parked on Main Street, an indication that prosperity had reached the country as well as the city. In the same issue, the editor detailed the assessor's figures for Dewey County. The average value of farm land was $8.22 per acre, and the 287 sets of farm buildings averaged $264.16 in value, while Timber Lake's ninety-six structures (the most elaborate of all the towns in the county) had an average value of $995.47. Dewey County residents owned 305 autos, 127 pianos, and 53 Victrolas.[2]

Although the regional economy grew shakier in 1920, Timber Lake's local boom continued. Timber Lake residents could watch workers constructing a 25,000-bushel elevator, a twenty-room hotel (with running water and sewer system), two garages, and two stores. Farm prices continued to hold firm at $10 to $40 per acre (including buildings); one farm sold for $45 per acre. When the assessor compiled his reports in August, automobile numbers were up by one hundred, and the number of phonographs had doubled. Pianos, the instrument of home-produced entertainment, had barely increased at all, however.[3]

Things were equally good in Kadoka, 135 miles to the southwest, on the wall of the Badlands. As 1919 opened, the editors of the *Kadoka Press* rhapsodized about their town's future. Upon hearing the town bells ring in the New Year, they had dreamed of a growing Kadoka, "a good-sized, lively, throbbing town." In these dreams the editors saw Kadoka "dotted with beautiful trees, casting their shade across rich green and well-kept lawns in front of the beautiful residence sections now building up, the darkened street thrown into a glow of brightness by a properly equipped electric light plant. The thirsty watered, not from a barrel but from a dandy little waterworks system." They also visualized a new and improved school, an enlarged and well-maintained park, and a Main Street lined with "neat and substantial fire proof buildings."[4]

Events in Kadoka seemed to bode well for their dreams. Agricultural prices remained high. A ranch on the White River south of Belvidere sold for $60 per acre. The *Press* included reports on prices paid at auctioneer C. L. Leedom's sales of ordinary milk cows: $124 in January, $155 by July. Demand for land remained strong. In one week in June 1919, out-of-town buyers purchased 3,280 acres of Jackson County land. Advocates of progressive agriculture had their hopes realized when sales of registered purebred stock became popular: a Kadoka man paid $235 for a bull. Houses were in short supply, and several residents announced plans to build in the summer. Several area men announced their intentions to form a home loan company to supply money for construction. Reports of home or business construction plans and estimated costs appeared frequently. (Stucco appeared to be the favorite finish for those building or remodeling.) The *Press* also endorsed a plan to build a new school to ease severe crowding in the old structure. When the bond election had to be cancelled due to a legal technicality, the town faced a crisis. Two grades had to meet in the Presbyterian Church when school opened in the fall. In November the school board authorized the construction of a 30-by-70-foot building to house a few classrooms and a gym. In May Kadoka reached an important milestone; the school graduated its first high school class. Four students had completed a twelve-year course and received diplomas. R. N. Rounds, a local entrepreneur, deciding that electrification was the wave of the future, began to build a light plant and contracted to wire businesses and residences in town. Residents also circulated a petition to encourage the town board to issue bonds for a water system. In February Kadokans voted unanimously to build a water system.[5]

Outside the immediate community there were other grounds for optimism. The state highway commission decided to build a large steel bridge over the White River, a few miles south of town, opening the Pine Ridge reservation and Bennett County to the south to Kadoka trade. "Finally, after years of waiting and with no cost to us," the *Press* commented enthusiastically. In July 1920 the Kadoka Commercial Club organized a dedication ceremony, picnic, and festival to mark the bridge's opening. In March 1920 a representative from the proposed Custer Battlefield Highway met with the Commercial Club to announce that the road would run through Kadoka en route to the Black Hills and to the battlefield site in Montana. The businessmen attending subscribed more than $500 in two minutes to help with promotion of the new tourist route.[6]

No one in Timber Lake or Kadoka expected the crash that came. In May 1920 the federal government dropped its wartime agricultural support policies. The Federal Reserve, alarmed at inflation, took immediate steps to create deflation. Agriculture was the first to feel its effects. The prices of important west river products began to plummet. Wheat, the wartime staple because of its ease of storage and wide range of uses, dropped from a high price of $2.65 in May 1920 to 98¢ one year later. By September 1922 wheat prices had fallen to 76¢ a bushel. Oats fell from a high of 94¢ a bushel in June 1920 to 18¢ in December 1921. Horses had brought an average of $135 in April 1918; by November 1921 the price was $60. Beef cattle prices plummeted from $10.70 per hundredweight in July 1919 to $4.40 in December 1921. Hog prices had peaked at $20 per hundredweight in July 1919; two and a half years later hogs brought $5.90 a hundredweight. Prices of other commodities, such as butter, eggs, and wool, dropped equally precipitously. Nonagricultural prices did not begin to fall as early, nor did they fall as quickly, so the difference between prices farmers received and prices they paid for the goods they needed to run a farm and support their families increased. Land values began to plunge as prices for goods produced on the land dropped. Farmers who had borrowed money for expansion or modernization during the wartime boom had no way to repay it. Small towns dependent on area farmers for business suffered as well. Banks that had financed the run-up in land prices saw their collateral badly devalued, and some began to fail.[7]

All of these developments were nationwide in their impact. Across the United States farmers, and the small towns dependent on them, suffered greatly during the early twenties. West river residents, however, faced a special irony. They lived in an area where settlement was relatively new, where reserves were few, and where the environment created uncertainties and impeded progress. They had believed, albeit briefly, that outside economic forces might be their salvation. Instead, their link to the national and world economies had condemned them to another round of failure and readjustment. The agricultural depression of 1920–1921 permanently damaged west river prospects and hastened the slide into regional oblivion. The hard times of the early twenties set the tone for the remainder of the decade and set the stage for the even harder times to come in the thirties.

How did the crash of 1920–1921 affect the west river country? What was unique about its circumstances? For farmers, the drastic decline in prices meant the loss of income that could have gone to pay creditors, especially those who had lent money on land, and money that could have paid taxes.

In 1917 the state of South Dakota, under the leadership of progressive Republican governor Peter Norbeck, enacted a state financial credit program for its farmers as a means of promoting the general welfare of state citizens. The Rural Credits program, as it was called, planned to make money available statewide, but it had a special importance for the west river counties, where credit was difficult to obtain and interest rates were high. The state sold bonds to raise money and in turn lent that money to farmers at 5.5 percent to 7 percent; the Rural Credits board oversaw the process. The rules for granting funds appeared to be clear and carefully drawn, and the money was lent quickly; it could take as little as a week for farmers to receive their money. The Rural Credits board took a first mortgage on the land as collateral and applied the loan payments to the state's bond debt. The Rural Credits loans were popular, and demand was extremely high. Between 1917 and 1922 the program lent $37,901,150. Although the loans were divided almost equally between east river and west river counties, the proportion of all west river farms involved with the program was significantly higher than in the east. The west river portion of the state had less than a fourth of the population but held 51 percent of the Rural Credits loans. Perkins County had the highest number of loans — 753, or 48 percent, of the farms in the county.

The system ran into trouble quickly. When the agricultural downturn began in 1920, the Rural Credits board began to grant extensions on repayment, although the state still had to make payments to the bondholders. The board was also inundated with requests for loans from strapped farmers who wanted to consolidate mortgage loans from local banks with a lower interest Rural Credits loan. The Rural Credits board helped when it could, providing loans based on the inflated land values of the pre-slump period. This was poor business on their part but kept farmers from feeling the drop in land values in the short run. By 1923 the Rural Credits system was clearly in trouble, and the state implemented stricter policies. By 1924 the system had begun to break down due to poor business judgment and alleged corruption on the part of some board officials. A third of the loans were in default. In 1925 the legislature voted to end the program, and the work of reorganization and collection began.[8]

The agricultural crisis of the early twenties is reflected in farm foreclosure numbers. The legal notices of foreclosure from all sources began to fill more and more of the local papers. The *Kadoka Press*, for example, listed chattel mortgage foreclosures on cattle and horses that involved sums of money formerly unheard of in the west river country. A Washabaugh County man owed a Minnesota corporation $14,700 on cattle and horses. A Bennett County man owed $18,237. Another rancher owed some Kadoka men $23,142 on cattle, horses, and machinery and owed the St. Paul Credit Loan Company $15,718 at the same time. Both loans were being foreclosed. This was at a time when most farm foreclosures concerned loans well under $3,000.[9]

For west river farmers, the big shakeout came in the twenties and not in the Great Depression a decade later. For sixteen of the eighteen counties, the years of highest foreclosures during the two troubled decades came in the 1921–1925 period. Hundreds of farmers lost their land. In Perkins County, 799 farms, or 51 percent of the 1920 census total, were foreclosed; in Harding County in 1921–1925, 389 farmers, or 42 percent, lost their farms; in Jackson County 53 percent lost their farms. Those foreclosed by Rural Credits, however, could make rental arrangements that allowed a family to stay on the land as tenants of the state Rural Credits board. That system temporarily prevented a wholesale migration from west river rural areas.[10]

The newspaper lists of delinquent taxpayers also began to grow. In 1920 the list of delinquent taxpayers filled five and a half columns of the *Kadoka Press*. In 1921 that figure increased to nine columns and included the names of prominent businessmen, a county commissioner, a barber, and several homesteaders who had survived the early days.[11]

The "adjustment" or the "reconstruction," as the depression of 1920–1921 was sometimes called, had profound effects on west river dwellers. Farm families suffered extreme hardship, towns stagnated, and banks failed. Delinquent taxes meant that county and town services diminished as local governments sank deeply into debt. The retrenchment of the 1920s left indelible marks on the west river country. Boosters and experts suggested remedies with little success. The dry plains environment and the distance from the mainstream of American economic life worked to inhibit real growth and successful development.

T. E. Hayes, a Perkins County farmer, explained the dilemma he and his neighbors faced in 1923. "I have so often read in the farm papers that the dairy cow will save Dakota. Most people in this community milk cows and yet the percentage of successful farmers is very slight, indeed, while the failures and foreclosures are great. All these men are not poor farmers or drones." He went on to complain about the quality and consistency of advice given to farmers by the so-called experts. "First we are advised to get into the beef cattle, the world needs meat after so many meatless days. Some of us do that—get nice herds started via the mortgage route and now the bottom has fallen out of the beef market." Farmers had followed the experts into the hog market with similar results, yet now the experts blithely told farmers to invest in sheep or dairy cattle. "I fail to see the salvation in any of these things," Hayes concluded, "with good cattle bringing so much less than they did in previous days and taxes almost double, with the farmer's dollar worth 69 cents and notes bearing 10% interest, it will take more than the dairy cow to save the farmer." [12]

A Pennington County farmer, who signed himself N.B., pointed out another problem. "The price paid to farmers here for grain by our local elevator is 29 cents below the Minneapolis market. This year farmers received from 39 to 55 cents [a bushel] for rye and about 69 cents for wheat. It takes no department statistician to tell that grain at such prices, with low average yields and high threshing costs can be produced only with agonies to the banker who holds the mortgage." A Ziebach County man reported on conditions in his area, Township 12, Range 21. There were only twenty-seven farmers in the township, and twenty-one were "at the mercy of creditors." Five had already left their farms. "The 1921 production or yield was low as well as prices and a bare living was realized. In 1922 the yield was good, but prices were so low it was only little better, if any, than 1921." High railroad freight rates added to the disaster. "In 1917," he commented, "freight was 13 cents per hundredweight on grain to our nearest terminal and today it is 28 cents for the same distance." In 1922 the *Bison Courier* reported what it hoped was just a rumor. It seemed a rancher from nearby Adams County,

North Dakota, had been unable to borrow further money from his bank to feed his large, heavily mortgaged herds. He had gone instead to the hardware store and bought bullets to be used in lieu of feed. While the editor surmised that the story was a rumor, it had been "prompted by the severe conditions that prevail everywhere in this west of the river country." In Haakon County a debtor farmer hanged himself before a scheduled court appearance.[13]

Farm women struggled to find ways to feed and clothe their families in the emergency. The "Home" and "Help One Another" columns of the *Dakota Farmer* provided a wealth of information on making do. One woman wrote in to ask the question, "How does one make something out of nothing?" and received encouragement and moral support from other struggling farm women in reply. The editor of the two sections received so many requests for discarded and extra clothes to make over that she decided to stop publishing them and established an exchange through her office instead. People with extra clothes were instructed to inform the *Dakota Farmer* of their willingness to share; the office staff would then send them the names of the needy families closest to them. A Harding County woman had a large supply of beef tallow and requested recipes for converting it to butter for home consumption. A Lyman County farmwife wrote to the *Dakota Farmer* to explain how she had made a tablecloth from flour sacks and had beautified it with rickrack and needlework designs in each corner. Other writers suggested a variety of economies, including the conversion of stoves from wood, kerosene, or coal burners into straw burners and the use of bacon drippings in place of shortening. The Perkins County agent, A. M. Eberle, summed up the situation: "The farmer is in about the position of a six foot man strolling in five feet of water and now sees it beginning to rain." He urged farm families to overcome their economic disadvantages through home production by the woman of the house. Their efforts to sew, can, and otherwise process food could make the difference between success and failure on the farm. The *Dakota Farmer* itself felt the pinch; by August 1921 the issues thinned considerably and featured far fewer ads.[14]

When farmers went, they took the small towns with them. The first signs of difficulty showed up in business ads: merchants announced the beginning of cash-only policies in their stores, offered "reconstruction" sales, or told their customers that they would work with them during these times of readjustment. Bonds for city improvements went unsold due to the confused economic situation. A Kadoka bank changed its hours of business due to a rash of robberies in the country and the "unsettled conditions." Residents of reservation towns, where payments on town lots to the federal government were overdue, tightened their belts. The *Timber Lake Topic*'s editor urged his readers to write to Washington for extensions because there was no money in the region. By late summer 1922, Kadoka appeared torpid. The editors of the *Press* noted the problem in an editorial titled "We Should Again Take Our Place Amongst the Leaders." After describing the drowsiness that seemed to prevail in the community and noting how unlike Kadoka this lull was, the writer named the cause: "It is true and the *Press* realizes as acutely as anyone that conditions are and have been extremely trying for our people, but not more so here than at other places, and we do not believe that this is any pattern of excuse." The editors concluded the piece with a list of projects that needed attention, including the promotion of the Custer Battlefield Highway. Because the Commercial Club had died, there was no forum for discussing issues or focus for action. The first item of business had to be the reorganization of the club.[15]

Such chiding helped spur action on several civic projects, but neither the reorganization of the Commercial Club nor the full support for the Custer Battlefield Highway could fend off economic forces besieging the region. In January 1924 the two banks in Kadoka merged in hopes of making one strong bank. In February a group of local men organized the Jackson County Agricultural Credit Corporation to help area farmers take advantage of new federal loan aid as well as "greatly relieve the pressure on the community and the local banks and business." They were not successful. In May a terse note on the front page of the *Press* announced the closing of the bank due to a "steady leakage of reserves since reorganization and an inability to realize on the bank's frozen assets." It would be two and a half years before the bank made its first payment to its depositors. Depositors recovered only ten cents on the dollar in this first issue, because two years of crop failure made the sale of assets—farms—difficult, and large sums had to be expended for upkeep of bank property, including taxes and maintenance on real estate. In the meantime, one of the two banks from Belvidere moved to

Kadoka to fill the gap. When that move was made, in November of 1924, the two banks in Belvidere were the only survivors of the six Jackson County banks in existence in 1920. Kadoka residents greeted the new bank "by just pouring their gold, silver and currency into the coffers." But the imported bank failed in 1927, and Kadoka was without a bank again until 1948, when a branch bank opened in the town.[16]

Another effect of the agricultural crash in 1920–1921 was pressure on county governments and other local units to maintain services with drastically decreased revenues. West river people paid a high price for schools, roads, and other government services in the best of times, because there were so few people occupying so much space. A serious financial squeeze only complicated an already difficult situation. County and school officials were well aware of the difficulty and struggled to hold costs down. Many counties paid their obligations with warrants (essentially IOUs) rather than with cash. When property owners began to renege on their tax obligation, counties had to issue more and more warrants at 7 percent interest. Indebtedness grew rapidly. Perkins County decided to issue bonds for the $120,000 debt that the county had accumulated. The taxpayers were asked to vote for such an issue, which would carry interest of only 5 percent and not be due for repayment for fifteen years. The county would then run on a cash basis, the theory went. The *Courier* ran a strong campaign endorsing the plan. The editor argued that the only other means of payment would be strict collection of the delinquent taxes. Real estate was a glut on the market. The county had purchased nearly all the land sold for taxes in the last two years. "To enforce collection of the personal taxes which are delinquent, against the residents of this county at this time would mean the destruction of many of the good citizens." "Our aim now," he concluded, "should be to give every protection possible to the residents of Perkins County, because they need it." Despite such endorsements, the bond issue failed.[17]

Schools also caught the attention of harassed taxpayers. A notice submitted by the clerk of school district number 46 in Glendo Township, Perkins County, requested that the county superintendent call a meeting to explain why Perkins County teachers' salaries were above the west river counties' average. "In consequence of the depressed condition of all kinds of business and especially the extreme low price of all farm products," the clerk wrote, "there should be a reduction in all public expense," including teachers' salaries.[18]

Likewise, in 1922 the Jackson County Board of Commissioners addressed the "huge problem and one always under discussion" by cutting the mill rates by .24, resulting in a tax reduction of $10,000. The Kadoka Town Board called a special election to vote on resolutions to lower the assessed residential and agricultural land values in the city limits because people could not pay. Those resolutions also contained admonishments for the board to encourage them to take "the utmost care" in using tax money. The tax problem became so vexing that in 1924 a group of western Jackson County farmers were rumored to be petitioning for an end to all county road work for two years. This was heretical. Roads were the lifeblood of any rural community or small town; without them trade became impossible and social isolation became suffocating. The *Press* fought the petition with vigor. The editor produced county budget figures to prove that roads were not a tax problem. He chose five quarter sections at random and listed the annual assessments against them. In all cases the road tax was the second smallest assessment, leading only the portion given to the state. The average road tax on the five quarters was $3.84. Roads were not the tax problems, the *Press* concluded. What the figures did show was the huge outlay for schools. For all five properties, the school assessment was the largest. The average school tax was $30.64. Jackson County voters by a narrow margin refused to support a county agent, and Perkins County commissioners voted to appropriate funds for an agent only after a hectic campaign that emphasized the potential financial benefits an agent could provide.[19]

The budget squeeze continued throughout the decade. Although farm prices stabilized to a degree (wheat, for example, sold for $1.45 a bushel in January 1926, and hogs reached $12.80 in June of that year), overall farm income was considerably lower than it had been during the boom years, while expenses remained high. Land prices and the total economic value of west river farms reflected the loss of agricultural earning power. Between 1920 and 1925 the average total value of west river farms dropped more than 42 percent. The value of the land alone dropped more than 30 percent at the same time. There was little improvement in the 1925–1930 time period; the average total value of west

river farms fell another 35 percent; the value of the land alone fell another 5.3 percent. Foreclosures continued but at a slower pace. In Perkins County another 385 farmers, or 30 percent of the number of farms
in the county in 1925, were foreclosed; in Harding County the number
was 245, or 34 percent of the number of farms in the county in 1925. In
Jackson County another 143 farmers were foreclosed.[20]

Such financial exigencies kept government institutions short of cash.
In 1928 Jackson County, a quarter of a million dollars in debt, decided
to issue bonds for the past due amount and run the county "on a strictly
cash basis." In 1929 the Mellette County sheriff won a judgment against
the county for $1,178 in back mileage and service fees he was owed. To
pay it, the county had to levy a special tax against the citizens. Two
months later, the Mellette County commissioners instructed the state's
attorney to begin legal action against those who owed back taxes or
who had defaulted on school land loans.[21]

The impact of the many bank failures continued to reverberate across
the region. Individuals, social organizations, and institutions lost
money and had to begin saving all over again. The state Supreme Court
ruled that government and tribal depositors had first priority when
banks were liquidated; individual and organizational dividends therefore could not be paid with any dispatch. The Kadoka banks had carried "many such funds," and local people felt the effects. The South
Creek Lutheran Ladies Aid, for example, had saved $1,500 toward the
building of a church (they met in a school building) but lost it in the
1924 bank failure. They could not again afford to build a church until
1934. The Gorum school district sued Jackson County for the money
the district had lost when the bank closed. A court ruled that the
county did not have to repay the district. The Kadoka school superintendent expressed his gratitude in the columns of the *Press* for the community's aid to the local teachers; the Board of Education had paid the
debts that many had incurred when the bank closed.[22]

The problems of the early twenties were the denouement of the
World War I boom years. The common denominator of both was that
international and national factors controlled the most fundamental
economic fact of life in the west river country — farm prices. The first
crisis of the west river settlement — the drought of 1910–1911 — was the
product of local, natural, indigenous forces; the second crisis of the west

river settlement — the depression of 1920–1921 — was the product of global, economic, exogenous forces. The response of the west river people to both crises, however, was substantially the same — reliance on self-help, thrift, and cutbacks in government services. The one notable exception — the Rural Credits program — ended poorly: the state-operated lending mechanism turned into a state-operated mass liquidator of farms. Even on the heels of the 1920–1921 depression, the *Kadoka Press* reaffirmed the faith that local resources were sufficient to deal with the problems. "Whether the coming year will be for us one of happiness and prosperity or otherwise," the paper noted, "is largely written within our own making, and if we but determine to make it the best year of all so it will be, for with that determination will come forth the effort to make it so."[23]

The effects of the agricultural crash of 1920–1921 lingered throughout the decade. But as an equilibrium of sorts returned to the west river country in the late 1920s, the basic frontier myth of self-reliance resolidified. The lesson of the 1920–1921 depression — that all the hard work, careful planning, and wise investment of west river residents could be reduced to havoc in the blink of an eye by forces far beyond the control of local people and local resources — was repressed if not forgotten.

2

The Cow, the Sow, and the Hen

Tractor farming on the Eugene Miner Young place in Corson County, 1924.

What is wrong with the west river country? Nothing. Do you know that
when you abuse anything it becomes stubborn? Don't you know that if you
whack a cow over the back with a milk stool she will hold her milk? Well,
that is what we are doing with the West River Country. . . . We are whacking
it over the back figuratively speaking, hence it is acting rather stubborn. . . .
Man must change his method in harmony with the nature of the country in
which he lives.
—A. J. G., Harding County, *Dakota Farmer*, April 15, 1922

To develop this western slope it will be necessary for us all to lift at the same
time. You might find a car turned over in the road with a family under
it calling for help, you might lift on the car with all your might then go away
and twenty others working individually do the same thing and those under
the car get no relief, but if they all lift at the same time, results are obtained.
To make a country of this, then, we should all lift at once. Summerfallow by
keeping the cornfield clean and raise winter grain, hogs, cattle and dairying.
—E. W. Laisy, Harding County, *Dakota Farmer*, February 15, 1922

FOR FARMERS, the west river country posed a riddle that they had
not yet been able to answer. Settlers had lived on the land for fifteen
years or so by the 1920s, but farmers still learned mostly by trial and error what their land could produce. One fact had become clear: agriculture was difficult west of the Missouri River and always would be.
Yields tended to be far lower than in more humid areas, and the plants
were shorter, making their care and harvest more complicated and lim-
iting the uses of the straw of grain crops. Agricultural techniques were
different, too. The focus always had to be the preservation of moisture.
West river farmers also had to learn to save hay and grain from fat years
to provide feed for stock in lean years. Those who refused to learn that
lesson found themselves deeply in debt as they borrowed to cover the
costs of feed. In spite of these difficulties, however, there was a strong
sense that solutions could be found to farmers' problems. Hard work
and proper techniques would provide a way.

Experts had helped build the faith. On the national scene, the twenties ushered in an era of well-funded social science research on the
problems of marginal farmers throughout the United States and in particular on the plains. Henry C. Taylor, head of the U.S. Department of

Agriculture's Bureau of Agricultural Economics, M. L. Wilson, one of his students, and others came to believe that progressive farmers on the plains must be encouraged to expand and mechanize their operations. Poorer, unprogressive farmers would have to leave the area both to remove their negative presence and to provide the land needed to enlarge the progressive farmers' holdings to what the experts considered a commercially viable size. The experts' message, when translated by the west river public, was viewed optimistically, as an endorsement of the region's potential; it also put a positive spin on the massive population losses that had occurred after the 1910–1911 drought. The experts appeared to be saying that farmers who had adequately sized operations and modern techniques could succeed on the plains.[1]

Certainly the county agents, the local representatives of organized, progressive agriculture, conveyed an upbeat message throughout most of the twenties. T. E. Hayes of Perkins County recollected that the county agents' "plan was to break up most of the original prairie sod and make the land produce two or three times as much as it was doing in its natural state." According to Hayes, the agents worked tirelessly to reach farmers at their homes or at community meetings, "always telling [them] this land that was so rich should produce such a lot more if certain methods were followed. Farmers took the advice given." The county agents' annual reports to their superiors at the U.S. Department of Agriculture in Washington bear out Hayes's recollections. While the agents were sometimes discouraged that more of their clientele did not actively implement the recommended improvement regimes, their reports reflect a belief that high quality stock, adapted and clean seed, and various tillage and crop maintenance techniques would bring conventional agricultural prosperity to the region.[2]

The west river country was the site of several experimental farms run in partnership with the South Dakota State College in Brookings. State farms in Vivian in Lyman County and Cottonwood in Jackson County tried many seed varieties over the years; their results were made available to farmers through the Agricultural Station Bulletin published in Brookings. In 1920 another station, the Office of Dry Land Agriculture in Newell in Butte County, published an important study, Bulletin 1163, *Dry Farming in Western South Dakota*. The *Dakota Farmer* published highlights for its readers.[3]

The bulletin summarized the findings of several years of research at the west river agricultural experiment stations. According to the experts, the west river country, except for the Black Hills region, was a land of deficient rainfall. Most of the rain that the country did receive (65 percent of it) fell between April 1 and June 30, which was good because it helped the crop establish itself. In the driest years lack of rainfall was teamed with hot winds and high evaporation of what moisture there was. Drought brought some crop damage almost every year. The author of the study advocated three steps to aid in successful farming: the choice of adapted crops, the use of efficient methods "which will give the greatest return for the labor expended," and the development of a system of farming "in which crop production supplements other lines of farm activities." The experts urged early seeding to give crops a chance to mature before hot weather or drought damaged them too greatly. Corn was the most widely grown crop west of the river, and the experts had found that it could be grown profitably in half of the years they had planted it, which they considered good. Alfalfa and brome grass were good hay crops, and the production of alfalfa seed was profitable in some areas. The bulletin advocated the cheapest methods of soil preparation to help insure a profit. "Grain planted on disced corn land or on any land where a cultivated crop has been grown, has given the most profitable results," the author concluded. More intensive cultivation or the use of subsoiling or deep tillage did not affect grain yields but added greatly to the costs of production. Listing corn, a solution often proposed in the west river country and used widely in Kansas, did not help in the region west of the river and in fact hindered the crop because it retarded germination and slowed maturation. (This finding contradicted the advice of many other farm experts.)[4]

The experts concluded that livestock was vital to the success of any farm operation west of the river. Grain farming alone and livestock production without growing feed crops were economically precarious operations at best. The bulletin urged farmers to raise only the number of livestock that could be sustained in the driest years, to plant enough corn to feed the stock in winter, and to produce small grain on corn ground for added benefits.[5]

Did west river farmers follow the experts' advice? According to the agricultural censuses conducted by the federal government in 1925, they did, at least as far as the kinds of crops were concerned and the diversification of the farm operation. Seventy-six percent of all west river farmers grew some corn, making it the most commonly grown crop. Hay, both wild and domesticated varieties, was the close second favorite at 75 percent. In eleven west river counties, farmers grew more acres of corn than any other cultivated crop. (Wild hay, natural grasses cut for livestock, filled the largest number of acres in fifteen counties.) One county, Corson, grew more wheat than corn, although wild hay remained the largest crop there as well. Only 31 percent of west river farmers grew wheat. Farmers grew other grains, however, both to feed their horses and other stock and to market for cash. Forty-six percent of all west river farmers grew oats, although it was never the largest crop in any county, and 22 percent grew other grains, including barley, rye, and buckwheat. Nine and a half percent grew flax for seed; the resulting flax straw was too short for use in linen manufacture. Given the difficult environment, the commitment to corn is surprising, but corn was a versatile crop with many uses, and it also symbolized "the farm" to west river residents, who tended to come from corn-growing states. Farmers fed corn to stock. Corn ground could also be "hogged off," or used as hog pasture, until the animals had gleaned the dropped corn and the stalks. The farm papers advocated the use of corn for silage for milk cows and urged farmers to build silos. The silo, in fact, became the mark of progressive, up-and-coming farmers in some regions. Only 1.2 percent of all west river farmers owned such a fine symbol of rural progress in 1925, and there was some contention over the usefulness of silos in a semiarid region. Some farmers claimed it took too much corn to fill a silo (one man said his "silo would never be filled as long as he lived on the place") and that it wasted corn better fed to hogs. Milk cows could thrive on alfalfa hay alone if they had adequate shelter from the cold.[6]

West river farmers took the message of diversified farming to heart. The *Dakota Farmer* and local newspaper editors frequently advocated "The Cow, the Sow, and the Hen" as the route to agricultural success, and farmers west of the river followed that advice. According to the 1925 census, 62.5 percent of all farmers milked cows, while 62 percent raised beef cattle. Hogs were even more popular, with 71 percent raising swine. Eighty-four percent of farm families kept chickens, and 97 percent maintained at least a team of horses. (Only 14.3 percent owned a tractor.) There was little single-crop cash farming done in the early 1920s west of the river.[7]

Farms in the west river country tended to be far larger than those in more humid places, although farm size varied by location within the region. Overall, the average size for a west river farm was 668 acres. In Gregory County, on the Missouri River in south-central South Dakota, the average farm size was 312 acres, and in neighboring Tripp County, which had the most farms of any county west of the river, the average size was 394 acres. Harding County, in the far northwestern corner of the state, had the largest farms; the average there was 1,765 acres. Averages, of course, obscure the wide diversity possible within a county and within a region. Gregory County did have large farms as well as many of average size. Thirty-one farmers in Gregory County held more than 1,000 acres, and two of these farmed more than 5,000 acres. Harding County, at the other end of the scale, had 167 farmers who farmed less than 500 acres, and 41 of these farmed less than 260 acres. Harding County had 48 farmers with farms of at least 5,000 acres. Gregory and Tripp counties, along with Bennett County, were the only west river counties to have more farmland in crop than in pasture. Usually the ratio leaned quite heavily to pasture. Washington County, populated primarily by Indian people, for example, had twenty-four times as much pastureland as cropland. Harding County, all of whose farmers were white, had ten times more pastureland than cropland. Eighteen of the twenty-one west river counties had more pasture than crops; thirteen had twice as much or more pastureland as cropland. This would insure that farmers had adequate grazing land for the stock they raised and for wild hay to cut for winter.[8]

As west river farmers continued their struggle to meet the conditions of the land in the 1920s, they also confronted changes in agriculture that were national in scope and created a revolution in work that ultimately would undermine rural community life. The most visible of these changes was the advent of machine technology to perform many farm tasks. The gasoline-powered tractor and the implements it could pull were widely advertised by 1920. Not everyone could afford a tractor, of course, especially west of the river where cash crops were relatively small. (In 1922 an average east river farm produced $5,475.75 worth of

commodities, while an average west river farm produced $2,199.80.)
But farm papers carried the advertisements in every issue, and the experts urged tractor purchases in their ongoing effort to make agriculture
a business as well as a way of life.[9]

The tractor advertisements aimed squarely at the hopes and fears of
American farmers. Moline Tractors, for example, advertised that their
product was "a powerful factor in keeping boys on the farm." The Indianapolis Tractor Company told farmers to stop farming for their horses
and farm for themselves instead. According to this advertisement,
farmers worked a month or two each year to feed and care for their
work horses, time that could be better spent making a profit for themselves. The Herring Motor Company of Des Moines, Iowa, manufactured threshing machines of a size to be used by individuals rather than
by large outfits or neighborhood threshing rings. With an individual
threshing machine, the company argued, there would be no need to depend on one's neighbor to help with threshing and no need to waste
time helping the neighbors in return. Every man would be able to work
on his own schedule to his own best advantage. The advertisements and
the experts equated the ownership of mechanical power with modernity
and progressivism. In the farm papers as well as in the small town
newspapers, to be termed "progressive" or "up-to-date" was a great
compliment.[10]

How did the trend toward mechanization affect west river farmers?
In the early 1920s, the inroads were small. Money was too scarce and
times too hard to make such large purchases. A Moline tractor cost
$650 in 1922, and other brands were similarly priced. Implements for
use with tractors were also expensive. The Sears catalog in 1927 advertised implements for use with tractors at prices from $34.00 for the
simplest, smallest models to $98.75 for larger, more sophisticated machines. Walking plows, on the other hand, began at $4.58 for the lightest equipment, and riding plows cost between $40.00 and $50.00 depending on the model. High prices often put modern machinery out of
the reach of farmers who still fed cattle in sheds made of poles and
straw or who had sod outbuildings. According to the 1925 agricultural
census, only 14.3 percent of west river farmers owned tractors. Yet they
knew that such luxuries existed, and over time the hum of machinery

would grow louder. While the hard times of the thirties complicated the process of modernization to a great degree, it resumed with a vengeance after World War II.[11]

In spite of the trend toward mechanization and modernization in agriculture, farming continued to be tied to nature and the changing seasons in very traditional ways. Although some techniques were new, farmers were linked to the cycle of birth, life, and death, and seed time and harvest, in ways that most Americans were not. For the most part, farming also remained a family occupation in the 1920s. Although there were a few exceptions, most west river farmers were married men with families. Wives and children each filled important economic roles of their own, besides helping with the press of field work when they were needed. Because so much of the labor was still performed by hand or with horses, it was tedious, strenuous, and time consuming. There was as much drudgery associated with the farmer's work as there was with the work of his wife; it was just drudgery of a different sort. Most farmers seemed to love their work, however, and in the west river country they hoped someday to measure up to the standards of farmers in more hospitable places. In working toward that goal, west river farmers combined age-old customs and patterns of life with the advice of experts and with new technology where they could afford it. That their labor would so often be wasted was nature's cruel joke on a hopeful people.

For farmers, the year began in late winter, when they assessed the previous year's performance, planned their crops for the coming year, and began to repair harness and machinery for the big push ahead. Planting time was hectic; the optimal time for seeding was relatively short, and the work required great concentration and care. Farmers who were up-to-date and in tune with the experts' advice chose their seed corn carefully from the field the previous fall, not at random from the bin. Commercially grown hybrid seed corn was not widely available until 1932. Small grain seed also came from home fields; the seed had to be cleaned carefully to remove weed seeds that threshing missed.[12]

The first step was proper preparation of the soil. The experts advocated fall plowing, but many in the west river country did not abide by that rule. An Iowa man, a recent arrival to Perkins County, wrote to the *Dakota Farmer* in some bewilderment about the lack of fall plowing. The *Dakota Farmer* expert explained that west river farmers often found it too dry to plow in the fall. It could be done, he suggested, with a heavy disc plow made even heavier with the addition of hundred-pound weights. The work would go much more slowly using this technique, but at least it would be done. Fall plowing had the advantage of speeding spring's work to a degree. It removed one step from the process at a very busy time. Farmers did it or did not do it according to local conditions or personal custom. Even if the ground was plowed in the fall, however, farmers had to perform several other procedures before the seedbed was ready. Again, this varied by custom and locality, but most farmers seemed to disc and harrow their land, sometimes more than once, before planting. If farmers used walking implements, they trudged eight and a quarter miles for each acre they worked.[13]

Corn planting was the trickiest operation performed during the spring season, and many farmers insisted on doing it themselves, without the aid of hired men or family members. Corn-planting implements generally seeded only one or two rows at a time and used long rolls of wire to establish the rows and the proper distance between plants. A farmer stretched the wire from one end of the field to the other and staked it firmly at each end. The wire contained knots every forty inches, and when those knots passed through the planter mechanism, the machine dropped two or three seeds at the proper place in the row. At the end of the row, the farmer had to move the wire and begin again. The idea was precision. If the farmer worked carefully, kept the horses neatly in line, and set the trap door in the planter boxes correctly, the corn would grow in forty-inch intervals in each direction and could be cultivated lengthwise and crosswise. Forty-inch intervals were the standard distance in the Midwest for corn rows, though some experts advocated forty-eight-inch intervals for dry land corn.[14]

Some farmers used walking planters that generally planted only one row at a time, but not everyone used a traditional planter. Gladys Leffler Gist remembered that, in Lyman County, corn was planted with a lister, a double moldboard plow that created furrows and ridges in the field. With an attached planter box, a farmer could plant corn in the ridges, which supposedly aided its growth in a dry country. Farmers who planned to use their corn for fodder (cattle feed made up of the entire corn plant) might drill their corn rather than "check" it. Checked corn could be cultivated in both directions; drilled corn resulted in closely spaced rows of corn that could be cultivated in one direction only. Of those farmers who advertised auction sales in the *Bison Courier* or the *Kadoka Press* in the mid-twenties, three advertised corn planters, two advertised listers, and three planned to sell both types of equipment. (Even those who did not have listers or planters to sell mentioned other corn culture equipment, such as a "Bradley corn plow" or a "corn cultivator." Some auctioned corn fodder as well.)[15]

Once farmers planted their corn, they began the careful work of tending it. Farmers cultivated corn as many as three times in a season, although some advocated fewer cultivations west of the river to reduce moisture loss. The primary purpose of cultivation was weed control; weeds brought yields down. The *Dakota Farmer* urged its readers to cultivate carefully and shallowly to avoid harming the roots of the corn plant. Three implements could be employed in the battle: the weeder, the spring tooth harrow, or the surface cultivator. Experts at the farm paper noted that "local conditions will decide which is best." Cultivating implements were generally equipped with seats allowing the operator to ride, although an earlier generation of farmers had walked while they cultivated. It was possible in 1925 to purchase cultivating equipment for use with tractors. These were hooked directly to the tractor; the farmer rode on the tractor seat and controlled the cultivator from there.[16]

Whatever method a farmer chose, cultivation was vital to the success of the crop. One west river farmer shared a tip with *Dakota Farmer* readers. "Don't plant too thick," he advised. "Fight the weeds like you would Satan." Once the corn reached a certain height, it was no longer possible to cultivate it with an implement. Farmers then turned to their trusty hoes (or turned their children to the hoe) to weed the fields by hand. In an age without herbicides, constant hand hoeing teamed with crop rotation (many crops choked weeds quite effectively) and intensive cultivation were the only methods available to eradicate weeds.[17]

Weed control was an ongoing problem. The columns of the *Dakota Farmer* almost always carried a letter or two inquiring about the best ways to eliminate such pests as sand burrs and especially bindweed or creeping Jenny. The Lyman County agent reported in 1926 that entire fields in his county had been abandoned because of bindweed infestation. An experiment there to determine the best equipment to use in bindweed eradication had failed miserably; the farmer who agreed to try the various implements decided he liked only one, refused to try the others, although all had been delivered to him at great effort, and disced his land up contrary to all instructions. Nevertheless, the agent held out hope for change. Corn smut was a troubling problem as well. Corn smut is a fungus; spores are spread through the air. The *Dakota Farmer* advised a Pennington County farmer to remove the smut from each plant by hand to save his crop. It would take the cooperation of all corn growers in an infected region to eradicate the pesky ailment, however. Farmers would have to treat their fields by hand at roughly the same time to eliminate the disease, or infected plants would continue to contaminate neighboring plants and fields.[18]

Farmers in the west river country also grew a variety of small grains on their farms. The most popular was oats, the gasoline of the horse-drawn agricultural era. Small grains were usually seeded in the early spring from seed chosen from the previous year's crop, although some experimented with fall sowing of so-called winter grains, which would be dormant during the harshest weather but mature for an early summer harvest. The experts advocated careful cleaning of grain seed to avoid infestation of noxious weeds. To insure a clean crop, wise farmers separated the grain seed from weed seeds with a fanning mill; many of these mills were hand operated, but the *Dakota Farmer* did carry ads for larger engine-driven models. Enough west river farmers failed to clean their grain seed that *Dakota Farmer* experts and county agents returned to the issue again and again. The Lyman County agent declared dirty seed "one of the biggest problems of the country."[19]

Farmers could drill or broadcast their small grain seed into the ground. Drills planted the grain in close rows; broadcast seeders spread the seed over the surface of the field, and a cultivator then covered the seed with earth. A stand of grain grew thickly and did not require cultivation. This dense growth habit made grain crops helpful tools for weed eradication when used in a crop rotation system. The *Dakota Farmer* advocated a three-crop rotation that put small grains last. Farmers were to begin with alfalfa or another pasture/forage crop, move to corn, and then to small grains.[20]

Hay crops, both wild grasses and those planted and tended by human hands, were also important; most farmers spent some time establishing new hay lands. West river farm families grew alfalfa for seed as well as for hay. As alfalfa became more popular, the market for seed grew, and prices were good. West river alfalfa was rugged because it had to withstand a harsh climate; the seed was greatly prized. Farmers had to master special tricks to grow alfalfa. They had to work the ground well with a double disc, but then, after planting, had to pack the ground hard again with a roller or else the seed would not start. Planting alfalfa on newly plowed ground did not work at all; some experts advocated planting it on corn ground that had been disced but not plowed. To maintain the crop, it was necessary to harrow it on occasion to cut back on the weeds. An implement for the purpose was available, but few west river farmers purchased one. Instead, they used their usual equipment, a disc or a conventional harrow, cautiously, to avoid destroying the roots of their alfalfa plants. E. E. Plympton of Dewey County strongly advocated growing alfalfa and corn "if we wish to arrive anywhere as farmers." He had had good luck with his crop, tended it faithfully, and hoped others would too. For those who wanted to sell seed, it was important to remember the unpredictable climate. The first crop of alfalfa in early summer should provide the seed, experts said; later crops might not mature in the dry weeks of mid or late summer.[21]

By the time the crops had been planted and cultivated, June had arrived, and it was time to make hay. A good hay supply insured proper rations for the family's livestock. Making hay was a family task, and it could be hot work. First the farmer, or a son or daughter or hired man, cut the hay with a horse-pulled mower. This implement featured a bar which extended from five to eight feet from the side of the machine. The bar contained serrated teeth which cut the hay when the horses drew the mower through the field. After a brief interval of a day or more, depending on drying conditions such as temperature, precipitation, and humidity, the workers then raked the hay into piles for stacking. This could be done by hand, but in the west river country farmers usually used horse-drawn hay rakes. The auction bills published in the *Kadoka Press* and the *Bison Courier* in the mid-twenties all advertised hay mowers of anywhere from five to eight feet in length and hay rakes, usually ten feet in size. After the farm family stacked the hay in piles, they used pitchforks to load it into wagons or hayracks for transport to

Making hay with a bull rake in Perkins County, 1923.

the barn or farmyard. This required that workers fork heavy loads of hay up over their heads to the waiting wagon. If the family had a barn with a haymow (a storage area for hay, usually on the upper story of the barn), and many did not, they then lifted the hay again, this time into the mow. A rope with block and tackle attached to a large metal fork aided this process; the fork bit deeply into the hay on the rack, and a team of horses guided by a family member then pulled slowly forward to lift the loaded fork up to the mow. Workers within the barn emptied the fork to the mow floor and moved the loose hay to the desired spot. Families without haymows might use pitchforks to load the hay into other outbuildings or might stack it by hand neatly in the yard near the barn. In a good year a farmer made hay two or three times.[22]

After haying season came the small-grain harvest. This, too, was a family operation. As Joe McTighe of Meade County recalled, "When the grain was ready we all swarmed to the field, from the oldest to the youngest we put up the shocks. No one was excused." The farmer harvested the grain with a binder that cut the crop in the field and tied it into bundles. Family members and/or hired help then shocked the grain—bundling the grain with the heads carefully arranged for optimum protection from the weather and wind, while allowing for necessary air-drying of the grain. Shocks might stand for several weeks until the threshing ring arrived at the farm.[23]

In the west river country where the grain was often short and the straw, therefore, unusable, farmers used a header to harvest the crop. Henry Miller of Perkins County described its use. "Horses were hitched to a pole that pushed the machine. The driver stood on a platform behind the teams and steered the header with a 'pilot pole.' A sickle in front cut the grain into a canvas that carried it up an elevator to a wagon pulled along side by another team." Headers generally cut only enough straw to insure that the grain itself was not cut or lost. The workers dumped the box of grain into a stack; the threshing rig then separated the grain from the chaff. Some headers could be used with a bundle attachment that tied the grain into bunches. In those cases, the header left enough stem with the grain to make a neat package.[24]

Threshing was the culmination of the small-grain season late in the summer or early in the fall. Threshing machines or grain separators were large, cumbersome, and expensive. Although the advent of the internal combustion engine and other new technologies made it possible for individuals to purchase threshing rigs for individual use, that option was not yet widely employed in the west river country. Instead, neighbors got together and arranged to have a professional thresher come to the neighborhood; the farmer agreed to help out with the labor. It was also possible to hire a complete threshing crew along with the rig in some locales. According to Thomas Isern, "In the Dakotas, both pure custom work and cooperative threshing were common." West river memoirs more often recount the shared labor approach to their hot, dirty, but vital task, and as late as the forties the rural newspaper correspondents told of women cooking for threshers.[25]

Threshing meant several days of intensive, dirty labor. Depending on the size of the crop, the rig might stay at the farm place for one day or three days or more. When the neighbors had threshed one farm's crops, the entire rig moved to the next place and the neighbors worked there and so on around the neighborhood. Threshing was an endurance test for males (and for females, who provided substantial meals for as many as twenty-five men at a time). Iola Caldwell Anderson remembered the work at her farm in Lyman County. "From early morning until dusk the old Case 'chug-chugged' while the thresher belched out chaff, and grain poured into the wagons. There was always friendly rivalry among the men who drove the bundle racks. Who had the best team? Who could pitch the most bundles?" The machine worked tirelessly while men struggled to keep up. "It took a line of bundle racks on each side of the big thresher, while the men pitched steadily to keep up with its hungry maw." The farmer saved the straw from the threshing operation to use as bedding and feed for livestock. As the threshing machine, or separator, as it was officially called, removed the grain from the straw, it blew the discarded straw out in a large pile. The blower could be set to move back and forth automatically, but farmers or their helpers had to help the machine create a neat stack. With a pitchfork, the worker shaped the dirty, dusty straw as the machine forced it out. With each pass of the blower, the workers were covered with forcefully propelled straw, chaff, and dirt; yet straw was far too useful as animal bedding to be carelessly handled. Farm families stored the grain gleaned from the harvest in bins on the farm. They hauled any surplus to a nearby elevator for storage or sale. For the Anderson family, elevators in Draper and Murdo served that important function. Horse-drawn wagons hauled the crop; in later years trucks took over the work.[26]

Delays in threshing could be serious. If a rig was delayed or if a person's farm was last in the neighborhood rotation, winds or rains could wreak havoc with the waiting shocks. When the elements damaged the grain, its value in the marketplace declined. Grain was sold by the grade. The grain buyers in town marked damaged grain down a grade or two; the price dropped accordingly. In the fall of 1924, for example, the *Dakota Farmer* reported that excessive, untimely rains had caused grain in the shock to sprout before the threshers could claim it. The need to depend on others for help with the vital work of threshing added one more element of risk and uncertainty to the west river farmers' already precarious existence and helped the slow but steady movement toward individually owned and operated threshing equipment.[27]

The next major field work on a farm came later in the fall with the making of corn fodder and, later still, corn picking. Many farmers used some of their corn crop for fodder, which was fed to livestock in the winter. It consisted of entire stalks of corn, including the ear, cut near the ground and stacked into shocks in the field. Because the corn was

Corson County threshing crew, 1920s.

cut when still green, it was heavy and the work tedious. Several stalks, as many as two dozen, comprised a bundle; fifteen or so bundles made a shock, which was held together with twine. In the winter farmers or their helpers retrieved the heavy, often snow-filled shocks and fed them to the hungry animals. The cows, however, often rejected much of the stalk, which made a mess in the barn for farmers to clean up.[28]

It was during picking (or right before picking began) that the best farmers chose their seed for next year. The choicest ears from the hardiest plants made the best seed, and farmers and their helpers handled those with special care, putting them into separate sacks or boxes as they were picked. These seed ears were then dried in an attic or kitchen until it was time to test their germination potential in late winter.[29]

Corn picking was the worst drudgery, but again it was vital to the success of the farm operation. Corn kernels were a major foodstuff for stock of all kinds. In the 1920s farmers still picked corn by hand, and it took weeks, depending on the size of the crop. Farmers and their helpers headed to the fields at daybreak and worked until dinnertime, rested briefly after the meal, and returned to the field until dark. They picked every ear of corn by hand. The workers, wearing husking gloves on their hands and old stockings over their jacket sleeves to protect them from the sharp leaves of the corn plant, cut the ear from the stalk with a sharp hook that was strapped across the palm of the right hand. They then pitched the ear into a large wagon equipped with a bangboard to catch errant tosses. Once the wagon filled, farmers or their helpers took it back to the farmyard and shoveled the ears into the waiting bin or corncrib. Henry Miller remembered alleviating the drudgery of corn picking with a bit of roughhousing. He and his brother, Lonie, lobbed ears of corn at each other on occasion instead of tossing them into the wagon. Corn picking had its own distinctive sounds. Iola Caldwell Anderson recalled her childhood memories of the season. "With the coming of daylight the crisp autumn air was filled with sounds of creaking wagons, of pickers hollering 'giddap' and 'whoa,' and corn ears hitting the bangboard."[30]

Corn picking could be miserable work. Some stalks might be broken or bent, and workers had to lift them to retrieve the ear and then step over them. Frost dampened the fields when it thawed, and snow frequently fell as well, making clothing and gloves wet and uncomfortable. In regions with heavy corn yields, farmers had to hire workers to help. West river farmers sometimes went east to pick in years when drought limited their own crops of corn. Until mechanical corn pickers became widely affordable in the late 1930s, corn picking remained the most labor intensive of the many farm chores.

Farmers juggled the seasonal routine of field work with a regular round of daily chores. They had to feed and care for stock of all kinds, milk cows twice a day, maintain their equipment, buildings, and home, as well as perform a myriad of duties now lost in a technological age. As with the field work, family members helped with many of the routine chores. At all levels, farming was a family enterprise, but the husband and father had ultimate responsibility for the barnyard work. It was he who supervised children and hired men, decided which tasks were to be done in what order, and in general managed the enterprise.

In the west river country of the 1920s, horses remained the foundation of farm work; their selection and care were vitally important to the family's welfare. In the earlier years of settlement, west river farmers also raised horses to sell, but the market collapsed at the end of World War I. Horses had unique personalities, and farmers quickly learned which horse could best perform a certain task. Driving the teams of horses took skill. Farmers often reserved the liveliest for themselves but taught their children to ride and drive the tamer horses at an early age. The horse herd was frequently replenished by births and by purchase; old horses that had served their purpose were sold, often to the disappointment of the children, who had become attached to the animals and treated them as pets. Farm families had to take good care of their horses because they were so vital to the family livelihood. Early spring work moved somewhat slowly to condition the horses and lessen the chance of injuries. Farmers cleaned horse collars carefully to prevent the creation of sores on tender shoulders and doctored any injuries with great care. The letters to the experts at the *Dakota Farmer* indicated the concern with which farmers handled their stock. They wrote for information quickly if an animal developed an unfamiliar problem that the farmer could not handle with the usual tried-and-true remedies. The solutions offered generally included the purchase of medications available through local drugstores or by mail order and detailed instructions for the farmer to follow in their application.

Farmers worked in close contact with their teams. Together they were a biological entity linked to the soil they worked. Critics of the new technology like tractors pointed out the loss of this important relationship when farmers mechanized their operations. Farmers rested their horses at noon; farm work came to a brief halt while the animals regained energy and strength. Farmers then had a rest as well. With a tractor, there was no need for a break. It roared on endlessly, refreshed with gasoline in brief breaks that gave farmers no chance for repose. The biological link was broken, and farming became a different thing. In the 1920s, however, that change was only beginning in the west river country. Farmers and their horses worked in concert; a well cared for herd was the hallmark of a good farmer.[31]

In a diversified agricultural community like the west river country in the 1920s, the care of other stock was important as well. Dairy cows took the most labor but were a dependable source of cash. Farmers who sold whole milk for home consumption received the most money, but whole milk was highly perishable and difficult to handle; its sale depended in large part on proximity to a major market. In the west river country, for example, the farmers of Pennington County, where Rapid City is located, sold the most whole milk. Fall River County, which also borders the Black Hills with its market towns, was second.[32]

Farmers at a distance from such markets sold their cream for its butterfat content. Although there were very few creameries west of the river (eleven in 1926, which includes three in Black Hills communities), there were cream buyers in every railroad town. Cream buyers tested the cream for its butterfat content and paid the seller accordingly; they then sent the cream by rail on its way to be made into butter. Although cream also needed careful handling (proper cooling was especially important), it was not as touchy as milk and would keep considerably longer, allowing farm families to store it for several days before taking it to market.[33]

Farm families also manufactured thousands of pounds of butter at home. The decade of the twenties was a time of transition as far as butter manufacture was concerned. The quality of creamery butter was often more consistent and dependable than that made at home and was therefore becoming more popular. But for farm families at a great distance from a rail line, butter manufacture was a means of converting their labor with their dairy herd into spendable cash. Small town stores still took butter in trade for items farm families had to purchase. West river farm families manufactured 1,968,210 pounds of butter in 1925.[34]

One by-product of twenties dairying was skim milk. The liquid left over after the cream was separated was virtually fat free. There was no real market for this because buyers paid according to fat content. Agricultural experts urged farmers to feed the skim milk to their calves and hogs. Even without fat, the nutritional value of skim milk was high and could be recycled back into the farm operation. With the advent of the bulk milk hauling truck after World War II, dairying would undergo major changes. That was in the future, however. In the 1920s west of the river, older patterns still prevailed.[35]

Much of the work with dairy cattle remained hard, dirty hand work in the twenties. In the summer, dairy cattle had to be brought in to the barn at milking time, both morning and night (in the winter, cows stayed in the barn much of the time, removing this step of the process), locked into stanchions (often homemade wooden contraptions), cleaned of manure and mud, and then milked by hand by a person seated on a stool. Flies buzzed busily about; the cows tried to protect themselves with their tails. Those engaged in milking often found themselves in the path of the swatting tail.[36]

In every season someone had to keep the barn clean. The most modern barns of the twenties were equipped with gutters located behind the cows to carry wastes away from the animals. Farmers shoveled the wastes from the gutters into mechanical carriers, which hung on overhead tracks. They then pushed the carriers outside and dumped them a distance from the building. This kind of equipment was still a novelty. More likely, the farmer, family members, or the hired man scraped manure and soiled straw bedding from the floors, shoveled it out the door or window, and put down new bedding around each animal.[37]

The resulting piles of manure and dirty straw accumulated, sometimes for months, before being disposed. The best use for manure, of course, was soil improvement. The experts advocated the frequent spreading of manure on croplands and pastures. Their advice was not always followed. In 1922 A. M. Eberle, the Perkins County agent, was amazed to discover that the "oldtimers" in his county were disposing of manure in creeks, draws, and holes in their land. They claimed that manure dried the soil. Eberle was heartened by the fact that new arrivals seemed to use manure more wisely for soil improvement. Frequent manure removal was important for good sanitation and fly and pest control. A female fly lays two hundred eggs at a time. The eggs become adult flies within a week. Farmers who cleaned up all manure on a twice-weekly schedule during the fly season could remove breeding grounds and break the cycle. This was not practical, however, for hardworking families with little time for extra effort. Manure, odor, and flies remained an ever present fact of life for west river farmers in the twenties.[38]

One element of change in the dairy business was the advent of the milking machine, which replaced tedious hand labor. Because the machines were new and their practicality still unknown, few farmers invested in them right away. Some who did wrote the *Dakota Farmer* to say that their cows did not mind mechanical milkers, but also that the machines required proper care and that cows had to be manually stripped of the last few ounces of milk. Another problem related to power. On farms without electricity, and that included most west river farms in the 1920s, milking machines ran on gasoline engines that sometimes provided power erratically and had to be properly vented. But they did save labor and allowed farm families to milk more cows in less time. A farmer from Jackson County, who signed himself "E.G.L.," was satisfied with his automatic milkers. He related the question most commonly asked of him: "How fast can you milk?" He provided the answer for *Dakota Farmer* readers. "We timed ourselves frequently, in fact almost habitually, and our average time for milking the 12 cows, weighing and recording each cow's milk separately, separating the milk, running and putting away the cups and tubes in sterilizing solution was 40 to 45 minutes." He and his wife worked together in the dairy barn and were quite pleased with their success.[39]

Historically, hogs have been called "mortgage lifters" in the Midwest; their potential profitability as well as their use for the home table made them a frequent, if not popular, presence on west river farms. The traditional mode of hog raising was not labor intensive. The animals were slopped twice a day with a mixture of table scraps, refuse, and true feed stuffs and allowed to root and wallow in the mud and manure of the barnyard. This regimen left the animals susceptible to disease and limited their potential for gain. Most west river hogs were so-called fat hogs, raised to be as large and fat as possible to increase the lard supply. (This is in contrast to "bacon" hogs also bred at the time, which were leaner and less able to thrive on the pen feeding and foraging common on the typical farm.)[40]

The experts hoped to change the traditional method of hog raising to insure greater survival among litters and better health and gain among adults. The new methods required cleanliness and substantial available pasture for exercise. The *Dakota Farmer* spelled out the method in detail in the May 1, 1924, issue; the Perkins County agent's report of his program, written in 1926, is similar. Farmers were to supply their sows with clean pens for farrowing and keep the indoor quarters clean until they moved the pigs to pasture about ten days after the piglets were born. (Farmers were to haul the pigs to pasture, not walk them, to keep them from dirtying their feet and spreading disease.) Farmers were also to place litters and sows in pastures according to the age of the babies. Too great a variation in age led the larger piglets to attack the smaller ones and take their food, whereupon the small ones died and the thieves were in danger of scours (diarrhea) from too much food. The *Dakota Farmer* reminded farmers to give their sows enough to eat while they were nursing. Apparently it was not uncommon for sows to lose seventy-five pounds while raising a litter; maintaining their regular weight should be the goal. Farmers should provide clean, dry shelters for their pigs while in pasture, preferably portable wooden houses. Because these were expensive, the *Dakota Farmer* writer suggested straw sheds as acceptable substitutes, but only if, after the litters were raised, the straw was burned or tilled into the fields with the manure. Reuse of the straw threatened to spread disease.[41]

Obviously, the experts' advice threatened to make hog raising a considerable effort. Some farmers balked. The Tripp County agent reported that eight of twenty-six farmers trying a new hog lot sanitation method gave up because it was too much work, although the remaining eighteen were rewarded with a bigger pig crop. A North Dakota man wrote an angry letter to the *Dakota Farmer* when one of its articles suggested that farmers stay up at night to help their sows farrow. "There is a limit to the number of hours that even a North Dakota farmer can stay up and work"; he went on to say that he was broke, worn out, and tired of articles on prizewinning animals and crops achieved with state money at the agricultural colleges. But those who followed the experts' advice usually profited. The Perkins County agent reported "amazing results" when farmers raised hogs with the new methods.[42]

A diversified farm also raised chickens, but in the twenties this remained largely women's work (see chapter 3). In 1920 the Office of Extension Work surveyed farm women in the northern and western portions of the United States. In that year, 85 percent of farm women were in charge of the chickens. The work was important to the welfare of the farm enterprise. In 1925 west river farms produced 5,830,945 dozen eggs and 1,824,918 chickens, with values of $1,383,965 and $1,100,041, respectively.[43]

Beyond the stockyard there were countless other tasks that farmers performed or oversaw day by day and season by season. Iola Caldwell Anderson remembered her family's efforts as they helped her father run the farm. Her father never attended the county fair, for example, because of the press of seasonal chores. "The house had to be banked, fodder cut and stacked, there were always fences to mend and wood to haul." Her father dug postholes with a spade after a rain when the ground was soft. He banked the house with dirt plowed up from the yard south of the house. With the help of his son, Mr. Caldwell hauled loads of dirt to the side of the house and shoveled it to a height of several feet against the outer walls to help keep out winter's cold. All winter the family hauled feed and chopped wood for the stove, except when the severest blizzards kept them indoors. Mr. Caldwell also mended his own gloves, repaired the children's shoes, and, after 1923, when Mrs. Caldwell returned to teaching, cooked meals for the family. All was part of life on the farm before mechanization and specialization changed farm life forever. The hours were long and hard, and, west of the river, rewards were frequently small. Yet the work was honest, and the struggle had a peculiar appeal. West river farmers hoped to make something of the country with their labor and, in the process, prove that they were farmers the equal of any.[44]

3

If a Woman Is a True Companion

Cleve and Jessie Berry, Mellette County, 1920.

I figure by the time I've taken care of my 4 kiddies, raised a garden and chickens, canned hundreds of quarts of food, patched and darned clothes and made them, and made $25.00 or $30.00 cash in various ways that I've made a big step toward the living.

If hubby can't go unhampered by the care of any little folks and with his two own hands make the rest of the living, well I suppose we'll just have to do without, but I still feel I've done my share.
—Mrs. C.F.D., Jackson County, *Dakota Farmer*, October 1, 1932

M EN MAY HAVE been the economic mainstays of west river farms in the twenties, but women filled important roles as economic producers, wives, mothers, and as hearts of the homes of the region. For women, the "home," broadly defined, was the center of their duties. "Home" meant the dwelling, of course, where women carried out their traditional duties as the processors and preparers of food, as manufacturers of clothing and products such as soap, as housewives, and as mothers. But on the farm, "home" could also mean the yards and gardens, the poultry houses, and even the barn and the fields, depending on the family's circumstances and the woman's likes and desires.

Because the west river country was relatively poor and sparsely settled, scarcity of resources and a plentitude of space shaped women's lives. They made do with less and worked hard in partnerships with their husbands to build the country. They were very much aware, however, of the technologies and consumer goods available in richer, more densely populated areas, and they had to grapple with the changing ideas about women's roles as producers on the farm, as wives, and as mothers. West river farm women did what they could to work efficiently, to be companions and partners to their husbands, and to be loving but firm teachers of their children. They did this within a framework of individual circumstances shaped by their economic status, their values, and a myriad of other variables. For west river farm women in the twenties, hard work and change were the hallmarks of the decade.

The farmstead, especially the house and yard, was the center of the farm women's world. Farm buildings and their layout, of course, varied widely due to the family's economic circumstances, interests, tastes, and energy level. (Tenants had to endure whatever conditions their landlords cared to provide. Often, facilities on rented places were far poorer than on those occupied by their owners.) In spite of the diversity in farmsteads, it is possible to describe in a general way typical west river homes. In 1935 the South Dakota Agricultural Experiment Station published a bulletin on standards of living in selected South Dakota counties. It included illustrations of farmsteads "typical" of three distinct South Dakota regions. The southeastern South Dakota farmstead was located in Yankton County. A large, white frame Victorian home graces the picture with a massive, painted hipped-roof barn and several neatly arranged outbuildings, also all painted, complementing the scene. The yard has several trees and a windbreak of sorts, which protected the farm's inhabitants from winter's blasts. The photograph of a representative farmstead in central South Dakota was taken in Faulk County. The home on this farm is a newer bungalow-style, painted white, with a porch and neat front steps. A smaller barn and lesser number of outbuildings make up the yard, but all appear to be painted. There are no trees on the place. The west river photo was taken in Perkins County. The farm that the Agricultural Experiment Station people chose as typical of the region is stark and poor. The house is a small, unpainted story-and-a-half box with a lean-to addition at the rear. The unpainted barn has a hip roof but is considerably smaller than the barn in Yankton County. Three small outbuildings complete the farmstead. There are no trees on this farm, and it looks practically abandoned. One thing that all three "typical" farms have in common is windmills in the stockyard. Water would have to be hauled some distance to the homes where the women worked unless the family laid pipe to carry it in.[1]

Pictures and descriptions of west river homes, included in other sources, show just how typical the Experiment Station example was. Leo and Mary Ann Abelt of Ziebach County posed outside their home in 1927 to show off their new car. The home behind them is a small one-and-a-half story building, covered with tar paper, with a tiny, enclosed entry porch. Mrs. Abelt had hung cheery curtains in the windows, however, and the trim around doors and windows appears to be painted. There is no tended yard visible. The Ziebach County home of Charles and Elizabeth Bennett in 1920 was "a 14 × 16 frame building with shingled roof with a dugout basement beneath." A photograph shows that the frame was slapped together haphazardly with torn tar paper held on with uneven lathwork covering one side. Many of the family's possessions lay "stored" outside the door. Again there is no yard, just worn prairie grass and bare dirt around the house. The barn on this farm was made of upright poles — small trees of various lengths that had been trimmed of their branches and stood on end. The Bennetts had stuffed straw against the poles to make walls.[2]

The inadequacy of many west river farm women's workplaces was reaffirmed in the reports of federal relief workers, who in the early 1930s visited the homes of applicants and evaluated their surroundings. Not every report described housing, but most did. Of the 157 farm applicants whose housing was evaluated, seventeen homes were rated "very poor" by investigators, one was "horrible," six were "bad," eleven were "poor," and twelve were "not very good." Eight families lived in shacks, seven in "unfinished" houses, one in a sod house, one in a barn, and one in a chicken house. On the other hand, eighteen homes were described as "good," eighteen as "very good," and three as the "best" local housing. The largest category of evaluation was "fairly good," with thirty-three homes described in that fashion.[3]

Ninety-one applicants provided the size of their farm home. Eight families lived in one room, fifteen in two rooms, twenty-one in three rooms, and the most families, twenty-six, lived in four rooms. Only one family had an eight-room house, but four had seven rooms, and five families had six rooms. The size of the home was bore little relation to family size. Ten or more people might be crammed into three rooms; space and privacy were often at a premium. Larger homes were no guarantee of comfort; one relief investigator described an applicant's five-room house as "very bad" with "no foundation, siding loose, cold air rushes through the cracks." Another investigator described "a rambling frame house covered in rusty tin, badly run down, windows broke."[4]

Good housing was available to most west river residents if they had the money and were willing to spend it on housing. Local lumberyards provided supplies for homes and outbuildings; families could hire local carpenters to do the work, could call on friends and relatives to help with the building, or could do it themselves. Several mail order companies also sold kits for ready-cut houses and farm outbuildings that arrived by train. Sears and the Gordon–Van Tine Company of Davenport, Iowa, were among the best-known and most successful merchants of the "ready-cuts."[5]

The Gordon–Van Tine Company was very much aware of the special needs of the farmwife and her home factory. While the company eschewed the fancy names for the houses that Sears employed, they clearly labeled homes designed specifically for the farm. Ready-cut homes for farm families tended to be larger, with as many as six bedrooms, than those marketed to city dwellers; all farm homes featured bigger kitchens with cabinet-lined pantries and a washroom area directly inside a back or side door, which would allow family members to clean up and shed work clothes before entering the kitchen.[6]

Substantial, well-built housing, whether locally purchased or prefabricated, required the expenditure of a considerable sum of money. Buffeted by unpredictable weather and uncontrollable economic cycles, families had to build or add on to existing homes as they could afford it. The problem of finances, along with the thrifty local custom of using abandoned claim shacks for ready-made home additions, resulted in the haphazard appearance of many west river farm homes.

Only in the *Dakota Farmer* were west river homes portrayed as up-to-date and comfortable. This farm journal advocated progressive, scientific farming and modern, egalitarian family life. The editors hoped that the information and inspiration they provided would help farm families improve their knowledge and techniques and motivate them to do more to improve their surroundings. To this end, the *Dakota Farmer* often included pictures of the best farm homes in the state to serve as examples. Two such west river farms appeared in the early twenties. One, a large bungalow painted in contrasting colors, had been built by a Tripp County farmer and was used to illustrate an article on the excellent prospects that could be found in the west river country. The second photograph was taken in Haakon County. It showed the house and barn of the Prairie Queen Ranch owned by Cyrus Thompson. The house was a classic, white, two-story, L-shaped frame house. Two screened porches complemented its entries. In the background, a large hip-roof barn, also painted, illustrated the obvious financial success of its owners. Photographs like those in the *Dakota Farmer* portrayed what could be and what should be in the west river country. Such examples

were used to encourage and educate families and to help promote
Dakota as a farming region generally. They showed that some west
river people lived comfortably; not all lived in shacks. But for most
women on west river farms, living and working conditions remained
crude by the standards of the day.[7]

The yard surrounding the home was generally the woman's domain
as well, but the concept of the yard as a groomed, landscaped, and carefully maintained area for family recreation and extension of the beauty
of the home was just beginning to filter into the west river country. Progressive papers like the *Dakota Farmer* urged their readers to provide
yards and improve the appearance of their properties to boost their own
spirits and to delight the eyes of passersby. The dry climate, however,
made it more difficult for grass, shrubs, trees, and flowers to grow without great effort on the part of the farm family. Poverty also played a
role. Nursery shrubs and trees cost money, and because the plants' survival was risky, many decided not to take the chance of failure. One
Stanley County woman, however, urged her neighbors to make the effort to beautify their yards. "So many farmyards are in a miserable, run-
down condition," she commented. "A broken doorstep, perhaps no
sidewalk at all, no fence to keep out the chickens and pigs and all the
filth that goes with them right around the house." She urged farmers to
clean up the old rubbish and suggested several inexpensive flowers and
vines that could be planted. "I hear so many farmers talking about what
they will do in the future to fix up their place—when they can afford it.
Don't wait until that time comes, because with a lot of us poor mortals,
that time never comes." The editor of the *Dakota Farmer* agreed. He
understood that, while the prosperity of the homesteaders had not met
their goals, they appeared, from the looks of their farmsteads, to be
"merely existing." While lack of money and the need to use available resources to "keep body and soul together" were good reasons, still, he argued, beauty was necessary, too, and he hoped that more farm families
would plant "trees, shrubs, orchards and flowers" to make their homes
more beautiful. A Harding County man wrote to the *Dakota Farmer*
about his innovative ranch home equipped with water, sewer, and electric lights from a battery plant. He had also planted trees and maintained a clean yard. "It hardly seems human to have old underwear,
overshoes, tin cans, etc., lying around the doorstep and yard, walking

over them everyday." These ideas about neat, well-landscaped yards were the wave of the future, but it would take time and effort for them to become institutionalized. The dirt paths and sparse prairie grasses, the scattered refuse, tools, and chicken droppings — all left an impression of squalor. Yet, for many women, this was the setting for their work and their family life.[8]

These poor houses and unkept yards were the centers of food production, processing, and meal preparation, which were the most important and time-consuming tasks farm women performed. Although canned foods of all sorts were available and most small towns had bakeries for bread products, homegrown and home-canned foods made up the bulk of the family diet. Some reasons for this are obvious. Canned goods cost money, and many families lacked ready cash or had to use their trade balance at local stores for items like kerosene, sugar, or coffee, goods that could not be made at home. Distance also handicapped farm families. Bakeries could be ten or more miles away; with families devouring huge quantities of bread, cake, and pie, it would have taken daily trips to maintain a fresh supply. But there was a less obvious reason also. An argument that began in the *Dakota Farmer* columns in the twenties revealed how rooted farm women were to their work as thrifty producers and providers. That is, like farm men, farm women to some extent viewed new and costly options to their traditional labors as wasteful and a threat to their status in the family economy.

The *Dakota Farmer* surveyed farm women on their use of canned food and other ready-made goods. The paper received in response a long letter from a west river rancher's wife, who advocated the use of all ready-made clothing, foods, and other products wherever possible, in an effort to emancipate farm women, as well as improve the health of the farm family through better nutrition and a wider variety of foods. In her letter, Jennie Haas attacked the "home factory" system, arguing that it made too much work for farmwives and drove families to the city to escape. "Homemade goods with their halo of romance and sentiment have so entwined themselves about the home life that any attempt to uproot them appears to threaten the home life itself," she wrote, "but those of us who are practical know that the picturesque ivy rots the shingles . . . and we also know that the picturesque custom of producing everything needed in the home with Mother's own hands is a parasite strangling all the joy out of Mother's life." Her family (her husband and five sons) lived entirely from factory canned and produced goods, including even canned milk and bakery bread. Haas claimed that purchased food and supplies actually cost less because they resulted in less waste, were more sanitary due to regulation of factories, and added variety to the diet that reliance on home produced and processed foods could not. Her attack on the home factory system was wide-ranging. She compared farm and town women in their use of toiletries, for example, and found farm women far behind. While a town woman of moderate means would have an array of products such as cold cream, soft soaps, talcum powder, and even makeup to use for her own comfort and beauty, the farm woman used homemade lye laundry soap on her face and kept on working. Her only reading was farm magazines; her money went for items useful in her home factory. The result? Farm women sacrificed everything for their work, wore themselves out, and moved to town to get away from the farm.[9]

Haas's manifesto set off a vigorous defense of women as home factory producers. Readers argued in response that home production was cheaper and that the products were of better quality, as well as items of pride. A Meade County woman asked, "I wonder what Mrs. Haas does with her time if she never bakes bread or cans anything?" The letters made it clear that, for most farm women, production, processing, and preparation of food continued to be a primary responsibility, although some allowed for factory goods in emergencies.[10]

The canning of home produce and meats was the most time consuming and difficult of women's home factory work. The vegetables that graced the family table in January began as seedlings grown on window sills in March or in the garden as the weather warmed. Although gardens could be as large as two acres, tending them was generally women's work. Men often plowed them in the spring, and many helped dig potatoes in the fall, but the time in between belonged to the women, who were aided by their children. The seeds and tiny seedlings had to be planted and carefully tended. Children picked potato bugs and other pests; weeds were hoed out or hand-pulled. Some families with access to a dependable water source rigged up irrigation systems to help promote yields. In good years, gardens grown on irrigated ground produced tremendous quantities. One family sold 350 muskmelons in

Philip and stored others for home use. Housewives routinely canned dozens of quarts of vegetables and fruits. The fruits were gathered from the wild, grown with irrigation at home, or purchased. A Pennington County woman reported canning two hundred quarts of jelly, jam, and preserves one fall, as well as three to four hundred quarts of vegetables. The "Help One Another" column of the *Dakota Farmer* often listed recipes for a variety of canned goods, including regular pickles and pickled vegetable mixes and relishes, and recipes that made use of leftover garden vegetables, like green tomatoes, that had to be picked when frost was imminent.[11]

The task of canning and processing meat was more difficult than canning vegetables and had a greater likelihood of failure. Meat was the mainstay of the diet and required the greatest ingenuity to make it an interesting addition to the table. Salted meats had been the summer staple for centuries; the advent of home canning in the late nineteenth century allowed farm women to preserve more cuts of meat in a manner that allowed more choice in preparation when the meat was used. West river farm women worked hard to preserve their home butchered beef for the table in the face of changeable weather that threatened the meat's freshness. Several of them wrote to the *Dakota Farmer* to suggest methods that had worked well for them. Mrs. Hans Sorenson of Butte County advocated two boilers per household; since each held eighteen quart jars, a woman could process thirty-six jars at a time using the same fire. It only took a morning to cut enough meat to fill the three dozen containers. After a break for the preparation of the noon meal, the jars could then be processed in the afternoon. She argued that this provided a reasonable day's work. "You can get them done in the afternoon," she stated, "and still not be too tired to feel pleased over a day's work well done." The glistening jars stored on the shelf would make all feel "duly rewarded" for their efforts. Sorenson used a similar method for pork and chicken but did not remove the bones of the chicken. She wrote her letter in April 1923 and planned in the upcoming week to can more beef "in spite of the fact that I recently canned 38 quarts of pork and 26 quarts of meat balls (part beef) besides rendering 8 gallons of lard." Her family also enjoyed pork put down in brine and smoked pork. She corned beef every March but watched it carefully; if it appeared to be spoiling, she canned the remainder. Sorenson simmered any bones left from the butchering and canning process in her large granite dishpan in the oven and made a soup stock of their juices. That she canned as well.[12]

A west river woman from Perkins County, who signed herself only as "Grace," provided *Dakota Farmer* readers with her recipe for processed pork. Several days before her family butchered a hog, Grace began curing a barrel over a smoldering corncob fire. Once the barrel had the proper smoke flavor, it was put aside in a clean place to await the hog. After the hog was butchered and cooled properly, Grace cut the meat into strips, hams, or steaks and rubbed it with salt. She packed it into the smoked barrel and poured in a brine made of salt, brown sugar, saltpeter, and water. After ten days of curing, the meat was ready to eat. Grace also canned some of her pork after it had been properly cured.[13]

A third west river woman suggested an oven canning method that she said won her compliments. She cut beef, pork, chicken, sausage, or other meats into pieces, packed the jars, and put the lids on part way. Then she roasted them in a dry pan in the oven for three to four hours. When they were done, she filled the jars with boiling water and sealed them. "Everyone who has tried this way will use no other," she concluded.[14]

One of Jennie Haas's criticisms of the home factory system was the lack of variety in farm family diets. Certainly it was difficult to prepare meals from the same stock of supplies day after day without monotony. Most women writing to the *Dakota Farmer* argued that it was possible to have variety with home goods. It just took ingenuity and a large recipe file. Women generally cooked three substantial meals a day and prepared a morning and an afternoon lunch. If they had children in school, they had to pack a cold lunch or, in cases where the teachers prepared hot lunches for their students (a growing, although controversial, trend at the time), ingredients for the class's menu. In the fall they fed threshers, the biggest test of culinary skills. Cakes, cookies, and breads were staples for the farm table, along with the meats, potatoes, and vegetables. By the twenties fruit or vegetable salads were popular, although some farm women thought them too difficult or expensive to make for large families. While rural people tended to be traditional about their tastes in food, not all of it was dull fare. The *Dakota Farmer* recipes submitted as family favorites by farm women included a chow-chow liberally spiced with onions and hot red pepper, a special rabbit flavored with cloves, allspice, and laurel, and oyster and corn souffles.[15]

West river women cooked these meals on a wide variety of stoves. The old-fashioned wood stove remained popular. It could be filled with wood or corncobs. Kerosene stoves, oil burners, and gasoline stoves, many with easy-to-clean enamel finishes, were widely advertised. New stoves had temperature gauges, which allowed cooks to monitor their foods more closely and rely less on intuition and experience. Some stoves ran on more than one fuel, enabling farm families to switch to cheaper or more readily available fuels. The oil and gas stoves added an element of individual whim and comfort to cooking that the wood stove did not allow. The newer stoves had individual tanks for each burner. A woman could turn on just one burner and brew herself a cup of tea without firing up the whole stove. Cooking became a cooler activity and permitted people to satisfy their wants more easily.[16]

Keeping foods refrigerated was no easy task before the advent of Rural Electrification Administration–supplied electricity. Families with their own supply of ice could use the icebox, an upright wooden chest lined with metal with one large compartment for blocks of ice and one larger or several smaller compartments for food. To supply one of these with ice, farm families had to have an icehouse and a water source, such as a dam or pond from which to cut ice in January. Even with the best construction, 50 to 64 percent of stored ice would be lost to melting. Even with such waste, iceboxes were a better alternative than cellar, cave, or well storage, but many people had only that. Lack of refrigeration, of course, made meal preparation much more difficult.[17]

Although food processing and cooking involved many hours of hard work, other indoor jobs demanded attention as well. Washing clothes was especially difficult. By the 1920s gasoline engine–powered washers were available, but they were difficult to start. One woman occasionally exerted three hours of vigorous effort before hers would fire. By that time, the water she had heated was cold, and she had to reheat it and go through the process again. Other women had their husbands start the engine before they left for their chores or field work. The engines had to be placed at a distance or vented outdoors because of their dangerous fumes. Nonetheless, women with power-driven washers, however balky, were far better off than those without. Women used washboards well into the thirties. Others used hand-powered agitator washers that were only marginally better than the scrub boards. No matter what kind of technology was employed, water was the most difficult problem associated with wash day. Women who had to depend on rain water filling cisterns or water barrels might not have water when it came time to wash. Those with wells had to haul water in and haul it back out. It took between twelve and twenty-four pails of water to do the wash for a large family. Most wells were between seven and fifteen rods (115 to 248 feet) from the house. If a woman could carry two pails—or up to fifty pounds of water (six gallons)—per trip, the distance traveled might equal a mile or more, all before the washing started. Then, once the laundry was done, the water had to be carried back out and dumped.[18]

Doing the laundry, generally, was an all day affair. In the summer, clothes dried quickly on the line and could be brought in and prepared for ironing. In the winter, women had to wade through snow and brave cold winds to hang the clothes out, only to find them merely partially dry and as stiff as a board at day's end. The clothes then had to be hung indoors for several hours to complete the drying process. Family members had no choice but to dodge cold, clammy overalls and nightwear for a day or more. Only after the clothes were dry could they be ironed and put away.

Ironing was in itself a tedious and time-consuming task. In 1918 the *Dakota Farmer* asked readers to write in about their ironing techniques. Sixty-four farm women responded. Everyone labeled laundry chores a "problem and a big one," and almost all reported that ironing was among their most difficult tasks. Most farm women still used the infamous "sad iron," heavy blocks of metal with attached handles. The metal blocks were heated on the cookstove and applied to the clothes with vigor until the iron cooled. The changing nature of cookstoves affected the task of ironing. In the winter, when a fire was needed for warmth anyway, women heated their irons on a stove fueled with wood or coal; in the summer, when the last thing a kitchen needed was a steady, hot fire, women with the newer stoves could heat their irons with kerosene or gasoline fires which could be turned on and off easily.[19]

Very few farm women had electricity; the *Dakota Farmer* readers reported hardly any electric irons in use. Other types of self-heating irons
were employed, however. It was possible to purchase gasoline-, char-
coal-, and alcohol-powered irons, and some women swore by them.
Others complained that they were undependable. A west river farmwife
even wrote that she was "a little bit afraid" of her gasoline iron. The
self-heating irons required a high quality fuel to run properly. The liquid-
fueled irons included small reservoirs for the fuel; the burner was then
lit with a match. The charcoal-fueled irons were quite large, in order to
encompass the reservoir for the hot coals. In spite of complaints about
dependability, the *Dakota Farmer* "Home" column recommended gasoline irons as the best alternative for women without electricity.[20]

Many of the women urged readers to loosen their standards a bit
when it came to ironing, as a means to lighten their work load. D.B.G.
of Fall River County wrote: "Personally, I iron only shirts, dresses
and table linens, believing that the girls will need a mother 10 or
15 years from now more than starched and beruffled clothes today."
Mrs. E.M.L. of Meade County concurred. "I iron nice things that are
not in daily use and the Sunday clothes and the best of the everyday
clothes but nothing that is not worth wasting time and fuel on. . . ."
This represented a reduction in her standards, however. "Before my
family came, I used to iron even Mr. L's socks and overalls, in fact every
article in the wash." Some women still did that kind of ironing, according to the letters in the *Dakota Farmer*, but most seemed satisfied to
compromise. Women still allotted as much as six hours a week for ironing, depending on the size and gender distribution of their families.
(Girls' clothes required much more labor to iron.)[21]

Women's home production skills were also applied to clothing.
While men's wear was generally purchased ready-made, women frequently made their own and their children's clothing. The pressure to
buy ready-mades was there, however, and by the twenties women who
believed that their skills were lacking or that their time could be more
profitably spent elsewhere ordered their clothes from the mail-order
houses. The columns of the *Dakota Farmer* carried strong arguments
both for and against the ready-mades. Jennie Haas claimed that almost
all the women in her neighborhood now ordered their clothes because
the prices were low, yet the material was of good quality and the styles

Jessie and Marian Berry, Mellette County, 1920.

attractive. Haas believed such purchases were wise. "Those who buy the factory-made clothes admit that they fit and look better than did the old-fashioned homemade dresses. We do not realize just how grotesque many of the dresses we women wear are because crudely made garments are still the rule with us." A Haakon County woman agreed. She had been sewing for her two-year-old daughter, but the end product disappointed her. "As there is no more time for sewing I have had to buy some things ready made to keep us going. The ready-mades are tricky little things with much more style to them than I could put into the clumsy things I have made."[22]

Those on the other side of the question were sure that factory clothes were far more expensive than homemade and lacked quality. Mrs. Hans Sorenson of Butte County attacked the quality especially. "I have sometimes sent for ready made dresses . . . all too often they are so poorly made that one almost has to make them over to begin with or repair them in one place or another after each time they are worn." She advocated teaching all daughters to sew so that they could know "what service there is in a well-made garment" and "the comfortable satisfaction of knowing that it will not rip out or come apart while we are wearing it."[23]

For many west river women, the question of ready-mades was irrelevant. Poverty led them to cut corners in every way possible. Their skills and ingenuity at making something from nothing might mean the difference between survival and failure. These women used flour sacks for their own and their children's underwear, for tablecloths and towels, and sometimes for dresses and shirts. The same women made over men's worn overalls into children's wear and gladly took relatives' and neighbors' hand-me-downs and converted them into useful items for their own families. Mrs. A.F.A. of Meade County wrote: "We wear out our old clothes and what we are sent by near relatives. Then we pass on everything useable at all to neighbors with larger families and smaller sizes and trade patches and swap troubles." In 1921 the Marousek family in Meade County asked east river relatives for help. Not only would they miss their Christmas visit home because there was no money, but Helen Marousek "asked for old clothes she could make over for the girls."[24]

Housecleaning was another of the farm woman's duties. Techniques for handling cleaning chores varied from household to household. Some women devised a schedule of daily work and followed it except in cases of real emergency. Others were more flexible but still tended to do set chores on set days, even if they did not predetermine the hour of the day the work would be performed. A daily work plan incorporated into a weekly work plan helped organize the endless chores and led to occasional stretches of free time that a farm woman could fill with reading or other hobbies. Several women wrote to the *Dakota Farmer* to say that they timed themselves at their many tasks to see which took the longest or which were being done inefficiently, so that they could better manage their time and create realistic schedules for themselves. The work of efficiency experts in business and industry apparently influenced even those on isolated prairie farms.[25]

Housewives confronted many problems when they tried to maintain high standards of cleanliness. The close proximity of barns and animal pens meant that flies created a constant nuisance. Jennie Haas described the problem. "My kitchen is flyless in the morning but just let the beef begin to boil and the jelly to send forth sugary fumes and my screens are black with flies, and then the children come in for lunch and the men for dinner and, watch and scold as I will, before night I am canning in surroundings that would put me behind bars as a law breaker if I was canning for the general public." The problem was worsened by the custom of banking houses with used animal bedding, consisting of straw and manure from the barn, in the fall. Any bedding not quickly removed in the spring would attract flies in droves. In the early twenties the *Dakota Farmer* frequently cautioned against the use of unsanitary materials, which indicates that the custom was lingering. (Manure had other uses. One family in Meade County used a manure and clay paste to seal cracks in the outside walls of their home.) [26]

Bedbugs presented another problem for farm women, one that few families cared to admit they had. A letter from "Mother of Five" in Corson County raised the issue in the *Dakota Farmer* "Home" pages. "When we came to this place," she wrote, "I discovered that the house had bedbugs and I just must find some method of getting rid of them before they get worse with hot weather. It is just a shack house and the rooms are covered with building paper and lath." "Mother of Five" knew several other families with bug-infested houses, "but they said they wouldn't write, for they wouldn't want anyone to know they had bedbugs." Several women responded to her query in the next issues of the paper. Most recommended highly flammable remedies, kerosene and gasoline being most popular. Mrs. V.M. of Pennington County wrote to say that she had lived in three houses infested with bedbugs. After failing to eradicate them in the first two houses, she finally succeeded in the third, "but not until the beds, especially the mattresses were full of them, but I killed them, too." Her method was a popular one. "I just soaked every seam in the wall with kerosene. . . . Then I soaked the joints in the bedstand and the seams and tucks in the mattresses." Mrs. V.M. repeated this treatment weekly until the bugs were gone. (The use of highly flammable substances for pest control, as well as stain removal and sweeping compounds, may help explain the problem of home fires. Too frequently, a farm home would be swept with flames and all personal property would be lost, with no explanation of the cause of the fire. Flimsy wooden structures whose walls were soaked with kerosene or gasoline, whose floors were sometimes swept with sand and kerosene compounds, would have been virtual matches waiting for a spark.) [27]

Other housecleaning problems were related to the nature of farm life. Family members worked in mud or manure and tracked it into the small homes. In houses not yet modernized, water pails, wood boxes, and other necessary items cluttered the already limited space. Animal odors sometimes permeated clothes and hair. Fuel, like corncobs picked from the hog pen, perfumed the home when burned in the range. Poultry might be raised in the house if the spring weather turned vicious and chicks were hatching, or other young livestock might have to be warmed temporarily at the home fire. Even food processing could taint the air. Lard rendering was especially noxious. Although some liked the odor, others found it heavy and cloying as it clung to clothes and curtains. The lack of water and a sewer made cleaning difficult. A home expert in the *Dakota Farmer* urged that farm families devise some sort of system for garbage and water disposal rather than use "the ever over-flowing pails, which are so hard to keep even reasonably sweet smelling or clean-looking." Families dependent on ponds that dried or froze or wells that failed had no water at all for laundry or cleaning.[28]

Besides the endless round of indoor work, farm women also often worked outdoors. The poultry yard was generally under a woman's control, and many women did other barnyard chores and worked in the fields as well. There was no unanimity of opinion on the necessity of outdoor work. Some women loved it and gladly left their housework behind to help their husbands. Others refused to go beyond the boundaries of the garden and the chicken house. Individual desires and family circumstances dictated the level of outdoor work women did.

Poultry work, most commonly with chickens and turkeys, was still a woman's task on the west river farms of the twenties. Advertisements for various disinfectants or insecticides for poultry houses that appeared in the *Dakota Farmer* portrayed a woman using the product. The poultry columns of the *Farmer* featured letters from poultry raisers, frequently women, and also provided special features on successful growers, again frequently women. In February 1922 an article on the start of the new poultry season addressed itself to "many farm women." In the same issue, four women wrote to the poultry department about issues of concern to them as poultry raisers. In March 1922 the paper included complete instructions on turkey raising, illustrated with a picture of a woman's flock. Chickens provided food for the table, and their eggs provided a tradeable commodity. Farm families processed turkeys for the holiday markets in big eastern cities. The family worked together to kill and dress the flocks and shipped them by rail to market, which could be Chicago or New York or anywhere in between. Poultry production provided cash. A woman billing herself as "Survivor of 1911" urged farm families to add poultry production to their other endeavors. "See how interested your wife will be in making the eggs pay for what she would like to buy."[29]

Iola Caldwell Anderson remembered that her family's chicken house was a dug-out, built into a hillside to conserve lumber. The furnishings were makeshift; the family used poles for roosts and wooden boxes for nests. Their flock included several breeds and a multitude of colors. When chicken mites became a problem, the Caldwells used creosote to combat them, thinning it with water or lime. Laying times were most critical. A setting hen was secluded from the rest and given a dozen eggs on which to set. The hen had to remain on the eggs for three weeks, leaving the nest only once a day for food. At the end of that time baby chicks began to hatch.[30]

Turkeys were another cash crop for the Caldwells. They started the business with a gift of turkey eggs, which they put under a chicken. Turkeys take a week longer to hatch than do chickens, so convincing the brooding hens to stay and complete the task was not always easy. A few of the eggs produced turkeys the first year. The following spring the family bought a gobbler and began regular turkey production. Baby turkeys were kept dry and fed chick feed and cottage cheese during their first weeks. "After a few trials and errors, we discovered that turkey farming was not an unprofitable occupation. They supplied meat for the table, plus a few dollars to the income."[31]

The Marousek family in Meade County also raised poultry. Their farm was located forty miles from Wasta, the nearest railroad town. To get to town the family had to cross the Cheyenne River and traverse several steep hills on poor roads; therefore, the sale of their poultry products was difficult. In one of the letters to her family east of the river, Helen Marousek reported one trip to Wasta in mid-March 1921, in which they carried eighty-two dozen eggs and made twenty-five cents a dozen. In March 1926 she wrote about her turkey operation. Forty-six of the fifty-one birds had survived, but all had lice, and she had to powder them with an insecticide. At Thanksgiving time in 1928, the Marousek family, with the help of their neighbors, picked thirty turkeys and shipped them in three barrels to Chicago. They sold for $114. The next year the family earned $132 for thirty-two turkeys. In December 1930 Marousek wrote, "We dressed 48 old hens and roosters last week. Got $27.00. Express [shipping cost] is high." The Marouseks had sold some ducks for seventeen cents a pound and two old cows. "That's all we have to sell except a few eggs and a little cream and that's cheap," she noted. "Five gallons brings $3.13." Women's poultry and dairy work often made a vital difference in family finances during hard times.[32]

As far as other outdoor work was concerned, farm women decided whether or not to do it depending on their interests and circumstances. Some of them reported that, since their husbands helped them with the indoor work, it was only fair that they help outdoors. "Mother of Five" in Corson County wrote the *Dakota Farmer* to express her belief that women should help outdoors in the busy season. "If a woman is a true companion, I believe she will be not only willing but anxious to help with the milking, etc., I take great pleasure in it myself." She went on to note that the help was reciprocal. "When he is not so busy," she stated, "I enjoy his help in the house or in the garden; in fact my hubby can, and does, help with all kinds of the work, except, as he says, making the pies." "A Farmer's Wife" from Ziebach County argued that women should help outside. "I think every wife, if she be called wife, should help with the chores. It doesn't hurt any woman to help her hubby once in a while or oftener. I don't believe in a woman being too good to do outside work." A Lyman County woman who signed herself "A Farmer's Wife on Bull Creek" told of her three children under age five who filled her time handily but concluded, "I also help hubby do the chores and feel better for it — he helps me in the house and on wash days." Women helped with haying, bound and shocked grain, and plowed and disced the fields. The crucial issue appeared to be the limits on these endeavors. Women should help, the feeling was, but not be run ragged with outdoor work. A Haakon County woman stated it clearly. "I believe in women helping their husbands, but there is a limit to what a woman should do. I think a woman can milk cows and do a lot of little things on the farm and still be a lady. But I have seen women work until they look so worn and bedraggled that how they can even look or feel like a lady again is way beyond me, and I don't think that's right."[33]

On the opposite side of the question were those who believed that women had enough to do indoors with their homes and children and those who believed that it was not a woman's role to do outdoor work. The first opinion was most common. These *Dakota Farmer* readers did not think that it violated any kind of natural law for women to do "men's work" outside, but they argued that women's work indoors was the more important and demanded their full attention. They emphasized the need for care and consideration for growing children and leisure time for women to rest and read or do their hobbies for enjoyment.

The second point of view reflected adherence to rigid gender roles. A Perkins County man most clearly expressed this attitude about women's place. "I do not think a woman has any place in the barnyard. Her sole place is in the house and no place else. I would give the liberty to go out and gather the eggs at the chicken house if she desired to do so, or pluck flowers from her house lot flower plot but nothing more outside." He also held strong beliefs about his own place on the farm. "The man is the sole proprietor of the barnyard and whatever he has out there is his own business. The trouble is that most of the men have come to rely upon the women for everything and they have lost their backbones of responsibility." A Lyman County woman complained about a common hybrid of behaviors in rural areas. Men were perfectly happy to see women go beyond the boundaries of their gender roles but clung tenaciously to traditional definitions of men's work. She wrote: "There is many a man that wants the woman to do his work, yet when he comes in the house he doesn't want to do anything to help her with her work. He sits down to rest while she does the housework, and then when she is through she has to go out and help him again, and she never gets any thanks for it. It is a mistake to start to help."[34]

Farm women varied in their interest and ability to do outdoor work. For some it was a welcome break from indoor routine, while for others it was more drudgery added to an already heavy work load. Individual circumstances shaped attitudes and possibilities. Women with helpful husbands enjoyed helping in return. Even some of those without

helpful husbands believed their men to be more severely overworked than they were and were willing to do their part to alleviate
the load. In the worst of cases, wives did not feel understood and appreciated by their husbands. These women resented their situations
and were quite obviously unhappy with these circumstances. Each marriage was different. What was universal, however, was the sense that
women doing outdoor work were "helping" their husbands and that
men performing indoor tasks were "helping" their wives. Each gender
had its own distinct responsibilities, which were not diminished by
the fact that each sometimes needed help from the other to get the
work done.

Once children joined the family, women had the primary responsibility for their care. That entailed the usual tasks: changing, bathing,
feeding, and amusing infants and teaching growing children to become
responsible members of the adult world. Because farm families lived
and worked in the same place, both parents trained their children in the
necessary work daily by example. Both boys and girls did chores indoors and out from an early age. If the oldest children in the family
happened to be daughters, they helped with the outdoor work as well
as the indoor work. Many mothers worked hard to train their daughters to be good housewives. Women who had not had such training
in their youths wrote to the *Dakota Farmer* to encourage mothers to
teach their skills to their daughters at a young age. A Ziebach County
woman wrote to tell of her method of instruction. She felt that she had
been poorly trained in cookery and did not want to repeat the mistake.
"When [my daughter] was 10 years old I started her at making one dish
a day on Saturday during the school term and one every other day during vacation, the alternate day being given to some other branch of
housekeeping." The girl was now thirteen, and her mother proudly
noted that she could "cook and keep house better than many experienced housekeepers." The family planned to send her to high school
the next year. She would have to work for a town family to earn her
board, but her mother was sure of her ability. "I can confidently send
her into any home and feel that she can more than pay her way and at
the same time keep up with her studies." Similar training went on in
the Marousek family. Esther, the oldest, learned to sew at age six, to
care for her newborn brother at age ten, and to cook for her father

The view from the Berry home, looking south, Mellette County, 1920s.

at age twelve, while her mother stayed in Rapid City because of her troubled pregnancy. When Esther moved to Rapid City to attend high school, her services on the farm were sorely missed. She was able to use them in Rapid City, however, because she worked for a family there in exchange for her room and board.[35]

West river mothers confronted special problems that were linked both to their roles as producers and to the region of the country where they lived. The child-rearing ideas of the day emphasized rational, scientific approaches based on the developing field of child psychology. The experts defined the techniques mothers were to use, with the common theme being the vital importance of raising children correctly. There was a right way and a wrong way; mothers who did not place the proper emphasis on their children, understand their needs and fulfill them, would damage them, perhaps irreparably. Yet, how was a farm woman to find the time, amidst the production and processing of foods, the daily cooking, the separating of the cream for sale, the sewing, the laundry, the gardening, the egg gathering, and the outdoor chores, to follow the experts' advice in child care? The urban middle classes could afford to place the child at the center of things; farm families, especially in the west river country, could not.[36]

The distances of the region compounded the worry. Growing numbers of young people attended high school in the 1920s nationwide. Progressive farm families west of the river hoped that their children, too, could enjoy such advantages. But high school programs could be found only in the larger towns. Farm children would have to board away from home for nine months of the year. How could mothers instill the proper moral values in their children from a distance? How could they train children in the ways in which they should go? And how could these mothers teach their children to accept and even enjoy the hardships and privations of farm life when they spent so many of their formative years in town? Few farm children, especially the boys, attended high school because of the distance, the cost, the demand for their labor at home, and the problems of boarding. But for those who did and for their families, it was an important lesson in the social costs of space.

For west river farm women, the decade of the twenties was a time of challenge and change. The exigencies of the environment continued to shape their lives; the hard times of the decade sometimes stretched their resources to the breaking point. Their ability to make something from nothing or to make something into even more often kept the wolf from their families' doors. Yet the decade also challenged women's role as a fundamental factor in farm production. New standards of diet, dress, and housekeeping made thrifty homemade goods seem shabby and backward in comparison, out of step with the march of progress. Wondrous new technologies that promised to make farm life easier remained tantalizingly out of reach for most west river residents. Even their role as mothers was affected: new standards of education accentuated the inadequacies of local rural schools, and mothers with ambitions for their children would have to send them away at a tender age if they were to keep pace with the march of progress.

In spite of these difficulties and tensions, there remained a sense of deep satisfaction in a day's work well done. In the west river country, it was understood that empires were built one family, one farm, and one town at a time.

4

Not a Young Chicago

Kadoka's Main Street, 1920s.

KADOKA in the 1920s was a town caught, like the countryside around it, between its ambitions and its realities. Although the *Kadoka Press*'s editor freely admitted that the town was "not a young Chicago by any means," the people who lived there knew what a live town should be. They were well aware of the latest trends, ideas, and fashions in the world beyond Kadoka, and they did not want to be passed by. Kadokans did the best they could with what they had. The result was a community that blended the old ways with the new, combining disappointment and frustration with hope and commitment, and alternating between periods of torpor and vigor. As with all small towns, a few energetic, involved individuals disproportionately shaped the social world. The pillars of the community, men and women with a vision of the good life for all community residents, struggled to make Kadoka a better place to live.

Struggle was the continuing subtext in Kadoka's social world. The constant struggle for economic stability undermined community life in many ways. Kadoka was able, but barely, to sustain most of the important social institutions necessary for a satisfying community life. The severe economic disappointments of the early twenties, coming as they did after the hopeful months immediately after the war, created a kind of lethargy in the town. Organizations started with energy and hope, then languished or died. An occasional lone voice would call for resurrection, and a flurry of activity ensued; then malaise again would settle in. The only exceptions to this pattern were the women's organizations, especially those affiliated with the churches; they maintained an energetic and committed involvement in good times and bad.

Struggle was reflected as well in Kadoka's effort to be "modern." The term "modern" in rural areas did not so much mean urban or sophisticated as technologically advanced. A modern house was not one of the latest design but one of any style that had electricity and indoor plumbing. These amenities were associated with up-and-coming places, quickly becoming necessities rather than luxuries in more prosperous areas. Kadokans recognized that there were new standards for the good life — the ambition of residents in every town from Kadoka to Chicago — and that Kadoka did not measure up.

Another force shaping Kadoka in the 1920s was the town's cultural ties to the outside world. The modernization of American society generally was, of course, reflected in Kadoka life. Movies, radio, and the music and mores of the Jazz Age were all felt in the town, and all helped to make Kadoka a different place than it had been in 1910. Structural changes in American society, including the movement of women into the work force and the changing pattern of work in general, extended to Kadoka. The trend toward a more structured sociability also shaped Kadoka life. The informal, inclusive community of yesteryear was fading, and in its place appeared planned, exclusive activities that tended to project people into defined social rankings. Even school activities became highly organized; this was the era that spawned high school athletic and activity leagues, proms, class banquets, and parent-teacher organizations.

But in spite of the changes in Kadoka life, the town remained, in comparison with larger and older towns, a highly personal place to live. Anonymity was impossible in such a small community; the success or failure of an individual was known to all. The newspaper still reported illnesses and injuries, celebrated births and marriages, and mourned deaths and other misfortunes. For good or ill, individuals still had a place in the community. The town shaped their lives and they, in turn, shaped it.

Kadoka in the 1920s was still a young town. The railroad had reached the infant community in 1906. Kadoka formally incorporated in 1908. When Stanley County voted to divide into three separate counties in 1915, Kadoka was chosen as the county seat of the newly formed Jackson County, assuring its future survival. In 1910 Kadoka had 222 residents. In 1920 its population had grown to 341. By 1930 the town had 385 residents. When William Schwictenberg made his census count (slowed by an outbreak of the flu in town that closed schools and canceled public meetings), there were seventy-one married couples in Kadoka; fifty couples had children under eighteen living at home. Twenty-one couples had no children at home when the census taker called. Eight of the childless couples were under thirty and may not have started families yet. Another eight were over forty-five and may have had grown children living elsewhere. Several families included grown children living at home — seven had children over eighteen at home and two others had children over twenty-five at home. Sometimes widows or widowers lived with adult children; one man and one woman had adult children with them. Other relatives also figured in the lives of married couples — nine couples had mothers-in-law, nieces, nephews, sisters, or other relatives residing with them.[1]

Eighteen percent of Kadoka's population was single in 1920. Of that number, thirty-five were single men, including four divorced and two widowed men. There were twenty-seven single women in Kadoka; four were divorced and four were widowed. Four Kadokans, three men and one woman, were listed as married but did not live with their spouses. Two of the men lived alone, the third boarded at the hotel, while the woman lived with her twenty-six-year-old son and a seventeen-year-old grandson.

Like the town itself, Kadoka's population was still quite young. In 1910 55 percent of the population had been under thirty. In 1920 59 percent were under thirty, with another 16 percent between the ages of thirty-one and forty. Children under the age of eighteen made up 38 percent of the population; almost 10 percent were three or under.

The town was small by urban standards but competitive by west river standards. The shakeout after the great drought of 1910–1911 left Kadoka with two churches, one Catholic and one Presbyterian, an independent school district which gradually added all four years of high school, a railroad depot with regular stops by the Milwaukee Railroad, a Main Street in constant flux, and two banks. The depression of 1920–1921 destroyed both banks. The postwar insecurities also led to business troubles on Main Street; the drugstore, for example, went bankrupt and was sold by the sheriff in 1925. The rise of the auto as the main source of transport allowed residents to get the things they needed and wanted elsewhere, a fact that threatened the town.[2]

Sometime in the late spring or summer of 1928 an unknown photographer climbed to the top of the Kadoka grain elevator and snapped a portrait of the town. The handful of trees are in full leaf and grass is visible in the yards and on the prairie. Just a few cars are parked on Main Street. Perhaps it was a weekday. Farm families still shopped on Saturday, and their presence would have made the town look busier. Or perhaps it was early in the day and few residents or visitors were yet out and about. Although the town looks quiet and peaceful, Kadoka still would not have fit most people's notions of a midwestern farm town. Residences to the west of Main Street remained scattered, with considerable distance between some of them. There were quite a few more new residences in 1928, however, than there had been in 1910, and in the area at the north end of Main Street the houses were fairly close together, more like a traditional neighborhood.

The downtown area was filled with business buildings, wedged shoulder to shoulder, facing the street with false-fronted bravado. Almost all of them were simple one-story buildings. The two hotels each had two stories, as did two of the business buildings. Behind the stores were lean-tos, storage buildings, outhouses, stored equipment, and assorted odds and ends and junk. The lots for each business ran deep, finally ending in a narrow alley that paralleled Main Street. The poles and wires for the town's electric system followed the alley. It is easy to understand why the *Press* frequently waged strongly worded campaigns for community clean-up and modernization.[3]

As late as 1927 the editor commented that tar paper, "the swaddling clothes" of "every new western community," was still visible in the town. He hoped to "speed the day when the 'shack' ceases to be a home or the place of business." The editor urged clean-up days. In April 1927 he remarked that many storefronts were "eloquent testimony to the fact that paint has been high-priced." Storefront signs also hung unpainted and askew. The state fire marshall inspected the town in October 1928 and told the editor that the backyards and alleys in the business section were so clogged with refuse that he had to rank it among the worst he had seen. The *Press* requested that merchants solve the problem as a matter of pride and of practicality; insurance rates would rise dramatically if the marshall reported the mess. By November 1 the editor reported real progress in clean-up and repair.[4]

The residential section of Kadoka had much in common with the business district. Most houses seem to have been simple one-story dwellings with little ornamentation. Three two-story houses appear in the 1928 photograph, two of which were modified bungalows, the rage in the late 1910s and early 1920s. Several homes were painted nicely with contrasting trim, while others were unpainted and shabby. Yards still occasionally contained outbuildings for a cow or two and a flock of chickens. The C. L. Corrington family, for example, residents of the town's nicest home (an "eight room, up to date house, with bath and ample storage and closet space") kept a cow; their young son was injured while taking it to pasture one day when a dog startled the cow and it bolted, dragging the child behind. The *Press* occasionally ran notices warning Kadoka residents to keep their stock from running loose in town. There was enough roaming stock in town and on the nearby prairies that the town fenced its town park to keep livestock from trampling campers. Sanitation remained a problem. In another of its periodic calls for a clean-up, the *Press* provided specific advice for homeowners: "If every home was provided with a suitable place for depositing all garbage it would go far toward keeping down the number of flies which make life miserable for all of us. Another suggestion is that those homes which have 'outdoor plumbing' provide suitable covers and keep them in place."[5]

Residents tried to add beauty to their somewhat crude surroundings. While there were few trees (the 1928 photograph indicates only four within camera view), homeowners tried to beautify their yards as best they could. The *Press* praised these special efforts. The Roy White yard bloomed in glory during the short time White and his new wife (a florist's daughter from Rapid City) resided in town. The P. L. Simon yard drew accolades for its peonies and honeysuckle in 1928. Olga Rounds grew roses in her tourist park during the height of the drought, until vandals cut them down. The community hired a landscaper, Stamford homesteader and famed lilac grower J. W. Canney, to landscape the courthouse, and schoolchildren named and planted trees at the school yard on Arbor Day. It took incredible effort to grow things in such a dry and windy climate, but several people tried. "Plowing and making gardens" marked the arrival of every spring, along with other familiar activities — boys playing marbles, Indians camped on the edge of town, and the arrival of tourist cars on the streets.[6]

Electricity was the first modern innovation to come to Kadoka. The concept of electricity had been understood since the time of Benjamin Franklin and his famous kite; it took until the late nineteenth century to put electric power to use. In 1879 Thomas Edison created the first complete electrical system that managed electricity from the point of generation to the lighting of the bulb in the lamp. Edison Electric Company became General Electric in 1892. During the same decades, George Westinghouse perfected the use of alternating current, which was more easily transmitted than direct current over long distances.

The work of both men and their growing companies helped to promote the use of electricity, first in business and industry and then in homes. In 1912 only 16 percent of American homes had electric service. In 1920 34.7 percent of American homes (approximately half of the nonfarm dwellings) had electric wiring. By 1930 85 percent of town and city homes had electricity, although only 10 percent of farms were electrified. Women's magazines advertised the benefits of electric service, including bright, steady light in every room, cleanliness (no fuels to spill or dirty lamp chimneys to clean), and the convenience and thrift of the numerous small appliances that proliferated rapidly in the first two decades of the twentieth century. Irons, vacuum cleaners, and curling irons became the most popular household gadgets in the 1920s, but companies marketed a wide variety of items, including toasters, hot plates, and heating pads. With the advent of electricity, civilization moved one step farther away from the natural world and the rigors of hard labor. Few people looked back with regret. To have electricity was to be modern. To be modern was the hallmark of an up-and-coming family and an up-and-coming town.[7]

The creation of an electrical system provided opportunities for energetic entrepreneurs. In towns like Kadoka in 1920, electricity was a business, not a utility to be regulated by the state or local government. Kadoka's venture into the technological age began with the work of a new up-and-comer to town, R. N. Rounds. Rounds moved to Kadoka in 1918 after several years' work with an east river local telephone company and with Bell Telephone in Sioux Falls, in Utah, and on the West Coast. He was born in Tyndall, South Dakota, the east river town of origin for many pioneer Kadokans, and he had homesteaded in the area during the boom years before 1910 but left following the great drought. Rounds returned to town to operate the telephone company and from that business made the logical leap into another new technology, electricity. He became the local sales representative for Delco light plants. Delco individual light plants consisted of an engine run by kerosene or gasoline, a "dynamo," or generator, and several glass-enclosed batteries for the storage of generated power. These became popular in the late teens; several companies produced individual light plants and marketed them aggressively as the solution for problems of electrification on farms and in towns too small for the high-line wire connections to large central generating plants that urban areas could afford. J. L. White, a local hardware store owner, had the franchise for Alamo plants and had wired his two buildings and one of the local banks at the same time as Rounds began his work with electrification. Rounds's entrepreneurial spirit, however, allowed him to seize the day. In late June 1919 he began to build a powerhouse on Main Street, from which he planned to supply power for three businesses and one streetlight. By September he had wired several more businesses, and by November he had plans to do the entire town. His equipment at first consisted of one extra-large Delco generating plant. In March 1920 he acquired a second extra-large Delco plant and proceeded to solicit the residential wiring business. By July he was stringing wires to the houses at the north end of town.[8]

Rounds's energy and entrepreneurial spirit could not overcome the basic problems of his limited technology or the economic marginality of the town. Early in 1923 Rounds announced that he planned to discontinue all electrical service. His equipment had worn out and could no longer supply consistent power to his subscribers; he did not earn enough profit on the operation to buy new machinery. By this time, of course, those families and businesses served by the plant had become very accustomed to electricity.[9]

With great solemnity, the *Kadoka Press* noted the "grave inconvenience" to come. The demand for a dependable source of power moved the Kadoka town board to action. In February 1923 they voted to hold a bond election to finance a plant large enough to serve the town. This did not mean that the town planned to run the electric plant. Instead, the town leaders decided to sell the improved outfit back to Rounds, who would make the monthly payments on the bonds, the whole plan supposedly costing the taxpayers nothing.[10]

The voters approved the plan ninety-seven to fifteen, and Rounds began work on the improvements. Once the new machinery was installed, he promised, Kadoka would again have twenty-four-hour power. In the meantime, one homeowner and two large businesses installed their own private plants, apparently unwilling to wait for the promised improvements. The lack of dependable power tried the patience of all. The following week the *Press* published late because the electricity was off, and the backup gasoline-powered generator had also failed. There was no quick solution. In August the *Press* noted the need to keep oil lamps handy, and by September the editor lost patience. "This bull must be taken by the horns and so trained that our good people will know when they can expect to have light, and for how long," the editor complained, "so that we won't have to apologize to our visiting friends when the 'juice' goes off at nine or ten or any old time it pleases the arbitrary powers that happen to be." "Permission to dig post holes along the city street and string wires anywhere at all," he continued, "usually carries with it certain other obligations that are satisfactory to those who foot the village bills." The *Press's* editor concluded that it might be better for Kadoka to return to "the days of reliable kerosene lamps." Small town life being what it was, disagreements could become personal. A week later, when Rounds appeared in a new car, the editor remarked that he hoped it would make Rounds work faster.[11]

The problems with the light plant continued throughout the 1920s. In the winter of 1924 an engine exploded when a plant employee started up the machinery for its evening run. The resulting fire leveled the light plant and threatened adjacent businesses for a time. Both sets of engines and dynamos were destroyed, as was the auxiliary light plant used to run the moving-picture house in emergencies. Rounds suffered a terrible loss in the conflagration. The fire consumed $4,000 worth of equipment; he held only $1,500 of insurance. The town confronted serious hardship without the plant. "Kadoka is without light," the *Press's* editor despaired. "Just now the moon will have to do its full duty."[12]

The next issue of the *Press* contained a bold headline: "Kadoka Wants Lights." The story implied that the town planned to take charge of the electrification problem. A local committee had convened and begun to investigate the types of machinery that might provide good service to the town. They did not plan to rush their decision, the implication being that careful consideration and wise choices might have avoided the difficulties that Rounds had faced. The committee apparently never followed through. In March the *Press* reported that Rounds was doing his best to provide some power when he could and that he was tearing down the burned hulk of the electric plant to avoid injuring passersby. By April Rounds had begun to rebuild and had purchased a new Fairbanks-Morse engine. In May he resumed full production of power.[13]

The beleaguered Rounds sold the plant to Dakota Public Service in October 1926, and the *Press* announced plans for extensive improvements; there were hopes that the town's travails might finally end. By November that deal had fallen through because the company had been unable to find financing. The reason reveals the ongoing struggle that Kadokans would face in all of their public works. A Dakota Public Service expert had visited the town and reported too little business for the investment necessary to build a proper light plant. Rounds found himself back in charge. To improve service and undoubtedly to cut some of the intense personal criticism he had received, Rounds invested in two new engines and new generators. One engine, a twenty-five-horsepower Fairbanks-Morse semidiesel, was due shortly. The larger engine, a thirty-horsepower Hart-Parr, had already arrived, and workers were busily preparing its concrete base and a new building to house it. The *Press* reported, without comment, that Rounds believed that he would be amply fixed for power and could care for all the needs of the town once both engines were in place. Less than a year later he sold the plant to another individual and left the electric business in Kadoka for good.[14]

The new owner, James Craig, continued to have problems with the power plant, although the citizens must have become somewhat resigned to them. Occasional items appeared in the *Press*. In June 1928, for example, when the South Dakota Hardware Dealers Association met in Kadoka at the Hotel Dakotah, Frank Hafner, the hotel owner, strung his own special electric line because the lights had been going out unexpectedly. Finally in 1929 Craig built a new and very modern electric plant offering alternating current and the promise of dependable services for the first time. This plant included a larger oil storage tank for fuel and could put out sixty kilowatts of power, adequate for the town's needs, including any extra customers that would be gained by the addition of dependable service. Craig sold the plant to a St. Paul man, Paul Kerfoot, who owned a similar plant in Philip, in 1930. Kerfoot promised reduced rates in exchange for a twenty-year franchise with the town. The citizens voted to grant such a franchise but were disappointed with the outcome. By August 1930 Kerfoot had not lowered rates or improved service as he had promised. The *Press* urged its readers to demand action, to the point of refusing to pay their bills. The number of electric refrigerators in Kadoka was growing, but their owners were discovering that low voltage caused their motors to burn out; any electric machinery was "rendered useless" at low power. To add insult to the situation, July bills were higher than ever before. "No patron can be expected to pay his light bill goodnaturedly," the *Press*'s editor complained, "when he has to buy ice because he can't use his Frigidaire; light the gasoline lamp when he wants to read in comfort; and turn on the Victrola when the radio won't work — all because of poor power and light."[15]

The solution to Kadoka's light problems finally came with Kerfoot's sale of the local plant to Central West Public Service Company. Based in Philip, one of the larger west river towns, with a population of 786 in 1930, Central West shut down the local operation and ran a high line from the Philip plant to Kadoka to serve the town. The new owners then had the necessary customers to make a profit and provide good service. In late 1933 the *Press* commented that "our light service has been very satisfactory, and it is very seldom that it is interrupted."[16]

Another element necessary to the creation of a comfortable and modern town was a water system. Again, the urban world outside Kadoka was moving toward modern water and even sewer systems. Most larger cities in the United States had some kind of rudimentary waterworks by 1860. At the turn of the twentieth century, almost half of the U.S. population was served by some kind of basic public water supply. The wealthy, of course, had more sophisticated plumbing systems than did the poor. Indoor bathrooms and running water became common for the well-off long before 1900; the urban poor were lucky to be served by a single faucet and a dirty privy in a crowded tenement yard. Farm families dug their own wells or, in poor and dry areas like the west river country, hauled water from stock dams or the places of more water-rich neighbors. In towns like Kadoka, individuals dug wells if they could afford it, or they purchased water from the water-wagon man. In Kadoka in the early 1920s that was N. P. Nielsen, who lived in the north part of town and had his own deep well on his property. Nielsen sold water for 25¢ a barrel or fifteen barrels for $2.50. Residents then had to pump or dip it from their cisterns.[17]

In July 1921 the *Kadoka Press*'s editor urged the town leaders to try to market bonds for a local water system. Kadoka had been talking of such a system since the teens, but the depression following World War I stymied their efforts to find financial backing. Although the town voted to issue bonds, no one would buy them at the acceptable rate, and the water system idea languished. As the depression lightened, the *Press* argued at length that the city should try again to market the bonds. The people had voted for water, the editor noted, and the construction of the plant would provide needed jobs in a depressed economy. The summer had been dry and hot, and the *Press*'s editor believed that work as well as amenities were needed to encourage residents. "We want water," he concluded, "and what's more, we want every person who has located here and established homes to remain." [18]

The wishes of the town for the comfort and convenience of running water began to be realized in the summer of 1922, but their full fruition took time. In June 1922 the town board let the contract for construction. In October of the same year the bonds were issued, and the money finally became available. Work began the following summer, and in July 1923 the *Press* found it necessary to caution townsfolk to watch for the trenches in the streets; a horse had fallen into one and had been badly injured. By August, when the workers began testing water pressure, anticipation ran higher. "He who has lived in a waterless western town appreciates the fact when he can turn on the faucet and have Adam's ale forced into his drinking cup," the *Press* noted. On August 21, 1923, the workers filled the water tower for the first time. Although not all service mains were laid, the contractor hoped to finish that job within weeks, which would allow residents to begin tapping into the system. In September the contractor finished the system, and town officials accepted it as properly completed. Individual property owners began to tap into the system at once, a practice the *Press* encouraged because it would shorten the time during which the streets remained disrupted. The paper listed the families and businesses tying into the system. It seemed as if all the troubles were over and Kadoka could take its place among the modern and progressive towns of the state. [19]

Of course, it was not that easy. The waterworks created nearly as many problems for residents as electric service had. The first problem developed in January 1924, when the entire system froze in a cold snap. Apparently the heating system installed to protect the pipes connecting the tank and the underground mains was defective and allowed the conduits to freeze. Kadoka had to do without water until warmer weather arrived and the burst pipes could be thawed and replaced. (It was during this time that the electric plant exploded. A water system worker had to run a mile and a half to the well to supply direct water for the firehoses.) By mid-March the problem had been solved and a working stove installed to heat the pipes when the weather turned cold.[20]

A more difficult problem developed in the summer of 1925. The wells dug to provide water for the town's water system began to run dry. This introduced a problem that became chronic. By November 1925 three wells had been dug, but drought dried them up. The water superintendent planned to dig a fourth. In May 1926 the town board issued a notice requesting water conservation because of dry weather and increased demand. In June the *Press* headlined an "alarming water shortage" as increased use, hot, dry weather, and poor flow into the wells reduced the amount available. "Just as we are getting thoroughly used to the convenience of a city water system," the *Press* noted, "we are confronted with a scarcity." By November 1926 the problem was acute, and residents offered suggestions at a town meeting. Some urged that mains be laid all the way to the White River, eight miles away. Others requested short-term solutions that could be implemented immediately at minimal cost while plans for the White River project were developed. The major roadblock to the White River plan was money. Kadoka was deeply in debt, and any major project would cost more than the town could afford. The town board appointed a committee to investigate both plans.[21]

The town tried to solve its problems by digging more wells. The plan was temporarily successful. In May 1927 the town board told water customers to go ahead and use as much water as they wished because there seemed to be plenty. But the summer of 1928 brought another shortage, and town leaders called for bids for a new well to be drilled on the Nielsen place. In March 1929 the *Press* declared the new well "a good one." It, along with two other wells in operation, allowed the water superintendent to pump 10,000 to 12,000 gallons a day. The solution to the water problem was temporary. The extremely dry years of the 1930s caused repeated problems. In 1934 the town went completely dry. The Milwaukee Road hauled in free water from Rapid City to fill Kadoka's needs.[22]

In spite of the ongoing difficulties with city services, life proceeded apace in Kadoka. Each family had its own routines which fit into the broader scheme of the community. Daily life had much in common with life in 1910; at the same time, signs of modernity were visible. The lives of both men and women incorporated elements of the old and the new.

Married women's work at home in Kadoka varied according to the circumstances of each family. Two worlds existed side by side. Women without modern services like electricity and city water followed old patterns. Those fortunate enough to have modern services, such as they were, were able to buy appliances to lighten their work load and enjoy conveniences that made life easier and more comfortable. Electric refrigerators, for example, replaced the old iceboxes in some homes. Iceboxes had worked fairly well when there was a good supply of ice, but in the 1920s the local ice seller frequently ran low of block ice by September. Only businesses could be supplied; private homes had to do without. Electric refrigerators solved this problem but created others when electric current was too weak. Maytag washers, equipped to operate either with electricity or with gasoline engines, were popular. The local dealer ran ads listing recent purchases, and many Kadoka families were included. This may have added more work to some women's schedules and deprived others of employment. Before the advent of the home machines, the town had supported local laundries, and it was not uncommon to pay to have the laundry done in someone else's home.[23]

Food production remained primarily women's work. Canned goods were readily available, but home canning continued. On one occasion the *Press* noted that most families were gathering fresh fruits from the prairies, which the women converted to jams and jellies. Another social note indicated that local women were engaged in canning apples shipped in by the train-car load from Rapid City. Many families had gardens and ate fresh produce in season and probably canned surplus for winter use. Farm women sometimes believed that town women led lives of ease, but letters to the *Dakota Farmer* from hired girls in town or town women themselves refuted that notion. Only a few town women "lived out of tin cans." Most gardened and processed much of their own food and cooked from scratch.[24]

Some homes had hired help to assist with domestic chores. Generally these hired girls were young women of high school age or a bit older. Sometimes families took in country girls who did household work in exchange for room and board while they attended high school. This allowed the girl to receive an education and the family to receive help with the domestic work load.[25]

More married women worked outside the home, at least on an occasional basis. In 1920 the census taker indicated that seventy-one married women were housewives, with fourteen of these holding paying jobs as well. The fourteen women ranged in age from twenty-two to sixty; six of them had children still at home. One woman, Gertie Corrington, ran the abstracting business so necessary in a county seat town; her children were six, four, two, and seven months. Her husband was a teacher at the school in 1920 and later held other positions in the town, including postmaster. She continued to do the abstract work until the family moved to Custer in 1940. The county treasurer, Ida Sharon, had a seventeen-year-old son and a six-year-old daughter at home. The *Press* reassured people that she had not sought the office out of any need for personal gain but had been drafted by the public. (It was Ida Sharon's death from typhoid in 1920 that started her husband, Otto, on the road to suicide.) The telephone operator, Olga Rounds, had an eight-year-old son at home, but the switchboard was very likely in or near her house. Her husband was the ambitious modernizer, R. N. Rounds, who brought electricity—sometimes—to Kadoka.

The other married women with children included a cook with eight- and six-year-olds, a hotelkeeper whose fourteen-year-old son was still at home, and a private-duty nurse with two older teenagers, one seventeen and one eighteen. The married women without children included three teachers, a stenographer, the assistant cashier at one bank, a cook, a waitress, and a salesclerk at the drugstore.[26]

The 1920 census provides only a snapshot of Kadoka women's work in that particular year. The decade to follow saw increasing numbers of married women enter the workforce, at least occasionally. There is no systematic way to chart these somewhat informal changes, but a close reading of the *Press* furnishes evidence. Small towns being what they were, the newspaper noted the comings and goings of its residents. If someone was ill, injured, or on vacation, a substitute worker might fill in, and the *Press* told its readers about the event in its social notes. From these social notes, it is possible to gather information about married women's employment.

The *Press* social notes provide numerous examples of women at work. A listing of school personnel in 1922 included the names of Mrs. Ira Johnson, an assistant principal, and Mrs. C. J. O'Connor, Mrs. J. C. Steele, and Mrs. F. L. Hafner, schoolteachers. Mrs. Johnson was married to the county agent, and Mrs. Hafner and her husband, Frank, owned the Hotel Dacotah. Mrs. Steele's husband's employment is unclear. She had a diverse career in Kadoka, sometimes teaching, occasionally operating a confectionery or a notions store, and ultimately ending up as editor of the *Press* in the 1940s. Mrs. O'Connor's husband was the school principal. In 1923 Mrs. O'Connor and Mrs. Hafner returned to the teaching staff, joined by Mrs. Woods, Mrs. Carlisle (an attorney's wife and former county school superintendent), and Mrs. Zimmer, wife of the new editor of the *Press*.[27]

Many women assisted their husbands at work. Eva Brugman retired as assistant postmaster to help her husband run his new café, although she occasionally returned to the post office to help out. In the February 6, 1925, issue of the *Press* the social news noted her work at the post office. In the February 20 issue the social notes included the birth of a daughter to the Brugmans that week. Mrs. P. L. Simon worked in her husband's meat market and grocery; her absence due to illness was noted in October 1925. Mrs. Fryberger worked in Fryberger's store from 1916 on. A replacement clerk filled in for her while the couple went on vacation. (Mrs. Fryberger also kept boarders throughout the twenties but usually had a hired girl to help.) The wife of a *Press* editor, Lucille Morrison, helped with the production of the paper and later became its editor for a short time while her husband was employed in the Black Hills. Her work was mentioned because she was injured when her dress caught in the shaft of the gas engine that ran the press. Her name later appeared on the masthead as editor with her husband, L. C., named as publisher. Examples of this sort can be found in almost every issue of the *Press*.[28]

A few married women went into business for themselves. In addition to Mrs. J. C. Steele, mentioned previously, there were others. Mrs. Frank Hafner opened a ladies dress shop in a building next to the

Hotel Dacotah in 1925 and cut a door in the wall to connect the two businesses. Mrs. A. S. White, wife of the local "land man," traveled to Sioux City to learn "beauty culture" and opened a shop upon her return. Mrs. J. R. Fowler operated the Home Cafe for a time, and Mrs. James Craig opened her own electrical appliance store, an appropriate business for her since her husband ran the electric plant in town. Mrs. Coye, whose husband farmed for many years but became an oil dealer in 1925, operated a millinery.[29]

The two Margulies women owned a large department store and ran it together while their husbands, who were brothers, engaged in over-the-road sales of Delco light plants and Frigidaire refrigerators. These Jewish families came from Sioux Falls. They purchased the store from Bertha Martinsky, a Jewish divorcée in business in Kadoka since 1916. At least one of the Margulies women had hired help at home; the *Kadoka Press* noted a replacement helper filling in while the usual hired girl vacationed. Martinsky took the store back in 1929 when the two Margulies families moved away and reopened it with the help of her daughter, Sara Hoffman, who became a pillar of the community active in a variety of endeavors.[30]

Other married women worked as temporaries on an occasional basis. Mrs. O. E. Stuart had to take a leave of absence at the bank, so Mrs. Corrington filled in for her. Mrs. Bob LaBau clerked at the Home Trade Store while it held a closing-out sale, and Mrs. Fowler worked at the Margulies store for several days while Mrs. Rumsey worked at the Tourist Cafe the same week. Many jobs appear to have been temporary positions, and women moved in and out of the work force according to demand and their own needs.[31]

Many unmarried women in Kadoka worked to support themselves. According to the 1920 census, there were seventeen single, divorced, or widowed women who held paying jobs. (The remaining twelve lived with family members and did not work outside the home.) The working single women ranged in age from a seventeen-year-old butter packer to a sixty-four-year-old private-duty nurse. They worked in a variety of occupations. There was a horse rancher, a nurse, a retail merchant, two assistants to county officials, the postmistress, two teachers, a dressmaker, a stenographer, a telegraph operator, a bookkeeper, and three salesclerks.[32]

Single women who held paying jobs rarely lived alone. Bertha Martinsky, the merchant, lived with three of her adult children on Main Street, probably in her store building. The sixty-two-year-old horse rancher lived with her daughter's family in their hotel building. The forty-eight-year-old dressmaker had her own home on Main Street; her niece, a salesclerk, lived with her, and the bookkeeper boarded there as well. The postmistress lived with her brother's family. One teacher and the telegraph operator lived at the hotel, while the other teacher, a fifty-six-year-old divorced woman, lived in her own house with a male boarder, a twenty-one-year-old "machinist," or mechanic at the garage. Four of the younger workers (the twenty-year-old salesclerk at the drugstore, the eighteen-year-old stenographer, the eighteen-year-old assistant register of deeds, and the seventeen-year-old butter packer) lived at home with their respective parents. The older county deputy, the forty-four-year-old assistant to the treasurer, boarded with the Fryberger family. The Fryberger hired help, twenty-two-year-old Carrie Olsen, lived in the Fryberger home as well. Only the sixty-four-year-old widowed nurse lived alone. She owned her house, free and clear of mortgages, on East Street.[33]

Throughout the decade of the twenties single women continued to work in Kadoka in a variety of occupations. A single woman was the office manager for the Weaver oil well project near town, and another single woman managed the White Eagle service station owned by her brother. Single women also held courthouse jobs. In the 1920s a single woman served as register of deeds for two terms before quitting to marry, and another served as county auditor. In the late twenties two widows served in county offices, one as register of deeds, the other as clerk of court. A woman usually held the county school superintendent's job as well, although the holder was not always single. Only one man held the office in the 1920s and 1930s, S. C. Edwards.[34]

Several young women left Kadoka in pursuit of further education or training. In 1923 the Presbyterian Ladies Aid and the Sunday school gave a farewell dinner for the young women departing for school or embarking on careers. Three of the young women planned to attend normal school to become teachers; two others would pursue degrees at Yankton College. One woman had just completed pharmacy school at South Dakota State College in Brookings and was starting a permanent job in a nearby town. Her sister, also honored at the dinner, became a missionary to Venezuela. In addition, in 1923 the Presbyterian minister's daughter moved to California to go to law school; two years earlier, another daughter had departed for Persia as a missionary. In 1926 a young woman moved to Minneapolis for "beauty culture" training. In 1929 a local telephone operator quit to go to nursing school, and the next year the daughter of a local farmer graduated from nursing school and returned to Kadoka to marry.[35]

The world of men's work had also changed by the 1920s, but for different reasons and in different ways. Men still worked in the kinds of jobs they had always filled, but changing technology provided more work and created positions that had not existed in earlier generations. The automobile and the truck played vital roles in the new world of men's work.

The 1920 census provides important perspectives. The largest category of work in Kadoka for males, married or single, was transportation—people and/or goods on the move. Twenty-five men, or 24 percent of those employed, worked for the railroad, on road building, in hauling or transport of goods, in the provision of oil and gasoline, or in the repair of automobiles and trucks. Retail and service occupations outside of transportation were each filled by sixteen men. In 1910 only 16 percent worked in transportation fields. The transportation business continued to grow in the twenties. Tourism became big business. P. L. Simon, who ran the meat market, built Camp Joy, the first paid tourist camp in South Dakota, in 1926. Other camps followed, as did the gas stations needed to fuel the tourists' cars. The world of men's work provided new opportunities for those with an entrepreneurial spirit and an eye for the future.[36]

The married men in Kadoka tended to be the owners, managers, and professional men in the town. Twenty of the sixty-six married men who still worked owned businesses, whether it be a store, a dray line, a livery barn, or an auto repair garage. Seven men managed the affairs of others; the lumberyards, for example, were chains with local managers hired by a distant company. Six men were professionals—doctors, lawyers, ministers, or teachers. Two were county officials, and four were in service occupations, such as life insurance sales or real estate. Ten of the married men were farmers or ranchers who lived in town.

Seven were salesclerks, and seven worked in such trades as carpentry or masonry. Only three married men were laborers.[37]

Employment categories were reversed for single men in Kadoka. Only five single men owned businesses, and that total includes two brothers who ran a restaurant for a short time and an elderly widower who ran the hardware store. Fifteen single men, or 44 percent of the total who worked, were employed as laborers. Three of the single men worked in professions (one was the Catholic priest whose work, of course, bound him to celibacy), eight in the trades, and three as clerks. Unlike the single working women in the town, however, almost one-third of the single working men (32 percent) lived alone. The remainder included nine men (aged eighteen to twenty-six) who still lived at home with their parents, three who boarded at the hotel, four who boarded with families not their own, and three who lived with their brothers. Two young men were farm laborers who lived with their employers. One forty-two-year-old hardware clerk lived with his widowed father, the store's owner. A sixty-five-year-old widowed house painter lived with his thirty-five-year-old single daughter; she did not work outside the home but kept house for him. Most of the single men who worked (almost 68 percent) were under thirty and working their way up to independence and better careers. Five of the laborers were over forty, however, and would very likely remain laborers. One of those, a sixty-six-year-old janitor at the courthouse, had been a veterinarian and important town leader in 1910 but was rarely mentioned in the *Kadoka Press* in the 1920s.[38]

In 1926 the *Kadoka Press* profiled the owners or managers of Kadoka's "progressive business houses." There were forty-six businesses, six run by women. The list of occupations illustrates the wide diversity available in the town in spite of its small size: a barber, a baker, two men who worked at the doomed bank, a hardware store owner, a druggist whose brother owned the drugstore in Murdo, a café owner who also did taxidermy, three lawyers, two hotel keepers, a railroad agent who also operated a truck line, a radio dealer, a butcher, two service station owners, a road contractor, two abstractors (one of these was a woman, Mrs. Corrington), a notions store owner, a lumberyard manager, a movie theater operator, two cream buyers, a pool hall proprietor, a bricklayer, a Standard Oil agent, a painter, two dray line operators, two general merchants (including Bertha Martinsky), a cattle buyer, a grain elevator manager, a milliner, the owner of a women's dress shop, two auto repairmen, several men with automobile franchises, a doctor, and a dentist. Some of the men wore more than one hat in the business world. Three men sold real estate, for example, but two of them did it in conjunction with insurance sales, auto sales, and cream buying. Not all men owned their businesses but instead represented larger companies or acted as managers. Both cream buyers worked for large companies as, of course, did the Standard Oil agent and the railroad agent. The elevator company was owned by local farmers and run by a board of directors who hired the manager. Some of the businesses reflect the transitional nature of the era. The dray lines used horses. In fact, Roy Dunmore advertised that his horses could easily extricate stalled autos "on dark stormy nights." Yet the two service stations, the auto franchises, and the presence of a local Standard Oil manager reflect the ongoing trend toward mechanical power. The radio dealer was the son of the frequently excoriated R. N. Rounds, owner of the electric plant. Hunt's Hardware also advertised radios, as did the drugstore. All three radio dealers offered installment purchase to make radios affordable to all.[39]

As in earlier years, Kadoka's business proprietors came from a variety of backgrounds and moved in and out of their occupations with some frequency. Frank Hafner, the proprietor of the Hotel Dacotah, for example, had previously been a barber as well as a rancher. The local painter, James Judge, had been "in the meat business," operated ranches for a while, and now painted and decorated Kadoka buildings. Several businessmen began as homesteaders. Only six of those in business in 1926 in Kadoka had been in similar positions when the 1910 census was taken, and only fifteen had been in Kadoka in 1920, although not always in the same business. At least eight other businesspeople, including two women, had resided on homesteads in townships near Kadoka in 1910. Those in business in 1926 did not necessarily remain where they were. P. L. Simon, owner of the meat market, opened a pay tourist camp and service station in 1926 and operated them in addition to his market. J. H. Fryberger opened a second store in the town of Wanblee. A. S. White, the "land man," moved away, as did B. L. McNally, another real estate broker, Morris Adelstein, engineer and son of Bertha Martinsky, and O. O. Snowden, the baker. The bakery opened and closed several times in the 1920s and 1930s; it was apparently difficult to sustain the business in a town of Kadoka's size, perhaps because Kadoka women continued to bake at home and the bakery could not compete. The business community continued to greet newcomers with open arms and say fond farewells to those who moved away or failed in business. It seemed as though there was always a new business or two ready to open, to fill empty buildings, and to try to make a go of it where someone else had failed or had grown tired. Even in the 1930s, businesses opened while others closed, as hopeful entrepreneurs searched for new starts.[40]

Businesses continued to be open long hours in the 1920s, continuing the tradition of earlier years. Farm families began their day early and ended it late; should they want supplies or parts, businesspeople wanted to be available to serve them. Saturdays remained the traditional shopping day for country folk, and stores might stay open until midnight or later, if customers continued to come. Many stores opened on Sunday for a short period at least. Business owners worked side by side with their hired help, although they had more flexibility in their schedules should they have other obligations. Men who were active in the local commercial club (when it functioned) might travel to a neighboring town on its business, and those with an interest in the school often took time to haul students to speech or music contests or athletic events. In their absences, family members or hired help kept the business running. People in business in Kadoka tried to adopt new techniques and carried new products to attract customers. Their businesses took much of their time and energy, yet those who owned them continued to be active in community life as well.[41]

The social scene in Kadoka was organized around the churches, the school, and formal social groups such as the various lodges or the women's clubs. It had much in common with the social structure of earlier years, but there were important signs of change. The churches remained mainstays of Kadoka culture but could not and did not live up to the hopes of the town's founders. Kadoka had two churches in the 1920s, a Catholic church and a Presbyterian church, and for a few years German Lutheran services were conducted by a rural minister at the schoolhouse. The Lutherans never acted as part of the community but seemed to have held services in town for its convenient location only;

Kadoka's Main Street, August 5, 1940.

their announcements of services offered cordial invitations for all, but they had no social gatherings or fund-raisers. They were quite active in the rural districts, however.[42]

The Catholic church was a strong presence socially, but little of Catholic religious life made the papers. Father Daley lived in Kadoka and offered mass regularly in town as well as in one or two neighboring communities an hour or two after the conclusion of the Kadoka service. A brief note of the mass schedule appeared irregularly in the *Kadoka Press* over the years. When Father Daley left town for extended visits to his family home in New York, Catholics apparently had no regular service. Father Daley seemed to be well liked; townspeople regularly entertained him for dinner. He, in turn, was interested in the community and offered scholarships for good students at the Kadoka High School.[43]

The most visible Catholic presence in Kadoka was the Catholic women's organization. At first the women called their group the Altar Society and sponsored events under that name, but in 1923 they organized themselves as the Ladies Guild and sponsored a variety of social events under the new auspices. Catholic women were an important factor in the social life of Kadoka. Every year they held a lucrative autumn bazaar and dinner to raise funds for the church; in 1920 they made $200 on the bazaar and the movie they showed in conjunction with it. In 1926 they cleared $400. During the remainder of the year they were responsible for a series of dances and card parties that drew a large attendance, as well as occasional food sales or dinners to mark occasions like St. Patrick's Day. The *Kadoka Press* greeted their activities with enthusiasm, and the events were widely attended. On one occasion the *Press* noted that the bazaar had been "patronized by practically everyone in the town and county." When the Ladies Guild events offered prizes, winners included Protestants as well as Catholics.[44]

The Presbyterian church had a much more visible presence in the town, and in the 1920s it was a church beset with internal difficulties. On the one hand, the church seemed to be on more stable financial footing than in previous years. Since its founding in 1908, the Presbyterian church had been dependent in part on funding from the national Presbyterian Board of Home Missions. In 1919, however, local finances were strong enough that the Kadokans themselves took up a collection to aid other Presbyterian churches that were unable to support themselves. Shortly after this, the Kadoka church was paired with the Presbyterian church in Interior. Pairing meant that the two churches shared a minister and therefore the expenses of his upkeep. The pairing of the two churches allowed both to be independent of the Board of Home Missions, at least briefly. Reverend Bryan noted that this "reflects great credit on the community considering the present financial straits."[45]

The pairing with Interior, however, caused dissension within the Kadoka congregation. Reverend Bryan had to serve both churches; because Interior was thirty miles away over rough badland roads, he could not preach in both towns on the same day. On the Sundays that Bryan preached in Interior, the Kadoka church had to make do with Sunday school and a service of some sort prepared by the congregants themselves. In 1925 the presbytery changed Bryan's assignment from the Interior and Kadoka churches to Belvidere and Kadoka. The pairing still required considerable travel, which meant the minister would be absent for worship half the time and would miss important religious holidays in Kadoka when he had to be in Belvidere. The situation apparently generated deep resentment if Bryan's pleading notes to his flock are any indication. He apologized for missing important services but tried to make his absence a virtue. Because he was not there, he maintained, the congregants had to take more responsibility for their worship, which was good for all. In several notes he argued that the success of the Kadoka church was due to his absence. On other occasions he chided his parishioners for their resentment of the situation.[46]

In 1926 a new minister came to the Kadoka church. Reverend Bryan, whose wife had moved to California in 1923 to live with a daughter attending law school, reluctantly gave up the post and moved west. The new minister also served Belvidere and for the first years resided in Belvidere. Although Kadoka residents did not like the arrangement, they had to learn to accept it. They were a dependent church, beholden in most years to the Board of Home Missions for financial aid.[47]

The Ladies Aid affiliated with the Presbyterian church was a happier organization. The women of the Ladies Aid worked hard to raise money for their church and to provide edifying sociability for themselves. They, too, had an annual bazaar and dinner and regularly conducted food sales, dinners, and other fund-raisers to outfit their church building properly. Their organization was stable and well run. Every month the *Kadoka Press* reported on their meetings and attendance ranged from twenty-five to sixty, depending on the weather and the location of the meeting. The country meetings were always the most popular; once or twice a year a rural member entertained the Aid on the farm and drew the largest numbers. Aid meetings took a variety of forms. Some were strictly social, others were devoted to sewing or quilting projects, and others were business meetings. The hostess, assisted by two or three others, always served a lunch of at least two courses. The money that the Ladies Aid earned went back into the church. In 1929 the women fixed the church basement and made repairs to the parsonage; in 1930 they reshingled the roof and redecorated the interior.[48]

An important offshoot of the Ladies Aid was the Missionary Society. This group usually met monthly. Any offerings collected or money raised from food sales or other activities went to mission work overseas. The program often revolved around foreign countries or "exotic" religions (the women studied Mormonism, for example). The Missionary Society was in reality a study group that acquainted its members with the broader world beyond the confines of the west river country.[49]

The school also played a central role in the life of the community. Its primary purpose was, of course, to provide a sound education for the youth of Kadoka and the surrounding area, but in doing so it provided a focal point for community attention and pride. (The conditions at the school were still primitive, even in the twenties. In 1922 the school janitor threatened to shoot stray dogs who were eating students' lunches stored in the hall. Also in January 1922 it was so cold in the building that the high schoolers exercised to keep warm; they "danced so hard that the lid [on the Victrola] fell and broke our favorite record.") The high school was especially important in this respect; high school students played on athletic teams, participated in music or speech activities, and sponsored the year-end ceremonies, such as the junior-senior banquet, which became a tradition during this era. The Kadoka school district employed only seven teachers during the 1920s. The accomplishment of the variety of tasks for a full extracurricular calendar required parents and interested members of the community to volunteer their time. Kadoka residents provided that help and seemed to enjoy the opportunities for interaction that school activities offered. The *Press* covered school events in great detail, and during most years each issue contained a half page or more of school news, consisting of short pieces written by representatives of each grade describing their progress and fun. But interest in the affairs of Kadoka youth did not automatically translate into interest in the management of the school. Very few contests for school board seats developed during the decade, and only a handful of people voted. By the mid-twenties women began to run, and it was not unusual to have women filling two of the three board positions and the clerk position as well.[50]

The school activities included both boys' and girls' athletics, an oratorical and field day contest, plays, an annual carnival, and the May activities surrounding graduation, including banquets, baccalaureate, and commencement. The sports teams provided several evenings of entertainment for the town each year, but there was no official league yet, and the schedule was irregular. Both boys' and girls' teams played on the same day to minimize transportation problems. Very often men from the town took time off to drive the young people to a neighboring town to play. If the teams were to play in Kadoka, local women's groups like the Ladies Aid made sure that the visiting teams were properly fed. The same patterns were followed for music contests, held in Rapid City. People from the town helped haul and chaperon students to and from such endeavors. At one music fest, the Kadoka students had been the only ones without uniforms, and a town drive began to insure that such an embarrassment would not occur again. Throughout the twenties there seemed to be a considerable commitment on the part of Kadoka adults to make their school a good one and to give their young people the attention they needed to grow into responsible adults. The paper helped the process along, urging residents to participate in the school and to make the new teachers feel at home.[51]

There were other important formal organizations in Kadoka that, while not as large as the churches or the school, still played important roles in making Kadoka a good place to live. The strong lodges provided both men and women with opportunities for sociability. There was also a women's club federated with a national system of women's clubs and two new organizations that ultimately became important forces in the life of the town, the American Legion and the Legion Auxiliary. The lodges continued a venerable American tradition of ritual and sociability. Kadoka had three sets of lodges: the Masons and the Order of the Eastern Star; the Modern Woodmen of America and the Royal Neighbors of America; and the Odd Fellows and the Rebeccahs. In each set, one lodge enrolled men and the other lodge enrolled mainly women, although the women's groups sometimes included males in their hierarchy.[52]

These sets of lodges tended to plan activities together and on occasion invited the public to attend. Early in the decade, a group of Masons calling themselves the Cinosam Club (Masonic spelled backward) organized public dances and held card parties. The Woodmen and Royal Neighbors sponsored an occasional dance or home talent play, as did the Odd Fellows and Rebeccahs. Lodges continued to mature in Kadoka in the 1920s, and many members of the community found their lodge activities to be fulfilling and worthwhile.[53]

The Women's Club was organized on September 29, 1922, and devoted itself to the education of its members. According to the *Kadoka Press*, "although the ladies are somewhat hampered as to numbers in a community of this size, nevertheless this lack is made up by cooperation and determination to carry out a program worthy of towns of far larger size." Their programs were ambitious. In 1924, for example, they planned papers on state government, the drug menace, conservation, fine arts, medicine, and home economics. Each meeting included a roll call organized around a theme, and most featured a musical number. The members included the wives of all the prominent businessmen (some of whom owned businesses or worked at least part-time themselves), the county school superintendent, and the county auditor. They took their mission of uplift very seriously. In 1926 Kadoka residents heard rumors that the railroad was mistreating its black and Mexican workers at a nearby railroad camp. The *Press*'s editor and several representatives of the Women's Club visited the camp to make sure that the workers were properly fed and housed. They reported good supplies of food and comfortable living quarters for the workers.[54]

The American Legion and Legion Auxiliary were new organizations created after World War I by veterans (or by their female relatives and friends in the case of the Auxiliary). Kadoka-area veterans organized their post in June 1919, the third such post in the state. Twenty-three men joined. The Auxiliary began operation in 1920. The organizations soon played an important role in the community. The Legion sponsored commemorative ceremonies on Memorial Day and Armistice Day, planned dances, and performed home talent plays for large, appreciative audiences. The Auxiliary served lunches at these events and generally aided the local post, while also working to help veterans everywhere. By early 1924, however, the post's energy had begun to flag a bit, and the meeting notice in the *Press* urged all to attend the next meeting with their dues in hand to "make this a real post." The *Press* continued to report successful Legion social outings, such as a picnic which attracted three hundred people, and social service activities, including the clean-up of the cemetery where Legionnaires filled in sunken graves and performed basic maintenance. In 1925 the organization apparently failed completely and disappeared from the columns of the *Press*. The following year L. C. Morrison took over the editorship of the *Press*. He had moved to Kadoka from Sioux Falls and as a veteran had a strong commitment to the Legion. With his strong leadership the Legion was reborn. The Kadoka post had lost its charter because of the prolonged period of inactivity but was granted a new one in December 1926. The Legion began again with twenty-eight members. The Auxiliary also came back in full force.[55]

The second organization of the Legion proved more successful. The Legion again took a place in the leadership of the community. Its officers in 1927 included an auto mechanic, the editor of the *Press*, an engineer, two local attorneys, the state banking official who lived in Kadoka for several years while he managed the assets of the area's many failed banks, and the one-time sheriff and local ballplayer who now farmed. The post organized a series of popular old-time dances, raised funds to benefit the baseball team, and provided a lively Fourth of July for the town. The Legion remained a strong force in Kadoka life well into the thirties, when it aided Red Cross relief efforts. The Auxiliary took on a life and importance of its own in the late twenties and into the thirties. The women met regularly and, as the crisis of the Depression broke upon the community, worked to alleviate suffering and distress, while maintaining their traditional interest in veterans residing in federal medical facilities.[56]

Beyond the organized and structured social life of the community existed an informal social world in transition. Kadoka remained a small town and its residents continued to follow traditional customs, but new ways and new ideas also emerged. Two important factors changing Kadoka's social world were movies and radio. Both of these new forms of entertainment required almost nothing of those who partook but their attention. Kadoka residents were more and more likely to be the audience rather than the performers as the twenties and thirties went on. When radio first arrived in Kadoka in 1922, people gathered around the few sets to listen in some amazement. As more individuals purchased sets for their homes, radio parties became common, with proud hosts demonstrating the variety and distance of the stations their radios could receive. After a nice lunch the guests departed full of wonder at what they had heard.[57]

Movies arrived in Kadoka in 1919 when Sever Texley decided to remodel the Scenic Theater to show films. (Prior to this date, traveling film outfits occasionally entertained Kadokans.) The Scenic was never truly successful. The owners had difficulty getting the best films, and the theater was closed for long periods. New owners would give the business a try but close again after a period of months or years. Yet films were a popular form of entertainment. *Press* social notes indicate that

Kadokans sometimes traveled to Philip to see the popular releases. When the Catholic Ladies Guild showed the western *Under Crimson Skies* as a fund-raiser, Kadokans turned out in large numbers. The Scenic's troubles may have been a combination of the town's small size and the Hollywood film distribution system of the time. Theaters signed up with a company like Paramount and had access to their films only. With a limited audience to deliver, the Scenic's owners might not have been able to contract with the better film production companies.[58]

The modern world intruded in other ways. Cards and Mah-Jongg parties, popular nationally, became popular in Kadoka as well. Social gatherings in the town became occasions for card playing. Card clubs with exclusive memberships, such as the Triple H Whist Club, formed and met regularly for social evenings around the card table. Women had their own nights out, playing cards at friends' homes. Jazz, the music of the twenties, wailed across the prairies to Kadoka. The trend toward jazz was not universally popular, however; in the fall of 1926 the town held a series of old-time dances, "back by popular demand." The dancers waltzed, square danced, or two-stepped to the local orchestra, while the women of the lodges served lunch. Large crowds attended, apparently pleased to hear "no saxophone sobs, or wailing trombones or trap drummers." Yet R. N. Rounds's Roof Garden dances, held on the dance floor he created on the roof of his auto repair business, also attracted large crowds that danced happily to the Henegar Orchestra of radio station WOAW in Omaha and other modern bands. In 1928 several Kadoka businessmen, following the national trend, formed a golf club and built themselves a course. Women bobbed their hair, shortened their skirts, and wore makeup. A beauty parlor opened in 1922 advertising that hair bobbing was the owner's specialty. Kadoka adults worried about "the boy problem" in town. Bored youths had vandalized the post office, leading the *Press* to call upon parents to reassert control. Within a month, the town organized a Boy Scout troop and shortly after that a Campfire Girls unit. Adults, too, had their peculiarly twenties' problems: one Kadoka businessman died and another became critically ill when they drank bad home brew. The circuit court held in Kadoka heard illegal alcohol cases routinely in the 1920s.[59]

Problems related to illegal alcohol in the area apparently led to the arrival of another peculiarly twenties' phenomenon, the Ku Klux Klan

(KKK). In 1925 the *Press* decried secret KKK meetings held at the Presbyterian church in Kadoka, and the Cottonwood social notes reported similar gatherings there. The *Press*'s editor spoke forcefully against the organization of such a group in the area. "Believing that we live in a free country," he wrote, "with a government of, for and by the people, there appears to us to be no room for the invisible empire, which operates as plaintiff, judge, jury and executioner, according to their own standards. . . . The *Press* sincerely hopes that this meeting may prove the first and last meeting of the hooded organization here."[60]

The KKK disappeared from the news very quickly; it is not clear whether they disappeared from the area completely or just went underground, out of sight of the watchful editor's eye. The Kadoka area was not the only west river region to entertain KKK notions; in Fall River County there was enough KKK activity to justify the manufacture of the characteristic white robes. The organization was short-lived, and the robes were stored away and forgotten. In the 1930s someone remembered them, and local women converted them into band uniforms for the high school.[61]

The styles, fads, trends, and social problems of the decade all made a mark on Kadoka. The town's residents probably suspected that their glorious future was already behind them. Yet they strove to be cosmopolitan and modern, unaware that achieving those goals might destroy the one thing they had going for them: a sense of community.

Kadoka in the twenties was shaped by forces largely outside its residents' control. The economic disaster of the post–World War I years shook the town to its very foundation, undermining confidence in the future and making it difficult to pay for improvements or to support the institutions necessary in an up-and-coming town. New standards for the good life established in faraway places much wealthier than Kadoka set the tone for the decade; Kadoka tried but often failed to measure up. Most fundamentally, however, Kadoka's problems, like those of the region, stemmed from underpopulation. There were too few people to do the work, pay the bills, and build the institutions every empire needs. For Kadoka in the 1920s, space was the final frontier.

5

The Social Costs of Space

Highway 18 in Shannon County, 1940.
Library of Congress, courtesy of the South Dakota Archives.

The people in this country have been disappointed so many ways and times and are so far from what is doing power.

— "West River Mother," Perkins County, *Dakota Farmer*, July 15, 1922

ONE OF THE fundamental problems confronting the west river country in the twenties was space.[1] There was too much of it—between farms, between towns, and between the region and national centers of power and influence. At a time when rural people were migrating to the cities by the millions and the national trend was centralization and consolidation in the economy, social institutions, and cultural expression, west river residents marched in stubborn opposition to the general direction of social change. They inhabited a land of blank space. This had not been their intention, of course; they had hoped to fill the empty places with farms and trees and good neighbors working together to build an empire. Although their dreams of empire had been seriously damaged, west river people continued to insist that they could conquer space, could bind their homeland with rail lines, telephone lines, roads, and bridges, and make it a comfortable and attractive place for the prosperous society they still believed could be built there. One of the most important struggles of the twenties was to combat the effects of space, distance, and isolation.

All west river residents incurred the social costs of space, but farm families, especially in inland areas at great distances from the railroads, faced the most difficult circumstances. Roads in the west river country were often primitive; in 1925 56 percent of farm families lived on "unimproved dirt" roads, which meant ungraded, undrained, and unmarked trails. Thirty-nine percent lived on "improved dirt" roads; this meant that the roads were graded but the surface was made of whatever nature provided. Only 0.5 percent of farm families lived on gravel roads. As late as 1933, when emergency government agricultural extension workers came to the area, communication and travel remained difficult and sometimes impossible. The agent assigned to Jackson and Washabaugh counties reported "few good roads in the District. . . . Washabaugh County has but 10 miles of all weather road . . . the remainder being gumbo." He could not reach his clients efficiently by mail because carrier service was not daily but three times weekly. So many lived away from mail routes that he could only contact them once a week or less, 93 when they came into town or to a post office and picked up their mail. Telephones were of little help. The agent reported that "very few farms in Jackson County have telephones." Washabaugh County was worse; that reservation county had only one telephone line, "a government owned one from Wanblee to Pine Ridge."[2]

Such impediments to travel and communication made it difficult for farm families to take products to market. The Marousek family lived in Meade County. Frank Marousek, a Czech-speaking butter maker from Wisconsin, homesteaded forty miles from the railroad in 1908. He and his wife, Helen, remained on their farm until 1946. Isolation and bad roads figured largely in their lives. The nearest town was Boneita Springs, a tiny inland hamlet seven miles away. The store there purchased cream (for its butterfat content) but at three cents less a pound than at Wasta, the nearest railroad town. The family sold most stock and crops at Wasta. Conditions of the roads, and the depths of creeks and rivers, governed the whole neighborhood's ability to trade. The events of late winter 1920 were indicative of the problems. Esther Marousek Letellier, the couple's daughter, summarized family letters from the period: "Spring thaws made the roads too muddy for cars and there was no mail for a long time when the river couldn't be crossed. The winter supply of flour was used up and flour had to be borrowed. . . . There were 14 fat hogs ready for market but roads and weather were too bad. The corn was gone so Frank fed the hogs ground rye and soaked barley, which wasn't very fattening." There were other problems as well. "The horses were about played out," Letellier recounted, "and there was no grain to feed them and there wasn't any available to borrow or buy. Frank needed more wire and posts to finish fencing and he couldn't fix the well [which had caved in] until he could get in town for lumber." The problems with transport were continual. Again in 1926 there were thirty fat hogs ready to sell and no way to get them to market. This time the neighbors were also out of food and coal as well and could not get more to tide them over. Occasionally a big loss occurred due to the delay. One year a hog died before the roads became passable, and the family lost the income it would have brought.[3]

Distance complicated other aspects of rural life west of the river. Health care was often difficult to obtain. The Marouseks, for example, lived forty miles from the nearest doctor. Another Meade County woman, who signed herself Mrs A.F.A. when she wrote to the *Dakota Farmer*, told of farm families in her county who were located "50 to 100 miles distant" from medical services. (She also wrote of "several thousand good citizens who need churches and schools, dentists and doctors, and just the common decencies of life which self-respecting people require.") Major accidents or illnesses required long trips to Rapid City, Pierre, or Mitchell for treatment. Doctors in the nearest towns might do the initial first aid work but referred most complicated cases to hospitals with better facilities.[4]

Childbirth was among the most common reasons that west river families sought medical care. In the isolated areas of western South Dakota, childbirth was made more difficult by long distances to doctors and hospitals. Many women gave birth at home with the help of a midwife, while others called a doctor who might deliver the child with the aid of a trained nurse, a midwife, a neighbor woman, or the husband. Other women went to stay with their parents or in-laws for the delivery or boarded in town homes for several days or even weeks before the due date to insure access to medical care.

Dr. George Mills practiced medicine in the Wall area starting in 1919. Obstetrics was an important part of his practice. He pioneered the kitchen table delivery in the region, which was greeted with some reluctance initially but quickly won acceptance. On several occasions bad roads slowed the doctor's trip, and he arrived after the birth: one family called too late during a dreadful winter, and Dr. Mills gave instructions for the delivery to the husband over the phone. The young father delivered the baby "with everybody on the thirty-mile party line listening in." In another case the doctor had to perform a "vaginal caesarean section" for a woman who was six months pregnant and in convulsions. A neighbor woman administered the anesthetic. The woman survived, but the baby died three days later.[5]

That doctors did their best to provide modern medical care to their obstetrics patients under primitive conditions is illustrated by a Kadoka-area case. Although sexual or reproductive topics were discussed only obliquely in the columns of the *Press*, it is clear from the coverage of the crisis at the Petersen farm that Dr. Hennings of Kadoka had performed an emergency caesarean on Mrs. Petersen. A doctor from Rapid City who was in the area with his nurse assisted, as did the doctor from

Cottonwood. The doctors performed the operation at the Peterson home on a makeshift operating table. The *Press*'s editor remarked that the mother's life was saved for her family by the doctors' actions, a fact that was "gratefully appreciated by the members of the community at large." Despite the doctors' efforts, the baby died.[6]

For most women, childbirth experiences were not as traumatic. They were worrisome, however, because of the poor roads and long distances. Families had to plan ahead to avoid being trapped at home with no help when the baby came. Women who already had children had to make arrangements for their care because a stay away from home to give birth could easily last a month. Frank and Helen Marousek had their first child after Helen underwent a three-and-a-half-hour labor at home. The nurse, who charged twelve dollars for her services, arrived only fifteen minutes before the birth. Helen wrote east river relatives that "we liked her fine." Although she was feeling well, the practice at the time was substantial bed rest of two weeks' duration. Helen wrote on December 10, 1914, that she had nine days left to stay in bed. Their second child was born in 1917. "I was alone when the baby came," Helen recounted. "Frank went to Strongs' as soon as I got sick (4 AM) so Harry could go after the nurse with the car but they were all gone so he came back. I knew he wouldn't have time to go 8 miles with horses so he was going to get Mrs. Rogers and Mrs. Haphner." When they were not at home, Frank went to another neighbor's home and told them to go help Helen while he took the team to the nurse's home. The baby came ten minutes before the neighbors arrived. Frank brought the nurse sometime later, and the Marouseks paid her five dollars, although "she didn't do anything." For the birth of the third child, Helen traveled to Rapid City, five or more hours away, depending on the condition of the roads. A neighbor took the two other children for the duration of her absence. She boarded at a home near the hospital for twelve dollars per week, which was fifteen dollars cheaper than a hospital room. After a five-day wait, the baby was born. Helen returned home shortly before Christmas after an absence of a month. She followed the same pattern for the birth of her fourth child in 1924. In 1926 when she was pregnant with her fifth child, complications developed, and she spent two weeks in Rapid City under a doctor's care. The baby was stillborn three months prematurely. Eight days later Helen returned home. Two years later, when pregnant again, she planned to go to Rapid City for the birth but did not make it that far. She delivered the child in the doctor's office in Wasta. Her final baby was born in 1931 at home while Helen was alone. A neighbor arrived shortly after, as did a nurse.[7]

Space and distance complicated the services of other social institutions as well. Attendance at high school was becoming the norm in urban areas, at least among the middle class. In the west river country, it was extremely difficult for young people from the farms to attend. Not all towns had high schools, and farm families often lived too far from high schools to allow their children to attend while living at home.

The alternative living arrangements were not very appealing. The student could board with a town family in exchange for household help. This worked best when the town family was already acquainted with the student's family and the situation. Oftentimes it was impossible to board with someone familiar, and the child had to work for strangers. Another alternative was boarding teenagers together without adult supervision. A third option was also used: the mother and children rented a room in town, and all of the children attended the town's school. The husband-father and any other children not in school stayed home to tend the farm. Sometimes neighbors of such a family sent their children to board with the mother and children in town, and in this way more students could be accommodated in a well-supervised way. Towns often suggested that dormitories be built to house rural children, and this was done with greater and lesser success in the thirties, with substantial government aid.[8]

The boarding system caused great hardship for families and the students involved. Esther Marousek was desperate to attend high school, although her parents needed her help at home. She stayed in Rapid City with relatives of some neighbors and attended the Rapid City high school. "It was a traumatic experience to go from a one-room rural school with two classmates and only 14 in the entire school to a class of 125 who were all strangers except one." Esther was able to return home for occasional weekends but only when the weather was good. It was sixty miles from the Marousek farm in Meade County to Rapid City. The second year she boarded with the Walter McDonald family. The McDonalds were strangers, but after Esther's parents met them and discussed the boarding proposition, they agreed to let Esther stay. "I liked it," Esther remembered, "and didn't have to work too hard for my room and board." The next year she was much busier. She boarded at a local doctor's home and cared for his children. Esther's final year of high school found her again at the McDonald's, living in a basement room because the family had two long-term guests staying with them. She had more work to do because of the extra people in the house, but the "McDonalds were very good" to her. "Mr. Walter McDonald even took me to school functions, to the library and to church." Trips home could be difficult and time consuming. After a Thanksgiving break in 1931, "Dad had to do a lot of shoveling to get us back. . . . The trip to Rapid took five hours. When we went home for Christmas the roads were terrible, and we made a lot of detours." The commitment to her education paid off, however; Esther graduated from high school in 1932 and enrolled at Spearfish Normal School that fall.[9]

The Batterman family of Pennington County also faced the problem of advanced education for their children. They lived five miles from the nearest high school in Wasta. Two of their children rode horseback to and from school every day for part of their high school careers. One daughter, Frieda, lived with her older sister, who worked at the Wasta bank. The two girls rented an empty two-room building and "did light housekeeping." Mrs. Batterman sent food for them every Monday and did their laundry on their weekend visits home. The second year of school Frieda took a job in a local restaurant to help with her support. She arose at 4:45 A.M. each morning in order to begin work at 5 A.M. She worked until 8 A.M., attended school till noon, worked a half hour at the restaurant at midday, and returned there again to work for three hours in the early evening. In exchange for this labor, Frieda received her tips and ate her meals for free. She graduated in 1931.[10]

That the practice of living away from home was common is indicated in the social columns of the area newspapers. The *Bison Courier* mentioned students, families, or parts of families moving in or out "to provide high school for the children." The *Kadoka Press* carried similar notations and, on one occasion, a more complete story. When William Porch graduated from Kadoka High School in 1925, the *Press* gave brief biographical sketches of William and his three classmates. His story illustrates the lengths to which some families went to educate their children. William had been born in Jackson County on a farm six miles from town. In 1910 his parents moved to Washabaugh County to ranch. He attended three years of school in Kadoka, then had "drunk from many fountains of knowledge." The young man attended school for one year in Missouri, spent one year "at an Indian school on the reservation," an unspecified amount of time at the Garner rural school, and several years at Philip, returned for his junior year back at Kadoka, took a year off to help his father on the ranch while his brother, Cy, finished school, and then returned once more to Kadoka to graduate. The *Press* praised the parents "who are this willing to skimp and sacrifice that their children may have an education better than they were able to secure for themselves." The Wanblee correspondent even noted the change in that town when May arrived and all of the winter residents in for school departed for their homes. In 1922 the Red Cross nurse stationed in Bison examined the high school students and noted that 43 percent boarded away from home to attend. (She urged the school district to provide bathing facilities for the boarding students because none of them had bathrooms and went the entire school year without once sitting in a bathtub.) [11]

At a more informal level, space and distance complicated social life. Farm families had to be willing to travel long distances to socialize. If it rained or snowed, roads and trails became difficult to navigate. Social notes often mentioned bad roads preventing attendance or the surprise of large attendance in spite of bad roads. It wasn't unusual for people to become lost when they tried to travel after dark. The correspondent to the *Kadoka Press* from the Brady neighborhood reported in March 1925 that a number of people planning to attend a Farmers Union meeting at a rural school got lost on the prairie and wandered for several hours before finding their way home. The writer urged the county supervisors to authorize some roads for the area, so travelers would not have to depend on trails. After a snowstorm, Kadoka-area residents resorted to horse-drawn sleighs to travel; the paper reported them "almost lost." The *Timber Lake Topic* noted "several lost" en route home due to the snow and the dark. [12]

It was not only farm families that struggled with distance. Inland towns had their own unique set of problems. As towns, they were supposed to offer a set of services: marketing and trade, education, worship, and even medical care. But located at a distance from the railroad,

Scattered farmsteads in Dewey County, 1942. Library of Congress.

their abilities to provide the services that people expected was limited. The cost and difficulties of transportation meant imported goods to be resold cost more, while farm products purchased for export fetched lower prices than in railroad towns. Even social institutions suffered. Camp Crook was located four miles from the Montana border in Harding County and sixty miles from a rail line. Bad roads often made life difficult. The spring of 1920 was very wet and followed a snowy winter. In late April a local freighter returned to Camp Crook with only a few hundred pounds of goods after a rugged two-week trip. His trucks were unable to carry more because the roads were too thick with mud. By the end of May prices in the town had skyrocketed. The local newspaper editor reported gas at sixty cents a gallon, potatoes at fifteen cents a pound, butter at eighty cents a pound, and eggs at seventy-five cents a dozen — exorbitant prices at the time. "Pay it and smile, smile, smile," he concluded. "They'd be higher if they came by airplane." In the same issue he told of "great excitement" in Camp Crook over the arrival of a freight truck carrying food. "Four quarters of fresh beef proved the greatest attraction for a meat hungry community, and two cutters and several assistants were kept busily engaged until the last scrap had been carried away."[13]

The events of spring 1920 may have been extreme, but that transportation problems were a constant is revealed by the Catholic priest's note to Camp Crook. He served mass at St. Ann's in Camp Crook the third Sunday of every month at 10 A.M.; however, "if the roads become impassable during the winter months, the priest in such circumstances will not attempt to come to Crook." The priest would answer sick calls if parishioners sent word; they were also to notify him if they needed a wedding or baptism service.[14]

It might appear that the railroad towns had the tools at hand to conquer space and therefore did not suffer the disabilities of the more isolated farms and inland towns of the region. Certainly they had the rail lines, and the railroad was a key ally in the effort to defeat distance. The leaders of the railroad towns, however, alternately loved and hated their corporate benefactor. Town leaders and merchants recognized their dependency; without the railroad they would be nothing. Yet they also displayed a strong sense that the railroad was betraying them through poor service and failing to help them in their fight to build stable, viable communities and therefore defeat space. The railroads, for their part, saw their operation as a business; they were interested in their own empires, not the hopeful empire of the west river people. After the drought of 1910–1911 destroyed the homesteading boom, it became obvious to the railroads that there would never be a large market in the west river country. The railroads thus cut back their services to the degree they felt was appropriate to the regions' long-term real potential. Town leaders believed that such limited service made the railroads' bleak forecast a self-fulfilling prophecy; without the full service granted to more populated areas, the west river country could never become a more populated area. Both parties were right according to their own perspectives. What resulted was a long-term struggle that was won by the automobile and truck—new players in the game.

The struggle to win better service and overcome distance began as early as 1912. Towns along the branch line of the Milwaukee Road between Mobridge and Faith filed a complaint with the state railroad commission about the poor service. Town leaders requested "a daily passenger and mail train, which would be able to get in on scheduled time," and a freight run two or three times a week. They didn't win that battle, but the railroad made concessions; the towns then withdrew their complaint. In 1914 the railroad asked the state railroad commission to allow them to reduce passenger service to three times a week. Town leaders were livid. James Stewart of the *Dupree Leader* reacted angrily: "After enjoying the prosperity incident to the opening of these reservations, they now propose to disregard their promises and the welfare of their patrons, many of whom came to this country as a result of the Milwaukee advertisement and have almost struck hard pan now." Stewart recounted the miserable service of the past (on one occasion it had taken "FOUR HOURS" to go twenty-two miles, while at other times "passengers were crowded into dirty and unsafe coaches" that "would not stand inspection") and railed at the betrayal implicit in the corporation's efforts to reduce service. "The company is unwilling to take the chances with the settlers . . . and seek to add to the hardships . . . by taking off half the train service."[15]

By 1916 the *Leader*'s editor could only resort to sarcasm alternating with plaintive appeals for respect and justice; his sense that the railroad really wanted to abandon them completely was growing. Stewart referred to the train as "our moveable bundle of scrap iron"; it had not come to Dupree for four days. He speculated that it was resting from its "terrible exertions," which had brought it to town six hours behind schedule in the recent visits. After four days without service, "the Mobridge authorities suddenly remembered us . . . and sent the snow plough lumbering down at 5 A.M." There was no snow, however. "A mythical snow drift would, therefore, seem to be as solid an obstruction as a real one," Stewart concluded, "as no train comes under either circumstance. It looks as if the railroad company was only too eager to seize upon any excuse . . . to deprive us of such service as we have." Two weeks later, when there was no train for five days, Stewart acknowledged that snowdrifts might be an obstacle but wondered "why we have to wait so long for the services of a plough or rotary." He argued that the settlers' efforts to build up the country "should win for us the favor of the company rather than their contempt."[16]

Rail problems continued after the World War I boom. In July 1920 the *Camp Crook Range-Gazette* reported that towns on the Faith branch of the Milwaukee Road planned to petition the railroad for better service because, as it was, the Milwaukee was retarding progress and growth. The Chamberlain to Rapid City main line of the Milwaukee also had its share of problems. Communities along the line resorted to almost continuous petitioning for better service. The primary complaints were the poor bridge at Chamberlain, which washed out at every sign of high water, the poor schedule, and the coupling of freight and passenger cars together into "mixed" trains, which west river residents found an affront to their dignity.[17]

The bridge at Chamberlain had been a horror story since early settlement. Passengers were still forced to cross on foot during high water as late as 1924. When the bridge washed out, as it seemed to do at least once a year, mail, freight, and passengers had to wait on the east river side or find alternate routes. Mail arrived late, and the post office had to open at odd times to distribute it. (Wagons and, later, automobiles, crossed the Missouri by ferry.) In 1923 the counties served by the Milwaukee main line decided to issue bonds to finance a decent highway bridge. Jackson County was the first to offer $10,000 to the cause, although Jones County argued that they should have the honor. In September 1925 the new bridge was dedicated with great pageantry, including a reenactment of Custer's last stand. West river residents thus circumvented the railroad to solve a long-standing transportation problem.[18]

Other problems were not easily dealt with. The railroad apparently made too little money on its line to offer the best service. In the summer of 1919 the *Kadoka Press*'s editor resorted to an uncharacteristic outburst of rage at the Milwaukee. Calling it "the damnable thing we are now given for a train service" and "the present hog train," he complained: "With the present service a passenger must travel with hogs and cattle, in cars hardly equal in comfort to those of the stock, and must stay over at Murdo, and if he can secure a bed at that place, all right, and if not, he can be damned." On another occasion he applauded the development of a mail stage between Kadoka and Philip to expedite service, a remedy required by the "toothpick bridge at Chamberlain" and the "Milwaukee teakettles getting stuck in snow banks." In 1921 the Milwaukee Road announced a new, more limited passenger schedule of one train each way, every other day. The success of even such abbreviated service "depended entirely upon the ability of the teakettles to pull the imitation coaches into Rapid," complained the

Press. The next year the railroad requested a further reduced tri-weekly service schedule. The *Press*'s editor was ready to give up. "If an arrangement such as is asked for by the Milwaukee is the best they can do," he said, "the outfit had better tear up their rails and let Henry Ford's Flivvers give us some real service"—a jeer that turned out to be a prophecy. In 1923 the paper noted the presence of the Milwaukee Railroad officials on a train that "passed through but did not stop," just one more insult in a long line of abuses.

It was not only small towns who resented the Milwaukee's failures. The Rapid City paper reported that its citizens would not stand for a mixed train. "Some declare that they have bought this line several times over," the editor noted, "and now want the service." In 1922 the governor of the state, William McMaster, decided to drive to Rapid City because the train service between Pierre and Rapid was so poor; the story made the news because he and his driver had an accident at a bridge and had to be rescued by passersby.[19]

Occasionally protests would bring results, and service would improve for a while. In April 1925 the Milwaukee Road announced that it would improve service to meet the competition presented by trucks and buses, which increasingly supplemented and supplanted the poor railroad service. This posed an obvious threat to the railroad. The *Press* noted that passenger traffic was very light in most trains; on some only a half dozen rode. The editor speculated that autos were replacing the passenger train for many. Yet the railway could not seem to arrive at a schedule that worked. In the summer of 1925, for example, it instituted a schedule that disrupted local mail service. Sunday papers would not arrive until Tuesday under the new program, and Kadoka residents again planned petitions.[20]

The automobile gave west river residents hope, offering liberation from the inflexible schedules and routes of the railroads. Individuals could choose when to travel, which routes to take, and where to stop. Trucks could haul freight on timetables set by local needs and conditions; the region would be freed from the indifferent business decisions made by distant corporate magnates. Cars and trucks promised to defeat the old enemy—distance. A west river editor toasted the auto as the "space annihilator."[21]

Of course, cars and trucks needed good roads in order to work their magic. In the twenties road building became a national obsession; it was especially important in places like the west river country, where distances were long, travel was difficult, and there was so much empire building yet to do. Unfortunately, the same problems of too little population and too much empty space haunted road building as they had haunted the railroad business. Those in the west river country found themselves at a disadvantage from the start and had to fight to get the roads they believed they deserved.

Road building west of the river was hampered initially by state policies. In 1916 the federal government passed legislation providing federal dollars for highway construction if states would match the funds. South Dakota had to pass a constitutional amendment to allow internal improvements before it could take advantage of the law; the amendment passed in November 1916. The 1917 legislature then created the State Highway Commission and placed a small levy on real and personal property to finance roads. Eighty percent of the levy was to be returned to its county of origin. In 1919 the legislature authorized a $6 million bond issue for road costs, with 75 percent of the money allocated back to the counties on the basis of their assessed valuation. The state thus completed highways in the smaller, more populous eastern counties first because of their higher valuation assessments. West river counties, with their lower valuations, struggled to get money for initial construction while richer counties east of the river that already had roads clamored for upgraded roads with better surfaces. Vehicle registration fees, begun in 1919, and the gasoline tax, begun in 1921, helped raise more money for roads, but the thinly settled areas had fewer people and vehicles to tax and brought in less. Only the state's interest in the promotion of tourism helped create a basic network of roads, which overcame, to a small degree, the disadvantages posed by a small population scattered over too much space.[22]

In spite of these impediments, enthusiasm for road building was high in many counties west of the river. The amazing equipment used and the sense of sheer power involved as men met nature head-on intrigued the public and made good newspaper copy. The *Kadoka Press* carefully described the "county road plainer and maintainer" and how it worked as well as the "monster Emerson tractor" and the big Caterpillar tractor. Kadoka residents could read in detail about the first bucket of cement poured for the Belvidere bridge over the White River and the test of the Kadoka bridge over the same river, where three men drove a tractor over it and "not a rod vibrated with the crossings." The men who built the roads in Jackson County became heroes, noble men working to connect the region to the world and bringing honor to the county by their labors. The *Press* celebrated "Mr. Buckmaster and his able crews" and suggested that they be set against the bad roads of other counties, where they could demonstrate their prowess for the advantage of all. "That Jackson County has the best dirt roads in the entire west" was a source of local pride.[23]

Not all counties were as proficient as Jackson. Harding County road-building and maintenance practices were the subject of considerable complaint. The county commissioners were slow to make decisions; as a result, Camp Crook was without a bridge over the Little Missouri River for several months after a spring flood washed out the original. When the county finally replaced the structure, the town believed it to be substandard. The *Buffalo Times* remarked on the poor condition of the road from Buffalo to Bowman, North Dakota. Harding County residents were "praying for the day we will have a highway commission who can see the advisability of maintaining the $70,000 investment," the editor exclaimed. On one occasion, a state highway official agreed and ordered the county to get its equipment working on the roads or risk having it sent elsewhere where county commissioners would use it wisely.[24]

One factor that aided the development of roads in the west river country was the rise of tourism in the 1920s. From the beginning, automobiles had been used for recreation. Because there were few good roads, tourists faced terrific challenges in their journeys to see the sights of America. Early motorists gloried in the hardships they confronted and eagerly shared their tales of adventure. By the mid-teens, however, the rising interest in auto travel and the spread of automobile ownership into the middle classes encouraged the creation of dependable roads. According to one historian of the road, "the farmer wanted to get to town; the urban middle class wanted to get out of town. The combination of the two forces produced a booster movement for improving highways."[25]

The west river country lay directly en route to much of the famous scenery of the West. The Black Hills and, later, the Badlands became attractions. Yellowstone National Park in Wyoming and the Custer Battlefield in Montana lay due west of the region, and thousands motored through to the parks. Tourist highway associations named and marked the best routes for motorists to follow to their destinations. The Yellowstone Trail (from the Twin Cities to Yellowstone National Park initially, later extended to run from Plymouth Rock in Massachusetts to Puget Sound in Washington); the Atlantic, Yellowstone, and Pacific Highway (from New York City to Portland, Oregon); the Rainbow Trail (from Chicago to Yellowstone); and the Custer Battlefield Highway (from Omaha, Nebraska, to the Custer Battlefield near Billings, Montana, thence to Yellowstone) all bisected the west river country. West river boosters and promoters helped support the development of such highway associations and built tourist camps to welcome visitors to their towns. West river boosters welcomed the contact it gave them with the broader world (the *Lyman County Herald* in Presho marked its editorial page in the 1920s with the slogan "Presho — on the Custer Battlefield Highway — Main Street of the World"), enjoyed the money the tourists spent en route to the sights, and hoped, usually in vain, that the tourists might encourage further migration to the region. That they might become just part of the tour, viewed by tourists along with famous graves and battle sites as remnants of the long lost West, rarely seemed to occur to them. When an Iowa tourist remarked loudly that "he wouldn't trade his section of land for the whole d——d state of South Dakota," the editor of the *Lyman County Herald* was proudly defensive:

> We would have been glad to show this gentleman from Iowa some of our Lyman County soil and just what it produces. . . . When we can grow wheat that will make 20 bushels to the acre . . . and corn waist high right now, we say we are living in a land of opportunity.[26]

Organized tourism came to Kadoka in 1920 when William Fisher, the executive secretary of the newly proposed Custer Battlefield Highway

(CBH), came to make his pitch. The CBH was set to run from Omaha to Sheridan, Wyoming, just south of the Custer battlefield site. Would the businesspeople of Kadoka help support the marking and publicizing of the route? The sixty people present subscribed $500 in two minutes.[27]

Every year for a decade, the CBH boosters' caravan, with cars of businesspeople from every town along the way, passed through Kadoka honking horns and waving banners en route to the annual convention at some city on the route. On other occasions, representatives of the Custer Battlefield Highway Association visited Kadoka while checking the signs along the road or collecting further funds publicizing the road. By the mid-twenties Kadoka had three tourist routes passing through the town. Besides the CBH, the Rainbow Trail, with its colorful markers, and the Atlantic Yellowstone Pacific road included Kadoka in their advertising campaigns. Kadoka businesspeople, in turn, gave financial support to the associations created to support the new routes. In 1927 Kadoka became the starting point for the "Wonderland Highway" running through the Badlands and on to Rapid City.[28]

The presence of the tourist trade did not spread the development of all-weather roads to every area of the west river country. In 1926 the state of South Dakota planned to build one general route from the Black Hills to Sioux Falls and chose Highway 30 (later U.S. Highway 14) as the shortest and most economical route. Kadoka was located on Highway 40 (later Federal Highway 16). In 1929 L. C. Morrison of the *Kadoka Press* complained that Highway 18, the east–west route across the Rosebud and Pine Ridge reservation country south of Kadoka, included treacherous stretches of gumbo and needed considerable work; the Highway Commission planned, instead, to pave east river roads.[29]

Thus, while tourism brought outsiders and their business to the west river country, it did not alter in major ways the distance and isolation of the region. Instead, tourists became markers of the changing seasons, occasional nuisances as they sped down the main streets and byways, and ready subjects for talk, as locals noted the variety of license plates, the styles of dress, or social faux pas.[30]

Tourists and locals alike traveled on the inadequate roads of the region, sometimes becoming companions in hardship. In dry weather the roads were dusty; in rainy weather mud became the problem and

Marian and Phyllis Berry ride to school on their horse, Scuffie, lunch pails in hand, circa 1930.

frequently made the roads impassable. Winter snow often drifted and blocked the way; snow removal equipment was not yet commonly employed to allow motorists to travel. The *Kadoka Press*'s editor regularly recounted weather-related travel stories, including one of his own. In August 1923 editor Zimmer and his wife arrived at the Badlands stretch of their journey right after a cloudburst. The road had dropped two to three feet in one section, and "a small river of mud and water" filled the roadbed. Thirteen cars were stuck there, but the "good-natured" tourists helped each other through. "We don't want to tell Pennington County about her roads," he concluded, "for she has none." During the autumn of the same year, there were two serious auto accidents in the Badlands when cars slid off the gumbo roads and toppled over precipices. In one, two Kadoka businessmen "had a spectacular escape from a short cut to glory" when their car "somersaulted" down a precipice. The two offered free road work to Interior Township to insure that the spot was repaired.[31]

In March 1924 a last minute court ruling allowed whites on reservation lands to vote in state and national primary elections. The Jackson County sheriff had only one day to deliver the election materials over "bottomless" Washabaugh County roads to all of the precincts, a round-trip of two hundred miles. No one would accompany him because the roads were too difficult. The doubters turned out to be right. After hours of travel, the sheriff had to turn back without even reaching Wanblee, the largest town, thirty-two miles from Kadoka. In May 1927 J. C. Steele, who ran a trucking company, reported using fifteen gallons of gas and taking seven hours to travel forty-five miles in mud. That same month, Kadoka high school students missed the regional track meet in Rapid City because muddy roads prevented travel. In January 1927 snow kept many interested Kadokans from a road commission hearing in Cottonwood. Eleven cars set out, but only four arrived after a five-and-a-half-hour battle. At one point twenty to thirty men were digging away at one drift. In that same snowy winter, regional mail carriers failed to reach the post office; one disappeared for a week. Some travelers resorted to horses to reach their destinations. The Kadoka doctor abandoned his car near Belvidere en route home from an emergency case and caught the train back to town.[32]

The automobile promised to conquer distance, but the mind-set it created — of unfettered freedom of movement, speed, and power — collided head-on with the realities of rural roads in the twenties. All rural areas struggled with the problem of dust, mud, and drifting snow, but west of the river where mud was not just mud but gumbo, where distances were long and people very few, the trials were worse and the need for resolution even greater. The promise of the automobile would take time to be fully realized and in time would come to be a mixed blessing. Autos and roads speeded trips to market, to church, and to the neighbors, but they also took people away permanently, to perceived opportunities elsewhere.

As a tool for overcoming distance and lessening isolation, radio appeared to have no disadvantages, beyond the initial cost of a set. Radio brought news, weather, market reports, music, comedy, and drama into homes, no matter their location, the existence or condition of the roads, or the state of the weather. People once isolated could have company in their daily round of chores. The silences of rural life were broken by voices other than those of family members.

The first scheduled radio broadcast in the United States took place in East Pittsburgh in November 1920, when KDKA broadcast the results of the presidential election. At the time, only a few hundred radio sets existed in the nation, but radio quickly became popular. At first, radio enthusiasts had to build their own sets, but by 1921 it was possible to purchase a radio. By the end of 1922, there were 1.5 million radios and 550 broadcasting stations in the United States. In 1922 as well, a radio station in New York broadcast the first paid radio advertising, solving the problem of financing the new innovation. By the mid-twenties national networks developed and broadcast standardized programming. The talent improved, programming became more sophisticated, and, because networks broadcast from coast to coast, broadcasters developed programs having a broad appeal everywhere in the nation. By 1930 the networks carried serials, comedies, and variety shows as well as music and talk, and radio stars had national followings. Radio was big business and an important step in the homogenization of national culture.[33]

The sounds of radio began to be heard in the west river country in 1922. In Kadoka, the *Press* reported that R. N. Rounds planned to establish a community radio receiver. He established a company to purchase a Westinghouse brand radio, "one of the larger and most popular" sets, in hopes that "people of the community will be able to gather round and tune in." His plan must have fallen through because the next report of "interest and excitement" associated with radio came in March 1923 when a local man, George Freemole, became the agent for Crosby radio and set one up in the Hotel Dacotah as a demonstration. "Large crowds" attended his radio concerts and reported hearing stations from Atlanta, San Francisco, Los Angeles, Dallas, and Portland, as well as three stations from Canada. The "first [radio] plant to be permanently located in Kadoka" arrived in late March of 1923 when J. R. Fowler installed a Westinghouse. In July of that year, Kadoka planned a "monster" Fourth of July celebration, which included returns from a boxing match in Shelby, Montana, via radio.[34]

By 1924 the *Kadoka Press* reported frequently that local residents had purchased sets for their homes, and some businesses had begun to use radio to attract shoppers. White Hardware, for example, installed a radio with a loudspeaker to lure customers, and the store quickly became "the big hangout." Charles Ray entertained his customers at the Ford garage in the same manner. R. N. Rounds treated part of Kadoka to radio — whether they wished to hear it or not — when he broadcast an Omaha station to downtown Kadoka by means of a large loudspeaker whose sound reached more than a block.[35]

People reacted to their first hearing of radio with awe. D. R. Perkins, the editor of the *Bison Courier*, heard his first radio at the home of friends in Lemmon. "The marvels of and the wonderful programs presented by the radio stations of the country were made known to us . . . last Friday evening," he wrote, using the language of the revelation of biblical miracles. "The marvels and the magic of the performers was made more realistic with the realization during the evening of who were listening" to the concerts. The announcer read telegrams of appreciation over the air and also passed along greetings from one listener to another. "The reports sent in this manner to isolated ranches in New Mexico and Oklahoma . . . was sufficient to make one stop and exclaim: 'What is this, and to what have we come in this age!'" Moreover, Perkins concluded, "We are told that this is only the beginning. . . ." In Kadoka, the town doctor, A. J. Hennings, became such a dedicated radio fan that he "listened every night and into the wee hours of the morning to the mysterious sounds extracted from the ether." W. C. Allen, the editor of the popular farm journal the *Dakota Farmer*, based in Aberdeen, also began to spend every spare moment tuning in to distant stations around the country. He often reported on his adventures and called himself "a great traveler — by radio." "Let me say right here," he wrote to his farm family audience, "that radio can hardly be believed by one who has not personally heard its wonders — and then many have to personally convince themselves that the things heard are not being 'faked' in some way."[36]

The enthusiasm for radio began to alter local social patterns. Newspapers reported numerous "radio parties" in small towns. Local families with radios entertained friends without one. They served a meal or a snack, depending on the hour, and used the radio for entertainment. Faye Merle Brown remembered that in his Jones County rural neighborhood the people held box suppers and pie socials to finance the purchase of a radio set. They installed the radio in the Westover Hall for all to enjoy. "Then for many weeks," Brown noted, "people from all over the community would congregate at the Hall in the evening to listen to the radio." Radio made it possible to justify missing church. Sermons quickly became common on broadcast stations, and farm families could listen to them on the radio instead of traveling long distances to hear them in person. Even residents of east river cities like Aberdeen did this on occasion. W. C. Allen reported that he listened to Sunday night sermons "and staid through until time to take up the collection when we got busy elsewhere — which is one of the advantages of going to church by radio," inadvertently revealing one of the potential threats of the instrument. Letters to the *Dakota Farmer* from isolated plains farmers as far west as Montana mentioned the joy of religious services by radio; residents of remote neighborhoods with itinerant pastors welcomed the opportunity for more regular worship, even if it was by long distance.[37]

Radio's potential for connection to a broader world was recognized and lauded. In Cottonwood, the local correspondent reported the acquisition of several radios for Christmas gifts and stated, "At the rate people hereabouts are buying this marvel of science, it will be only a matter of a short time until every home in Cottonwood and vicinity will be connected to the world at large, much to their enjoyment and benefit." The Brady neighborhood correspondent commented on another radio acquisition and concluded, "This community is continually coming in close touch with the entire world." Isolated individuals also saw the value in being connected to the outside world. A Pennington County man testified to the radio's importance in the *Dakota Farmer*: "This article is written by a farmer who is located somewhere in the Bad Lands of South Dakota and appreciates the value of radio to the farmers, especially those who live so far from town as to be unable to get away only a few times a year."[38]

For people swimming in oceans of space, radio provided more than mere entertainment. It also offered information that soothed worries and prevented tragedies. Radio stations in communities like Pierre, the centrally located state capital, quickly developed a program of service to the region. Many west river people traveled to Pierre for hospital care, and stays were typically long. The Pierre radio station broadcast complete medical reports for patients, so family members back home could monitor their progress and hear of their release times and need for a ride home. In bad weather, people stranded safely but far from home could assuage the fears of loved ones through radio broadcasts of their whereabouts. Radio also provided useful weather, market, and agricultural information. It helped farm families make decisions about crops and the sale of produce and stock. They were informed in advance of cold spells or blizzards that could endanger their families and animals. West river residents were no longer quite so alone or so dependent on the immediate community around them for advice, information, and recreation. Space and distance had been bridged to some extent by the "mysterious sounds extracted from the ether."[39]

Yet, in spite of its advantages, the impact of radio on rural life in general and the west river country in particular was, over the long run, ambiguous. Richard Schickel, in his book *Intimate Strangers: The Culture of Celebrity*, has noted that the electronic media of the twentieth century created an artificial, glamorous world that did not exist but seemed very real. People whose lives were hard or humdrum or disappointing began to hope that they could migrate to this fantasy "nowhere" that seemed so real. The "somewheres" they inhabited no longer held much appeal. As Schickel puts it, "the rewards and recognitions" of the hometown "seemed paltry. . . . It seemed to be very small potatoes." In the 1920s "nowhere" was becoming "somewhere and . . . somewhere was bound to be nowhere . . . a place where nothing good, interesting or important ever happened." For places like the west river country that were perilously close to becoming literal nowheres, radio helped point out the painful disjunction between daily life and the modern ideal.[40]

THROUGHOUT the decade of the twenties, west river residents waged an endless struggle against overwhelming space. Still convinced that they could, eventually, succeed in their venture to build an empire in the west river country, they applauded every new manifestation of progress, from roads to radio, not acknowledging that each new step in the march of progress left them further behind. When the initial "space annihilator," the railroad, lost hope and interest in the region, west river residents fought for increased regulation of the railroads and for better roads for the new "space annihilator," the automobile. Determined to shape their future and conquer space, west river residents faced the future with the conviction that they could and would succeed through persistent struggle. Their faith, based upon the experience and expectations of difficult times, was too harsh to be labeled "optimism," the faith of the weak of heart. But the disasters and punishments of the thirties would make even their willing acceptance of rigor and uncertainty insufficient for survival in the west river country. The drought and hard times of the Depression would redefine the meaning of struggle for west river residents.

6

Seedtime and Harvest Shall Not Cease

Governor W. E. Green (left) and other officials inspect grasshopper damage in Tripp County, 1931.

While the earth remaineth, seedtime and harvest . . . shall not cease.
—Genesis 8:22, God's promise to the faithful, often cited in the west river
   country

Lo! and behold, one day in June a collector arrived with a truck and without
preliminaries loaded everything up, leaving us stranded without milk cows,
work horses, or any means of subsistence. We weren't the only sufferers; in
two weeks this same company took over 9000 head of cattle in this county. . . .
Not one of those families affected can buy, borrow or in any way get a
foothold again in these times. . . . People are leaving their homes, piling in
with relatives only a little better off. . . . Here's hoping a good samaritan soon
passes this way.
—Mrs. Earl Harvey, Tripp County, *Dakota Farmer*, November 1933

THE OLD ADAGE that "it is always darkest before the dawn" seemed
to operate in reverse in the west river country. There, it was always
brightest before disaster. In 1909 and early 1910 settlement of the region
proceeded apace, and optimistic empire builders believed that they had
the tools and wherewithal to turn a desert into a garden. Then the
drought of 1910–1911 struck them down. Again in 1918 and 1919 the
high prices and rising land values of the World War era brought talk of
a boom and the long-delayed fulfillment of the settlers' dreams. The
abrupt contraction of the agricultural economy in 1920–1921 instead
brought bust, painful reconstruction, and disillusionment. It took nearly
a decade for a semblance of stability to return.

In 1929 a chastened and wary citizenry noticed increasing signs of
growth and economic health. The editor of the *Bison Courier* reported
the best hay yields in history in June. In that same month the city of
Lemmon held a celebration of the history and the community of the
west river country. The sponsors knew that most residents had come
into the region at the same time and believed that the shared hardships
of the past and the shared prosperity of the present had forged them
into one big family. Overalls and calico were the expected attire.[1]

In August and September there was more encouraging news. The
wheat and flax yielded well (although grasshoppers had started to
threaten). Because prices were also better, farm families had more
money; they came to the Perkins County courthouse to pay taxes not 117

due for two years. The *Bison Courier* also reported a "huge" number of cars and trucks licensed in the county in 1929. The Imogene correspondent told readers about a building boom in that region, "more building being done this fall than any time for years." In December a St. Paul, Minnesota, prognosticator predicted a cycle of ten wet years soon to begin in South Dakota. Bison-area residents even revived their hopes for a rail line. Railroad promoters held public meetings across Perkins County in December 1929 to build support for a bond issue. Hopes were high. "We have been sitting on the prairies here for the past twenty years, like the coyotes and jackrabbits on the hill tops, waiting for the railroad to come," the *Courier*'s editor explained. Finally it seemed that it would. The stock market crash in October actually improved their chances for a line, according to the *Courier*'s editor. Investors would now abandon the stock market and turn to the bonds that might finance their much needed rail line.[2]

There was no fear, no panic to mark the Depression's onslaught. Prices began to drop and work began to disappear, but few understood the implications. Drought, however, was a well-known enemy. It arrived hand-in-hand with the Depression and brought a new plague with it — the grasshopper. Beginning in 1930, drought, hoppers, and the Depression worked their will on the west river country. Relief of various kinds and from several sources averted actual starvation, but intense suffering shook the west river country to its core. The biblical scale of suffering in the area was brought to a close only when the immeasurable disasters wrought by World War II paradoxically left a wake of prosperity throughout America, including the west river country.

The first warnings came in June 1930. The *Kadoka Press* reported the first good rain in three to four weeks. It followed three days of hot, dry winds and "gave new courage" to area residents. The respite was only temporary. The next week the Ladies Aid had to meet at night to avoid the terrible heat of the day. The July 10 edition of the *Press* recorded six days in a row of 104 to 110 degree temperatures with hot winds. The local correspondents charted every hour of rain, almost to the drop. The South Creek correspondent told of rain for an hour the week of July 24 and wished for twenty-four more. The Kadoka and Wanblee correspondents reported eight drops in early August. The drought finally broke at the end of August. "Although coming too late to do the small grain any good, it will be a great benefit to the corn," the *Press* observed. "The water situation was also greatly relieved as many farmers have found it necessary to move their stock many miles to water." Good rains continued. In mid-October Jackson County farmers were cutting flax (generally harvested in late July or early August); it "lay dormant during the drought and sprouted later." There had not yet been a killing frost, allowing the unusually late harvest to proceed. The late rains had not helped everyone. Reverend Wackerfus, who served German Lutheran parishes in the Bison area, reported several needy families in his churches in December 1930. The Ladies Aid of his home church in St. Paul, Minnesota, shipped old clothes for him to distribute.[3]

Disaster was obvious early in the 1931 growing season. In May several neighborhoods in Tripp County held emergency meetings to discuss the grasshopper menace. In June the *Bison Courier* reported that "millions of tiny hoppers have been found in the alfalfa fields." Gladys Leffler Gist of Lyman County remembered 1931 as "the first grasshopper year, the beginning of bare earth farming." On her farm "the earth was alive with them . . . even the leaves of the trees were stripped. . . . There were so many piled dead in our potato patch that they stank."[4]

The counties distributed sacks of poison for farmers to spread on their land. The Gists and their neighbors mixed it with bran and spread it with the grain seeder. They barely made a dent in the number of hoppers. Grasshoppers so dominated west river life that the students at the Ideal high school named their school paper "The Grasshopper" and the Philip-area ball team called themselves the "Haakon County Hoppers." Motorists struggled with hoppers that hit them in the eyes as they tried to drive. A grasshopper bit a hole in the head of tiny Ruth Gist, and her mother found it to be "a hazard to wear rayon hose while driving the car." Hoppers "scalloped" the edges of the window shades in the Gist home.[5]

Drought revisited the land. In June 1931 the farmers of the Ideal and Westminster churches in Tripp County met to pray for rain. In July Bison-area ranchers were digging new wells to provide water for their cattle. The Ada correspondent reported that a light shower in July was "too late" for the grain. The River Park correspondent told of farmers cutting Russian thistles, a pesky plant introduced to the plains inadvertently by German-Russian immigrants in the 1870s, for feed. "If cut on the green side and put directly into the sack, it is said they will make fair feed." (Thistles provided some nutrition but made the cows unpleasant to handle. The cows developed a potent diarrhea; a Gregory County woman recalled it as "very powerful so a person stayed ten feet behind when bringing home the milk cows." Just one more burden to be borne in difficult times.) In the same issue the River Park writer noted 106 degree temperatures and "a wind as hot as though it came from out of a furnace." The merchants of Belle Fourche placed an ad in the local paper "for the general good of the community and in the general belief that anything that is worth having is worth asking for." According to the *Dakota Farmer*, which told the story, the type fairly screamed the message: "Wanted Rain . . . must be delivered soon to do any good. Will pay highest market prices." Prairie fires blazed across the land; Cottonwood residents fought several in July, while people from Kadoka and Belvidere worked together to control a difficult blaze in late August. Wanblee residents fought two fires in one week, also in late August, and four in one week in mid-September. By September the drought and winds combined to create dust storms in some parts of the region. In Tripp County the storms blew over small buildings. In Perkins County late fall winds "caused considerable damage — especially fences which were torn down for miles due to the Russian thistles blowing and piling up against them." At the end of the year, a high school student writing for the school page of the *Kadoka Press* told of "a certain family" who in the past year had "sustained life on bread and potatoes." The student concluded with a statement true for large numbers of west river residents in that painful year: "It is hard to see just where they will get the potatoes this year."[6]

Nor did 1932 begin auspiciously. Severe winter weather compounded the difficulties west river farm families faced. Snow blockaded roads, and people as well as stock ran very low on food. In the Cash area of Perkins County many families — and the town store — ran out of flour. The *Bison Courier* carried several stories of snowbound people struggling to find sources of stock feed and ways to get it to their animals. The Ada correspondent reported in March that the ranchers were out of feed, even thistles. "The cattle are very thin but if there are no more bad storms and little more snow they can perhaps pull through, that is, what are left." There would be no such luck. Two weeks later the

Cash reporter told the tale: "And didn't the elements just out-do themselves . . . ? In broad daylight, or under cover of darkness, it mattered not which, the old northwest wind did howl race and roar. Just one more terrific last whirl at the poorly fed, weak stock." The death toll was "shockingly large."[7]

Rainfall in 1932, however, was considerably better than in 1931. The primary agricultural problem was the heat and the presence of grasshoppers and other pests. In his annual report to Washington, the Perkins County agent wrote that the hot summer had brought "a plague of flies." Livestock "milled day and night and failed to put on flesh." The Lemmon area was "beset by rats," and the agent taught rat control techniques to the locals. In Tripp County the gardens were "mostly taken by hoppers," and crops were affected as well. The Dog Ear Lake correspondent recounted the damage: "All the blossoms are eaten from alfalfa fields and the cornfields are covered with the pests. . . . It looks as though the farmer has no show against them." In Perkins County in June cutworms ate both grain and gardens. In Jackson County farmers could try a fungus disease spore available at Hunts' Hardware that supposedly killed hoppers. In spite of these trials, the *Kadoka Press* was able to remark in October that 1932 had been a year of plenty (in contrast to 1931).[8]

Any hope that the relatively good year of 1932 had ended the threat of drought was dashed by June of 1933. During the weeks of June 4–20, 1933, the temperatures in Bison topped 90 degrees every day; two of the days saw temperatures of 100 degrees or more. Pessimistic crop reports began to appear. The *Kadoka Press* told of numerous grasshoppers. "They have practically destroyed all of the gardens and flowers in town. They are also doing considerable damage to what crops have not been burned by hot weather. Quite a drastic situation faces the people of these parts." The *Bison Courier* noted the presence of grasshoppers as well. In Perkins County the grain was also beginning to burn from hot winds and lack of rain. In July the paper speculated that the Bison area might get "a short half crop" while the northwest and northeast portions of the county would get none at all. People began to collapse from the heat. The July 13 edition of the *Press* recorded the first dust storm, "which raised the dust so high that it seemed like night time." In August the *Courier* registered the hottest temperatures yet: 104, 107, 105,

"Wind erosion scene in the Rosebud country," 1935.
Library of Congress, courtesy of the South Dakota Archives.

106, and 108 degrees, five straight days of misery. The heat wave brought wind and blowing dust with it. The dust "found its way into all homes. At times the wind rocked residences quite strong. . . . It was impossible to see beyond a few hundred feet." Prairie fires burned all around in August; at one point two raged at the same time, and farmers and townspeople traveled for miles to help fight them. Range cattle wandered far from home in search of water. The "water holes, dams, and creeks" were dry. In late August two inches of rain fell but did not fill the water holes "due to the extreme dryness." The rain led the trees to bud in August, which the *Press* welcomed, although the editor hoped that the grasshoppers would leave the tender leaves alone. In September the Kadoka area began to turn green again, "which is good after the complete drought of these months."[9]

But any hopes for a return to normality were dashed by the dust storms of the fall. They arrived in November and blew what little feed was left "to the four winds." The South Creek correspondent compared the storms to the "duststorms of the Sahara Desert" that she had read about. Correspondents from all over Tripp County wrote of severe damage to buildings on farms and in towns. Windows were broken and

roofs and walls blown down. When the minister left his Sunday services at Ideal, "we could not see across the road. . . ." He was sure the
storm was the devil's work. "Let us pray for protection from him who
would destroy our souls."[10]

Such extremities inevitably affected the business communities in
farm towns—that is, all of the towns in the west river country. The
biggest factor in business hardship was low prices paid to farmers. In an
economy so dependent on the health and productivity of the farm, low
prices were devastating. The Depression knocked the bottom out of
agricultural markets and made it impossible for farm families to acquire
the goods and services they needed. When farm families could not buy,
storekeepers had to cut back in a deadly downward spiral. A small note
in the *Kadoka Press* announced in 1931 the intention of the Standard Oil
Service Company to go to a cash-only basis "due to poor collections."
Two weeks later seven storekeepers published a joint notice of their intention to close up shop at 6 P.M. every night except Saturday "in order
to reduce expenses." In late 1931 the Cottonwood correspondent to the
Kadoka Press reported that all of the railroad workers on the Chicago
Northwestern, except the foreman, had lost their jobs. This added "to
the already serious unemployment situation." By the end of 1931 the
Kadoka-area stock buyer had to quit the business temporarily because
his banks in Sioux City had closed.[11]

Prices for all agricultural commodities were incredibly low during
the early years of the Depression. Mollie Moreland of Meade County
remembered selling cream for 10¢ or 12¢ a pound for butterfat and eggs
for 10¢ a dozen. Prices in 1926, in comparison, had been 38¢ for butterfat and 24¢ a dozen for eggs. Turkeys brought $1 a piece, not even
enough to pay for their feed. In Pennington County Peder Kjerstad
sold wheat for 16¢ a bushel (compared to $1.36 in the summer of 1926)
and burned corn in his stove because it was cheaper than other fuel. His
family had no income at all between November 1, 1931, and March 1932.
"Then we had a few cows come fresh and made 20 dollars that month,"
he remembered; "I thought that was great." Gordon Stout, a Kadoka-
area farmer, brought in the season's first wheat, for which he was paid
12¢ per bushel. With yields at four bushels per acre, instead of the typical twelve bushels, the *Press* commented, Stout was not "profiteering."
The *Press* reprinted a news item from the *Philip Pioneer Review* that

"illustrated conclusively how hard hit are the farms and stock feeders by the low prices." It seems that a Haakon County man shipped a load of thirty sheep to Sioux City. He received a bill from his commission firm for 5¢. The proceeds for the sale did not pay the full commission charge. The farmer still owed $8 for the cost of trucking the sheep to the railroad and received nothing to pay him for the feed and the work he had expended.[12]

Cash became so short by 1932 that both the *Kadoka Press* and the *Bison Courier* advertised their willingness to take wheat in exchange for newspaper subscriptions; the *Courier* noted that farmers could dump the wheat in specially built bins and could keep the sacks because "they are more valuable than wheat itself." The *Faith Independent* cut its editions to four pages, half its usual length, to meet expenses. The Bison barber cut the price of a haircut to thirty-five cents to attract more business. By late 1933 doing business on credit looked good. When relief money began to reach the region in large amounts, the Kadoka Department Store urged relief workers to "come and get your shoes and clothing to work in. We will outfit you and wait [payment] until you get your [relief] order."[13]

The credit that storekeepers were sometimes willing to offer played an important role in maintaining the pride and health of their customers. A storekeeper in Smithwick in Fall River County granted credit for the luxury of chewing tobacco to a formerly wealthy rancher who had lost all of his money when the banks closed. The same storekeeper also received a call from a farmer's wife who had been serving her family only pancakes for several days and had just killed her last chicken. The family had no money and did not know what to do. The storekeeper offered them credit. In Tripp County the Van Schaak family appreciated the credit the doctor offered. "Doctors were taking meat and vegetables for pay. We had neither so we paid what we could." When the doctor built a new office, Clair Van Schaak did some of the foundation work. "It eased the humiliation of not being able to pay," remembered Clair's wife, Rose. "Dr. Bouza never sent us a bill, not once."[14]

The drought, the decline in employment, and the collapse of farm prices soon put a financial squeeze on social institutions. Any organization that required dues began to lose members; larger, more official social structures such as churches and schools had to struggle to survive in the face of mounting debt. To stem the tide of decline, some social organizations began to cut dues for members. The Parent Teachers Association in Kadoka, for example, reduced its dues to twenty-five cents in 1931 in order to boost membership. Even the Kadoka junior class advertised reduced admission fees to its play "so that all can go." Some groups governed by distant national headquarters, such as the Masons, were unable to accommodate their struggling members, at least initially. One member of the Dallas Lodge recalled that many members were dropped because they had not paid their dues. In the mid-thirties the Lodge developed a plan to reinstate former members if they paid two years of Grand Lodge dues and one year of local dues. It helped maintain membership to some degree, but it was 1946 before Masonic membership actually grew again.[15]

Organizations that continued to function in the early thirties did so with lowered aspirations. Typical fund-raising activities such as dinners, bazaars, and socials continued, but without great expectations. People learned to be grateful for the small amounts that did come in. The Ladies Aid in Cottonwood received $100 for the goods sold at their annual bazaar in 1931, which the Cottonwood correspondent recorded was good "for trying times like these."[16]

The task of organizations such as the Ladies Aids that supported the workings of the local churches became much more difficult. The Ladies Aids doubled their efforts, yet progress was slow. In 1932 the *Bison Courier* reported that church collection plates locally had "given no indication that the bottom of the depression has been passed." Yet the same issue included announcements of a Lutheran church ladies circle bake sale, of another Lutheran Ladies Aid chicken dinner with prices of twenty-five cents for adults and ten cents for children, and of a Catholic ladies lunch to be served at the parish house. Rev. Holm, the pastor of several rural Lutheran churches, credited the Ladies Aid and the Luther League with raising the money to continue those churches.[17]

The effort to maintain the churches was continuous. A dramatic and desperate plea for community aid to the Presbyterian church in Kadoka appeared in the *Press* in late 1932. Written by the church trustees, the appeal thanked the community for its aid in hard times past but asked for more, to keep "open the doors of a protestant church in our midst."

The trustees pointed out that contributions had been declining in the face of the Depression. "It is no longer possible," they stated, "for a few contributors to shoulder the burden of even the most pressing expenses. . . . We need help in the form of regular and systematic contributions. They do not need to be large but they must come from more contributors and they must come with regularity." The alternative, the authors concluded, was the closing of the church and the loss of all the advantages it provided. Their appeal was successful; the church continued to operate. By mid-1933 the *Press* was crediting the Ladies Aid for its donation of a bit of luxury to the church, new rugs. "The ladies deserve much credit for their fine work of raising funds for this project, especially when the stressing times are taken into consideration."[18]

One community managed to build a new church. The people of South Creek, a Norwegian Lutheran neighborhood in Jackson County, had held church services in local schools since 1908. In that same year the South Creek women had organized a Ladies Aid with the goal of raising enough money, over time, to build a church. They held dinners, socials, and an annual bazaar for years to raise the needed funds. By 1924 the women had collected $1,500. When the Kadoka bank failed, the money was lost. Undaunted, the women again began to save. Depositors for the failed bank eventually received ten cents on the dollar, and the $150 helped the church fund grow. By October 1933 the Ladies Aid had accumulated $481, and they decided to build a basement church. Nine men of the parish, including the minister, dug the basement, and many volunteers labored to complete the roof and short walls. The Ladies Aid continued to raise funds as the project developed; they served the Kadoka Kola Club (a branch of the Kiwanis) dinner, for example, and earned $43 in one evening. The church was completed in the spring of 1934, at a cost of $716.75, and was completely paid for at the time of its dedication. The *Kadoka Press* report on this accomplishment commented on the struggle. "South Creek Church Is Fine Monument," the headline read; the subhead continued, "In the face of Depression and bank failures the men and women of community have finished fine edifice." The parishioners worshipped in their basement church until they closed it in 1953 and built a regular church building in Kadoka.[19]

School districts and school teachers also tightened their belts in the face of the crisis. When the economic disaster struck in the early thirties, the school system was especially vulnerable. Local taxes paid about 80 percent of the schools' operating costs. Taxes were high, especially considering the marginal nature of many farms in the region. When farm families and town dwellers could not pay their taxes, schools felt the pinch.[20]

The trials began early. In the fall of 1931 the Washabaugh County school board announced that it would open no new schools that year due to lack of funds. By 1932 districts began to cut wages. The Cottonwood correspondent to the *Kadoka Press* reported in February of that year that, while all teachers would receive contracts, wages would be drastically lower. This, the writer reassured *Press* readers, was not "a reflection on the teachers, but an indication of the serious financial condition of the school." According to one teacher at the Cottonwood high school, the school was so far in debt that the warrants the teachers received would not be paid for eleven years at the current state of school finances. The superintendent sold such warrants whenever he could and provided the cash to the teacher. Because the superintendent had lived in many communities in the west river country, he could generally find someone willing to buy the warrants. The typical discount, however, was 10 percent. The Cottonwood teachers received only $63 of the $70 per month their contracts specified, but at least they had access to cash; many other teachers did not. By mid-1932 the Cottonwood correspondent reported that the school board had saved $2,200 by cutting back salaries and coal purchases.[21]

The Kadoka schools, the largest and healthiest system in Jackson County, also cut salaries, but the district went one step further and cut teacher positions as well. In the spring of 1933 the school board announced that one teacher would be cut from the grade school, reducing the staff from four to three, and that a similar cut would be made in the high school faculty, also from four to three. Salaries would drop 10 percent for teachers who retained their jobs. The cuts reduced the salary expenses by $2,810. The board set the pay for grade school teachers at $81 per month. The high school faculty received $117 to $177 per month, depending on their duties.[22]

Small rural school districts suffered the most. Because they were so small—usually having only one teacher and bare bones buildings—they had the most difficulty cutting expenses. The only recourse for some rural grade schools was to close, although that was controversial. The editor of the *Murdo Coyote* complained that closing the elementary schools was a mistake. He argued that higher education was an unnecessary luxury. Society would benefit, he maintained, if the money spent on high school was instead spent on a solid common school education for all within easy reach. Parents in districts with closed schools sometimes sent their children to town for a basic education. The *Kadoka Press* reported a larger than usual enrollment in the Kadoka grade school in the fall of 1932 because of the closing of several outlying schools. Tuition varied by school, but it cost several dollars per month. Some common school districts recognized that paying transportation or tuition for their students to attend elsewhere might save the district money in the long run. The Little Buffalo district in Jackson County saved $1,000 in 1932 by closing one school and transporting children to its other school. The Thorpe district in Perkins County cut costs by limiting the school year to eight months and slashing salaries 30 to 40 percent. It did not close schools, although the average enrollment in each school was only six.[23]

The decision to close schools had troubling consequences for families too poor to pay tuition for school in town. Rose Van Schaak's children attended the South Ringthunder school in Mellette County. During the 1931–1932 school year the district closed the North Ringthunder school because it could no longer afford two schools. The children who had attended the northern school made the journey to the southern school for their education. (The teacher of the southern school taught "merely for his board and room as no warrants can be issued until the 1931 taxes are collected.") Then, in the fall of 1932, the school district closed the South Ringthunder school for the 1932–1933 year. Rose Van Schaak's parents operated the hotel in White River and offered to take her eight-year-old twins so they could attend town school, but neither the Van Schaaks nor her parents could afford the tuition. (Hotel rooms rented for fifty cents a day in White River at the time.) The Van Schaaks' six-year-old daughter should have started school that year but could not. Rose Van Schaak was not worried about the late start for her six-year-old but believed that "the missing of a year of school was a real setback for the twins." The next year the South Ringthunder school re-opened, but the teacher, for all practical purposes, worked without pay. She could not cash her warrants and boarded around the district, one home per month, "free of charge," to enable her to survive.[24]

The problem of schools was part of the larger issue of government costs, efficiency, and the tax structure as a whole. The issues here were not new; the high cost of providing government services to a sparsely settled region had been a cause of controversy since 1910. Hard times, however, gave the issue a life-and-death edge. By early 1931, for ex-ample, the Farmers Union convention in Jackson County opened the floor to members and nonmembers alike to discuss the troubling tax burden. The initial target was state taxes, but A. J. Granger, local stock-man and lawyer, pointed out the difficulty in exerting control over a distant state government. Instead, he argued, the problem of taxes might be more wisely managed locally. Granger illustrated his argu-ment with facts about the costs of maintaining townships, whose pri-mary role was road building and maintenance. The county, Granger suggested, did the same work much more efficiently; individuals would be far better off to abolish the township and allow the county to do the work. Granger wrote a lengthy piece for the *Kadoka Press* that provided hard figures for specific individuals. "Take the case of George Porch," Granger suggested. "If we were to abolish the state government en-tirely, George Porch would save $29.77, while by disorganizing Kadoka Township, George would save $59.54 on his taxes for the current year." Granger mentioned that his discussion of the tax matters at the local level had "struck a responsive chord" and that he hoped people would take concrete action to disband their townships at the next annual meetings. In May 1931 the South Creek correspondent reported that the men of that community planned to hold a public meeting "to discuss the problem of ever increasing taxes." Also in Jackson County, Cedar Township voters met to debate "a tax situation not to their liking," and in Perkins County a delegation of taxpayers informed the county com-missioners that they would have to cut the budget later that year. A large and enthusiastic audience attended a meeting of taxpayers at Seim. The Perkins County people went on to organize a taxpayer's league, which met frequently to debate the issues, pass resolutions, and publicize the tax problem. On occasion they held socials, including one dance at River Park where the Blue Ragadors Orchestra entertained. In June 1932 Jackson County residents also formally organized a tax league for their area.[25]

Angry taxpayers demanded major cuts in county and state expenses and substantial reforms in how county and state government operated. F. A. Ott of Ziebach County told the *Dakota Farmer* that he wanted lawmakers "to cut the wages of state, county and township officials to half" and to mandate that county commissioners "meet every 2 months for 1 day of 8 hours, instead of 3 to 4 days every month at only a 3 hour session a day." Ott demanded that mileage be cut to three cents per mile, "as our officials here spend more time traveling than they are in their office, and they make more from the mileage than a farmer will make on 160 acres of land." Ott also suggested that the positions of deputies to county officials be cut, that automobile and gas taxes be raised 10 to 15 percent, and that parents with high school age children be forced to pay their tuition to a town school so that taxpayers would not be forced to bear the extra four dollars tax. Joe Price of Meade County argued that taxes were unbearable and that a solution had to be found; however, he urged complainers to look to themselves for some relief. "Practice the pay as you go policy," he insisted. "Quit paying enormous prices for machinery, and live entirely within your means." Once taxpayers had done that, Price maintained, they could return to their present preoccupation with hunting waste, greed, and fraud. "Then outside of home," he concluded, "we can investigate the book company graft [the high cost of textbooks], the buying of high-priced public machinery, discourage the public bonding craze, scrutinize the mileage drawn by public officers, cut the number of public officers down to the minimum . . . eliminate the public charges and last, but not least, use common sense, good judgment and fair play in our work."[26]

One of the most controversial proposals for saving tax dollars came from several disgruntled residents of northwestern Jackson County in 1932. Led by two of the largest cattlemen in the region, this group proposed the merger of Haakon and Jackson counties, with the county seat at Philip, the present Haakon County seat. Proponents argued that because Jackson County was small, it was inefficient and operated with huge debts, all of which might be avoided if economies of scale could be employed in a larger governmental unit.

Opponents argued that a merger would not save tax money, that it would make it more difficult for citizens to reach their county seat and keep their eye on public officials, and that it would devastate Kadoka and its surrounding area economically. Merger opponents also characterized consolidation as a reversion to a more primitive state — an ominous prospect in light of the recency of settlement and the hopes for the region as a whole. Consolidation raised fears of history reversing itself in the region. Gordon Stout, a Jackson County farmer, pointed out that old time cattlemen were the leaders of those promoting consolidation, and he reminded his readers of their history. "Going back to the early days," he wrote, "men like these [ranchers] were in clover. They are cattlemen and to them the curse of this country was the plow and its resultant development." Stout claimed on good authority that before the farmers came, the county assessor would come out from Ft. Pierre, the county seat of old Stanley County, visit the scattered ranchers and enjoy their hospitality, and return home with only 10 percent of ranch property listed for taxes. "In the old territorial days before South Dakota became a state," Stout claimed, "there were no taxes at all and for ranchers like the above, you can bet they would be absolutely in favor of disorganizing the State." For Stout the danger of merger was clear. "Let's vote no for Consolidation," he concluded, "and not let our farms go back to the Indians and Cattle Men." The editor of the *Press* likewise viewed merger in apocalyptic terms. If the voters said yes, he forecast, "our fine courthouse and grounds would become a white elephant on our hands. In fact, our every institution, schools, churches, homes, business places, all would receive a stunning blow and the conveniences for which we have labored in the past will have been largely destroyed and emigration would shun us."[27]

The antimerger forces defeated consolidation, 1,029 to 319. Costs, taxes, and economic issues remained at the forefront of local consciousness, but the majority was not yet ready to abandon the hard won institutions that symbolized civilization and progress.

Victory over consolidation, however, did not resolve any of the problems that had sparked the debate. Jackson County operated under severe handicaps in the thirties, as did almost every other west river county. Although citizens were unwilling to abandon their county system, they were often unable to support it. Tax collections dwindled as money became increasingly scarce. Strapped families signed tax delinquency contracts that enabled them to pay their taxes on a delayed basis in installments. When times did not improve as planned, delinquent taxpayers were unable to pay the installments, and additional years of unpaid taxes piled up. The *Bison Courier* reported in August 1931 that because of lagging tax receipts, the mother's pension fund, the monies that went to indigent widows with children, had run out. Two weeks later the *Courier* noted that tax receipts were down 60 percent from the preceding year. By 1933 Jackson County could no longer pay the rent for the county judge's office and removed him to the courthouse basement. In November 1933 the Jackson County treasurer reported that 516 taxpayers had signed contracts to pay their taxes on a ten-year plan. (Jackson County's population at the time was 2,636.) The contracts and a tax collection rate of 54 percent were seen as reasons to be optimistic about the future "in the barren prairies." While schools were closed and costs reduced, the school system remained the same, as did the county and township structure. West river residents were unwilling to dismantle what the pioneers had worked so hard to build.[28]

Families, as well as institutions, suffered in the early thirties. It was the pioneer skill of "making do" that got many of them through the rugged days of the Depression. Because farm families often lacked the cash to purchase gas, oil, and repairs for their machinery, the horse staged a comeback as a source of power on the farm. The Cottonwood correspondent to the *Kadoka Press* noted the trend: "For the past several years there was always the hum and buzz of new tractors and power machinery being set up ready to be taken to the various farms at this season. In contrast, there is practically none of that this spring, but old Dobbin is being carefully groomed and made ready to furnish the power that will bring forth the world's sustenance. . . ." In Kadoka the local dairy deliveryman went back to a horse and wagon to save the expense of a car.[29]

Plain food and tattered clothes became standard. Rose Van Schaak remembered that her family's "food supply dwindled and clothes wore out and there was no money to replace them." She improvised with her

Dust drifts stall the "space annihilator" in Gregory County, 1936.
Library of Congress, courtesy of the South Dakota Archives.

menus, stretching meat and fish by creaming them and pouring them on bread or biscuits. A neighbor's potato soup recipe "made with diced, cooked potatoes, milk and a thickening of flour and egg" came in handy. "Breakfast was usually oatmeal, toast with hot milk, or a slice of toast with coffee and sugar over it."[30]

The Van Schaaks' wardrobe was meager. Rose had her work clothes (men's jeans and a shirt) and two dresses. A grasshopper ate a hole in her rayon dress, so she was down to one to wear away from the farm. Her husband, Clair, had a dress outfit of pants and a sweater besides his work clothes. The children wore relatives' hand-me-downs, which Rose made over. The family used flour sacks for underwear, especially for the children. "Everyone was making do," Rose remembered. "It wasn't so bad having to wear cheap clothes if all the neighbors were wearing the same kind."[31]

Ingenuity helped families endure. The Alex Olson family from Bennett County experienced the hard times and low prices of the early thirties but found ways to survive. In 1930 the family had forty acres of corn, and because of reasonable rains in their area in that year, the corn produced forty bushels per acre. The corn had to be picked by hand,

and the Olsons employed a family of five, who lived in a shack they had brought along. The Olsons provided several staples, including meat, flour, potatoes, ear corn, and wood for fuel. They traded pigs for the wood. The Olsons began to trade their picked corn for hogs but could not realize a profit; hogs sold at two dollars a hundredweight at the time. The Olsons hauled corn to Nebraska upon hearing of a market there. Many farmers in that region had been dried out and needed corn to feed their stock. They traded hogs and cattle in exchange. The Olsons took mostly cows for their corn (at an exchange of fifty bushels for one cow) and built up a herd of sixty, which they fed on hay composed largely of dried-up grass, thistles, and weeds. Because eggs were scarce in their area, the Olson family was able to sell or trade them for forty cents a dozen on the Pine Ridge reservation. That money kept them in groceries and paid for their truck's gasoline. At the local elevator the Olsons sold a load of shelled corn — about ninety bushels — for eight dollars. On the same trip they sold thirty dozen eggs for twelve dollars. The family always had something to eat but rarely had cash. The scarcity of cash, according to Alex Olson, was their biggest problem.[32]

By late 1931 it was clear that penny-pinching at the school and court-house and ingenuity and making do at home were not going to be enough. West river residents needed some kind of systematic relief program that could help them through the crisis. This posed a problem. The United States in 1931 was not a welfare state. Private agencies, such as the Red Cross, and local churches and communities provided relief from crises and disasters, acting to alleviate local or individual distress. This national emphasis on private or individual action was multiplied many times over in the west river country, where the ideology of independence, self-reliance, and the joy of the struggle prevailed.

West river residents had seen crises and struggles before. In 1910–1911, amidst the hardship of drought, they had asked the railroads for free freight on seed and feed, delayed payments to the federal government for reservation land purchases, and generated employment by having local units of government hire struggling farmers to build roads and bridges. These early efforts to provide relief were disorganized, short-lived, and ineffective. No sustained system of welfare ever emerged during the great test of 1911, and the region's pioneers resumed their customary faith in the future and in their own abilities to pull them through hard times when the crisis passed. When the agricultural crash hit in 1920–1921, calls for aid or relief were muted. Again, some land payments for reservation lands and town lots were delayed. Some, in debt to the state Rural Credits system for their farms or to other banks or private lenders, sought leniency and worked out individual solutions with greater or lesser success. Direct relief for physical want existed only through local, personal assistance. Thus, when confronted by a crisis as deep as the national Depression and the accompanying drought, the west river country had neither an organized relief system nor an ideology that would easily acknowledge the need for one. Trial and error characterized the delivery of relief during the early years of the crisis.

The first relief efforts were local and traditional, such as county road work. The Jackson County commissioners teamed up with those from Jones, Mellette, and Haakon counties to request aid from the state highway commission to finance road work projects that would aid the unemployed. They hoped to pay out between $25,000 and $30,000 to financially troubled farmers in exchange for their labor. In unorganized Washabaugh County, the highway board requested $5,000 for relief road work "due to crop failure and potential for suffering." Perkins County also devised a work relief program of road building and repair. The *Bison Courier*'s editor hoped that "married men and men support-ing families [w]ould get a share of this." That many farmers took advantage of the work is reflected in one correspondent's comment late in the fall that "not so many as usual attended [a local dance] on account of so many being in the road camps."[33]

County road work could not support all of the needy. As the De-pression deepened and the impact of the drought intensified, the Jackson-Washabaugh Red Cross chapter based in Kadoka decided to reorganize to meet the crisis. In a call for members, the *Press* noted that "the territory around Kadoka and throughout the county will see many families needing help this winter. County funds will not care for all of them." The editor urged those better off to help and reassured them that their aid would remain local. "It is necessary that the people of the county who have jobs should work together to relieve those who have no assurance of earning a living this winter. . . . All funds raised will be used in the assistance of home folks caught in the toils of the present hard times." In the first week of the reorganization effort, 41 people joined. The Legion Auxiliary also began relief work; the women held a card party with a 25¢-a-plate lunch to raise money for local welfare work, began a program of sewing for local relief, and packed boxes for needy families at Christmastime. Jackson County teachers donated $12.50 for the local food relief fund. "The donations would be larger," the *Press* commented, "but many are already donating stock feed for members of their own families." In January 1932 the local Red Cross, with a budget of $2,090 for January through March, reported 39 families in need of aid. The organization had enrolled 137 members in Jackson and Washabaugh counties. By March 1932 the Red Cross had aided 134 families.[34]

The Red Cross aided impoverished people by soliciting donations, which were used to provide food and clothing for needy persons in towns or on farms. In rural areas, like the west river country, where drought was a major problem, the Red Cross also assisted with feed for livestock. Local communities determined the need for aid and distributed it across their particular territory. In South Dakota the American Legion worked closely with the Red Cross to help distribute aid and keep systematic records. Recipients of Red Cross relief had to demonstrate that they could not supply their own needs and could not receive credit or loans to provide subsistence. In early 1932 a town family was allowed a 98-pound sack of flour no matter what the family's size. A farm family could receive anywhere from a 98-pound sack to two barrels, depending on family size, with families of nine or more receiving the largest amount. In April 1932, as national Red Cross drought relief operations drew to a close, the local Red Cross chapter received instructions on how to disburse the final food relief. Aid recipients were to take food orders to local merchants, who would then fill the order and bill the Red Cross in the client's name. The final order would be double those previously granted because it would have to last until gardens and crops matured, an event that all fervently hoped would occur. The *Press* printed the recommended groceries for an "average family": "20 lbs. salt pork, 6 lbs. coffee, 20 lbs. sugar, 3 boxes oatmeal, 9 lbs. lard, 12 bars laundry soap, 3 large bars Ivory soap, 2 large cans baking powder, 16 lbs. beans, 2 bushels potatoes, 2 gal. syrup, 2 doz. cans tomatoes,

No. 2 size, or 3 doz. No. 1; 2 qts. peanut butter, 6 large cans of milk, 10 lbs. rice, 8 lbs. dried fruit." The Red Cross also provided garden seed and seed potatoes to help local families rebuild their larders. By the end of 1932 the Red Cross had distributed $6,970 worth of food, clothing, and medical aid, 800 sacks of flour in 100-pound sacks, 100 packages of garden seed, and 150 bushels of seed potatoes to 702 local families.[35]

Because of the heavy emphasis on diversified farming and livestock production west of the river, the stock feed relief program was important. Red Cross rules for feed distribution warned local committees to crush or grind the wheat to prevent farm families from using it as seed or selling it on the grain market. No farmer was to receive more than 100 bushels of livestock feed wheat. Huge quantities of Red Cross relief feed poured into west river counties. In the one-year period between October 1931 and October 1932, Jackson and Washabaugh county farm families received sixteen railroad-car loads of hay and grains and more than 30,000 bushels of cracked wheat. The *Press* consistently supported Red Cross work and urged more area residents to join, especially as there were "ever increasing demands for service [and] constantly diminishing returns in local relief funds solicitations."[36]

Because the scope of the economic and natural disasters of the thirties was so broad, local relief efforts could not long meet the needs of the suffering. The Hoover administration in Washington recognized this reality and began to initiate federal programs that would supply some help without violating the standard credo of fiscal responsibility and self-help. The programs with direct impact on the west river country were a feed and seed loan program and the Reconstruction Finance Corporation, which provided employment for those without income.

The idea behind the feed and seed loan program was that farm families were only temporarily embarrassed by a short-term crisis and that they should provide for themselves. Therefore money to feed stock or to buy seed was to be loaned rather than granted outright. Farmers could thus be helped to remain on the land without the government encouraging dependency. The rationale was logical and might have worked had the Depression and drought been short-term developments and had the west river country not been economically marginal in the best of times. As it turned out, the programs caused farmers to incur large debts, which repeated crop failures prevented them from paying. The Gist family in Lyman County, for example, borrowed $500 for feed and seed in 1932; it took them fifteen years to pay it back.[37]

Applicants for relief under the feed and seed program completed a specially prepared form that required a description of the land to be seeded or of the stock to be fed. Farmers also had to state where they planned to purchase the seed or feed and how they planned to pay for it. The latter information was then forwarded to the county auditor. Each county had a local committee to oversee the loan process. In Kadoka, J. H. Fryberger, longtime merchant and community leader, sat on the committee and produced its public statements. The government granted feed loans up to $600; the average seed loan was $235, although farmers could borrow up to $400 for seed. The loans appeared on county records as a lien against the crop or the stock involved. Originally, the loans had a relatively short term; the government wanted farm families to pay up within the year. Conditions, however, thwarted that plan, and the government agencies extended the seed loan payments, provided that farmers pay 25 percent of the balance at the time an extension was requested. Farm families could not use their crop until they had paid the necessary percentage and had filed properly completed renewal forms. Such policies generated some ill will. As one angry recipient declared, "I was told that my seed loan for 1933, ¼ of loan must be paid and therefore was forced to sell 240 bu. of grain for $42.00. If I had refused to be so obliging I could have sold the grain in less than a year and cleaned up my seed loan and had money left." "Such practices," he concluded, "will keep us on relief indefinitely."[38]

The Reconstruction Finance Corporation (RFC), another creation of the federal government, provided loan money to local governments to enable them to create work relief projects that would alleviate unemployment. Federal field-workers audited the programs and repeatedly urged that only the very neediest be granted work on the projects. The newspapers also reassured their readers that "only those in actual need will receive this help." By October 1932 the RFC had loaned Perkins County $5,000 for relief work. In Jackson County the RFC financed the development of an artificial lake, under the auspices of the state game and fish commission, although the county highway superintendent oversaw the work. Each man employed received 30¢ an hour for his labor and an extra 10¢ an hour for each horse he worked, up to four horses per man. The men could live at the site; they paid $1 per day for meals if they did so. While such projects helped the unemployment situation, they were not large enough to help all who needed it.[39]

In spite of local and national relief efforts, the Depression continued to deepen, and the pattern of sustained drought developing in the region evaporated any hopes west river residents had that they could support themselves through subsistence agriculture. Desperation grew as more and more families faced privation and want. People in the west river country typically voted Republican, but in 1932, as the local and national situation grew grimmer, the voters turned to new faces, including Tom Berry, a west river rancher and conservative Democrat, who became the governor of South Dakota, and Franklin Delano Roosevelt, the Democratic governor of New York who was elected president. With the coming of the New Deal, the tone and pace of west river life changed. Before the Depression, national news rarely appeared on the first page of local papers, and there was little discussion of welfare or relief because none existed. During the Hoover years, relief became a more common subject, as the editors struggled to get the word out about the Red Cross, agricultural loans, and work relief projects. After the advent of the New Deal, the front pages carried weekly reports of new plans for relief, along with complicated rules and regulations. The initial response to the New Deal by editors and the public alike was tremendous gratitude and relief.[40]

In August 1933 the *Kadoka Press* carried word of the organization of the wheat allotment program for Jackson County under the Agricultural Adjustment Administration (AAA). This complex and controversial program required the creation of a new bureaucracy. The program's state administrator appointed temporary local committees to help oversee the work. They would assist the newly appointed emergency county agent (Jackson County voters had refused to support a county agent voluntarily since the hard times of 1920–1921). The committee would divide the county into districts with "approximately equal acreages of wheat" and would appoint subcommittees for each district that would be responsible for holding local meetings where experts would explain the wheat allotment program and answer farmers' questions. Participants would not sign up for the program until a second meeting, when they had had time to consider the ramifications. (The *Press* noted the desire "to avoid any so-called 'high pressure' methods.") Those farmers who decided to join promised to limit the acreage they planted to wheat in exchange for cash payments; they would then become members of the Production Control Association (PCA) of Jackson and Washabaugh counties. Finally, the PCA would formalize their organization with the creation of a board of directors and allotment committees to oversee the ongoing work. Temporary committeemen from Jackson County included Andrew Renning (a well-known progressive farmer whose wife, Katie, wrote the South Creek news notes for the *Press*), H. P. Gilchrist (a Kadoka attorney), and Frank Wray (a well-known farmer and officer of the Kadoka Equity Union Exchange elevator). Washabaugh County also had representatives. Farmers had to sign an "intention to join" card by September 25, although the new county agent, William Soule, assured them that they could still back out before they had to sign a formal contract. The farmers in Jackson and Washabaugh counties completed 528 wheat contracts and sent them to Washington. (There were 944 farms in the two counties in 1930; 56 percent participated.) The *Kadoka Press* published a complete list of participants, the total acres they owned or rented, the total sown to wheat in 1930, 1931, and 1932, and the bushels grown in those years as well as those sown in 1933. A formal statement at the top of the list asked the public to report any farmers' totals they believed to be inaccurate. Farmers would then have to prove the accuracy of their reports. (In Tripp County this provision led to at least one complaint; a farmer, angry that a competitor had rented land that he had hoped to farm himself, turned in the competing farmer.)[41]

Both Tripp and Perkins counties reported that farmers were anxious to participate. The Perkins County agent told his superiors that the farmers in his area "all are anxious, of course, to get their checks due to the stringent financial conditions." He vouched for their good intentions: "In return for this consideration they expect to do their part in putting the program across." The Tripp County agent reported that "most people are in such a state financially that they are anxious and willing now to study any plan whereby they may be able to get themselves above board again." Perkins County sent 765 contracts to Washington, including those from absentee landlords. Tripp County sent

The Civilian Conservation Corps workers at their camp in Butte County, 1934. This crew built Orman Dam.

464 to Washington and 919 directly to landlords, who had to approve their renters' participation. These would be sent to Washington once the landlords had signed. In October 1933 Secretary of Agriculture Henry A. Wallace announced a corn/hog allotment plan for producers of those commodities that would operate much like the wheat allotment plan. Farmers would promise to limit acres of corn planted and number of hogs raised in exchange for cash payments. Although aimed at regions that specialized in the raising of corn and hogs, farmers anywhere could apply. West river farmers began the complicated compliance process as soon as forms became available.[42]

Another kind of relief agency opened in Kadoka in September 1933. Every county in South Dakota organized a Reemployment Office in order to register unemployed persons who might need work on the projects the federal government planned to support. H. P. Gilchrist, a local attorney, was to head the Jackson County office. A committee of local businessmen would direct the work. Anyone who was already registered with the relief office would not have to re-register because the records would be transferred.[43]

The following month the program mandated by the Federal Emergency Relief Administration (FERA) went into effect. Congress passed FERA legislation in May 1933, but it took some time for the gigantic system to begin operation. In South Dakota, the state relief administrator coordinated the agency's work, appointing regional field representatives who served four counties and who worked closely with each county's relief committee. The proliferation of aid agencies confused a public, unsure what the purpose of each agency might be or how they fit together. In Tripp County, the field representative tried to explain her mission "by saying what it is not." Her agency was "not an employment bureau, neither is it a gift. It is to provide adequate relief to every deserving case." A deserving case was "one that has exhausted all means of self help." The *Kadoka Press* excused any sense of disorganization with its explanation that "the whole program is more gigantic than any one individual can conceive, and it has been launched in very short time." At one point the state poor relief local committee and the Re-employment Office local committee had to meet to "thresh out" responsibilities, a "matter that had never been understood." The flood of aid worried some strapped taxpayers in Perkins County, who had to be reassured that the money was "a direct grant from the federal government. The County had no obligations to repay it."[44]

To receive help under the FERA program, individuals were to apply at the relief office. Those able to work would be given some sort of employment to help pay for the aid granted. Those unable to work would be given help anyway. The newspapers urged any destitute people in need of aid to come forward; the *Kadoka Press* urged anyone with information on others who might need help to come forward as well. They would be doing "their country and their neighbors a favor."[45]

The aid records of one west river county provide some perspectives on those who applied for aid in 1933. Out of a total of 244 records, 28.6 percent of the applicants entered the recorded relief system in 1933. Of those whose residence is clear, 8 lived in town and 57 on farms.[46]

The severity of their circumstances is clear. Farm families had planted diligently, but of the forty-four for whom crop records were noted, only one harvested any wheat, a yield of 1.88 bushels per acre. Sixteen families had harvested hay, and one family had managed to grow potatoes. Interviewers wrote "no crop harvested" on application after application.

Relief provided the basic necessities. The office determined the weekly needs of the family and assigned the able-bodied to work projects to earn cash for necessities and also gave out commodities when available. If the investigators decided the weekly needs were $10.00 but the family had only $6.70 coming in, they would grant $3.30 in direct relief or work relief, if work was available.[47]

Often farm families owned substantial amounts of real estate but had high debts and little or no income. One family owned almost 1,000 acres valued at $6,400 but owed nearly $4,000 in mortgage, taxes, and seed loans. They owned considerable livestock but had only minimal forage. The relief investigators found that the family needed $10.00 a week to survive but had only $5.25 per week coming in. The farmer was assigned nine days of work. Another family of five lived in "a very nice home" and had modern machinery and a truck, but their only income from their 560 acres was what they could earn from the sale of eggs; they had participated in the wheat program and awaited a government check. The family received work relief.[48]

One other federal relief program began operation in the west river country in 1933. The Civil Works Administration (CWA) provided federal money for projects such as road building. Again, there was a state civil works administrator to implement the plan statewide and a county apparatus to operate locally. The CWA promised to pay ninety-nine of the neediest families in Jackson County fifteen dollars a week for three months, while another ninety-nine families, somewhat less destitute, would be given temporary work at fifty cents an hour. Anyone with projects in mind for the CWA to complete was to apply to the county relief director. The CWA quickly became controversial in the state because it forbade the hiring of property owners for labor on CWA projects. Rural states, of course, had large numbers of property owners—farmers—who were thus ineligible, even though their farms had produced nothing for them to live on. Disputes over eligibility for aid under CWA slowed its implementation. In spite of the high hopes of locals, the *Kadoka Press* reported only three CWA projects under way in the state at the end of 1933, in the cities of Aberdeen and Mitchell and in Codington County, all east of the river.[49]

The Depression and accompanying drought created the third great crisis of west river life. Residents met it as best they knew how by cutting back and making do. As the trials of the early thirties intensified, people turned to local relief efforts, such as those of the Red Cross, and welcomed federal help as a necessary route out of unprecedented disaster. If they had suspected the challenge that federal programs and their agents would pose over the long term to their fundamental ideology and their very history, the people of the west river country might have met the new waves of Washington bureaucracies at the Missouri River with guns. But the need for help was immediate, deep, and real. Like many others in many contexts, west river residents would later come to regret the days they had "signed on the dotted line"; but in 1933, they had no such regrets, only gratitude born of desperation. And they did not know, in December of 1933, that the worst was yet to come.

7

In the Last Days, Perilous Times Shall Come

Pennington County homesteaders in front of their dugout, 1936.
Library of Congress, courtesy of the South Dakota Archives.

Home on the range, where the dust and thistles roam, and the taxes not paid, and the skies are cloudy all day.
— Peter F. Cosgrove, Pennington County, *Dakota Farmer*, May 11, 1935

This know also, that in the last days perilous times shall come. For men shall be lovers of their own selves, covetous boasters, proud, blasphemous, disobedient to parents, unthankful, unholy. . . . Traitors, heady, highminded, lovers of pleasures more than lovers of God; . . . Ever learning, and never able to come to the knowledge of the truth.
— 2 Timothy 3, quoted frequently in letters to the *Dakota Farmer* to evoke the depth of the drought

FOR A farming people, the relationship with nature is fundamental. For west river farm families, the relationship with nature had always been problematic. Lean years were too common, and the struggle for sustenance was often hard. Yet, faith in the promise of Genesis for seedtime and harvest, and rain in due season, kept west river farm families at the work of wresting a living from an often unyielding soil.

The drought years of the early thirties posed a terrible challenge to that faith, but most people persevered. The mid-thirties would be different. Drought, hoppers, and blowing dust created conditions so severe that fifty years later, survivors refused to tell the tale in their reminiscences. Nineteen thirty-six was the nadir. Perhaps the most reliable indicator of its impact on west river folk is that tales of its cruelties replaced the legends of 1911 in west river lore, until then the benchmark of hard times. Many lost their faith and moved on, convinced finally that next year would not be better. Others stayed, like thousands of latter day Noahs floating in sea of dust, waiting for the wrath of God to subside and a new creation to begin. In the meantime, they lived on relief and government programs, not yet fully aware that the new world they looked toward would be very different than the old.[1]

In previous springs, newspaper editors and rural correspondents greeted the season with optimism and hopes for good crops and plentiful rains. In 1934 the papers told of drought and blowing dust. The winter had been dry and open. There was disagreement about the impact of such a winter. One rural correspondent was thankful because a snowy, severe winter would have brought "great suffering among the

146

people and the livestock." Others feared it portended a year even drier than 1933. The *Kadoka Press* welcomed a March blizzard for the moisture it brought.[2]

The dry winter brought dust storms. In March a statewide news service syndicated in the *Press* reported that cattle were dying when they ingested the dirt blown into their feed. April was filled with "disagreeable days as wind and dust blew steadily," according to the Wanblee correspondent. The River Park reporter posed a prevailing problem: "How to be cheerful in the continued dust storms, that is our task." In May a column from Pierre reported a haunting reminder that nature had the potential to bury civilizations: the severe dust storms were unearthing a rich trove of ancient Arikara artifacts along the banks of the Missouri. A week later the same Pierre reporter noted a dust storm that "blew away all but the mortgage." At the end of May the town of Kadoka ran out of water; the Milwaukee Railroad shipped free water from Rapid City, like a benevolent parent to its sometimes errant child. When a legislator in Pierre spoke of "the short grass country west of the river" in June, a listener corrected him: "Right now it's mostly no grass country." The Gist family in Lyman County remembered 1934 as "the year of the great dust storms. . . . Each day at sunrise the wind came up and was filled with blowing, cutting soil. . . . Each evening the sun set red and the wind died down and settled into a cooling peace, only to begin again the next day."[3]

Ray Gist worked on government relief projects "along with all of our neighbors" and helped his landlord (who "did not lose faith in Lyman County") build a new barn. The family sold some cattle to the government and bought feed for eight milk cows and raised their own meat. By the fall of 1934 "nearly everyone was dependent on government projects and aid," Gladys Gist remembered. "We refinanced our loans and kept as self supporting as possible."[4]

For the Van Schaak family in Mellette County, 1934 brought "a brutal struggle for survival." Grasshoppers had taken all of the feed crops they had tried to grow in 1933, their pasture had given out, and "there was no hay to be found anywhere. . . . The cows grew gaunt, their ribs showing beneath their loose hides." A tremendous dust storm blew out the large window in their house, took the roofs off the outbuildings, and killed the young turkeys, while the family huddled in their cave for protection. They sold their cattle to the government and tried to find new ways to survive. Clair Van Schaak heard of a road-building job in Nebraska and went there to find work, leaving Rose and the children on the farm. After an absence of several weeks he returned, disheartened. He had found work, but the sandy soil of western Nebraska had overworked his best horse and the mare died, a loss far greater than his meager wages were worth. He then went to work on a local Works Progress Administration project.[5]

In July the Van Schaaks had visitors from Wyoming who "could hardly believe the devastation" that had ravaged their once-productive farm. "He [the visitor] . . . looked over the barren fields, the bare grey stalks of corn in blown out lister rows, heat waves . . . the cracks in the earth . . . the sand drifts around the house and barn. Grasshoppers crawled up the sides of the house, hopping and buzzing in the yard." Rose Van Schaak remembered the visitor's words: "My God, Clair, how much longer can you take this?" Her husband replied, "Not much longer. We're just about finished." Within days the Van Schaaks borrowed a relative's car and went west to look for a new start.[6]

The Van Schaaks were not the only family to leave. By September 1934 the rural correspondents' columns recorded a growing number of departures, each presented with a tone of disappointment and dismay. Neighbors of twenty-five years, friends who had shared the hardships of the pioneers, had decided to leave it all behind for the greener pastures of Idaho, Oregon, and Washington. Rural communities held huge farewell parties for the emigrants, bittersweet acknowledgments of a shared experience now torn asunder by drought and depression. For those who left, there was relief blended with a terrible sadness. Rose Van Schaak remembered the day: "A feeling of panic clutched at my heart; I was leaving my childhood home. . . . The figure of my mother waving goodbye to us will be in my memory forever." Her husband told her how to handle her grief. "Don't cry . . . and don't look back. We have a whole new life ahead of us." (After they settled in Idaho, Rose often dreamed that she "was back again in the wind and the dust. Behind my eyelids, the dark clouds once again rolled toward me across the gray hills and blasted fields. I would jump awake, trembling.")[7]

The cattle were also leaving the west river country. With no feed and no water, farmers and ranchers could not maintain their herds. Livestock suffered terribly. Agnes Whiting of Gregory County wrote of her family's struggle to care for their stock. Her memories included "the bellowing of the hungry cattle that we could not feed, no hay except mounds of thistles which were the only vegetation the grasshoppers and drought had left us. The milk cows staggering and falling over barn door sills, following us, bawling for forage which we couldn't give them . . . cattle eating manure piles." Many of their cattle starved to death. The Cole correspondent in Perkins County reported that "believe it or not, the cattle are beginning to eat up the barns of our neighbors."[8]

In response to the crisis, the federal government established a cattle buy-out program, where farmers and ranchers could sell stock to the government. The program ran from June through September and helped depopulate the ranges. Private buyers also shipped great numbers of stock to the East. On July 26 the *Kadoka Press* reported twenty-one carloads shipped out by rail in a four-day period. In August the federal government opened a relief canning factory in Kadoka to handle some of the beef purchased. By mid-month women workers at the factory were canning "four beeves a day." When it closed in December, the workers had processed 10,213 cans of meat. The *Bison Courier* reported in October, after the government buying program had ended, that 25,473 cattle had been sold to the government in Perkins County. Farmers and ranchers received $376,376 for their stock, although Perkins County commissioners voted to list the county as first lienholder in cases where taxes were owed, in order to get much needed funds to run the government.[9]

The depleted ranges lent a further air of melancholy to an already tragic scene. The rural correspondents noted the departures. The South Creek correspondent saw "a herd of 300" driven by her farm. The Franklin writer told of "cattle driven away all the time." By September the Franklin correspondent reported that "the cattle range looks deserted." In Perkins County the River Park correspondent mourned for "the many folks [who] have to see their fine herds, the result of years of work, sacrificed for very little." It was a bitter pill.[10]

To add insult to injury, in August 1934 the federal government declared thirteen west river counties "submarginal" and established rehabilitation programs to move families out. The program and its director were the source of controversy. Dr. Elwood Mead, the federal reclamation officer, apparently stated publicly that both of the western Dakotas should be evacuated at once. According to the Pierre High-lights reporter, "He so irked state officials that an apology was forth-coming." Local people chafed at the "submarginal" label. The Wanblee correspondent reported many rumors floating about regarding the gov-ernment's purchase of the submarginal acres. "Many of the old timers seem to have faith in the productivity of this section of South Dakota," she noted. The *Bison Courier* and the *Philip Pioneer-Review* agreed. While the *Courier* understood federal reclamation director Mead's po-sition ("It's only natural for the specialist in his line to want to do his work. . . . Dr. Mead feel[s] like reclaiming"), the editor argued that good times would return "and would it not be a waste of time and en-ergy to leave, pack and baggage, just to have to move back again when good times come? We vote to save the cost of transportation." The edi-tor of the *Pioneer-Review* rejoiced to hear that few west river folks had taken the government's offer. "Most of them, although suffering terrific hardships, will stick it out in spite of hell and high water." He saw the plan as one created by people "who had no firsthand knowledge of ac-tual conditions" or by ranchers who could profit if farms were bought out and then leased at low rates to themselves.[11]

Federal agents worked to defuse local opposition. Oscar Hermstad, the project manager for the Badlands–Fall River submarginal area, told a "record number of interested guests" at a Kadoka Kola Club meeting that the "submarginal" label was incorrect. "Every land has its purpose," he explained. The Badlands had scenic value, and the west river coun-try would be good for grazing, but both areas were, he said, submar-ginal for farming. The program would aid three types of people now on the land. The first were the stock raisers, whom the government would ask to join voluntary grazing districts. The second were the farmers "who got off on the wrong foot" when they settled on high risk land. The third group consisted of "the man who always presents a problem, unable to manage himself." The program would relocate those in the second and third groups. Families in the second category would get better land elsewhere, while those in the third group would be placed in "supervised farming" projects where they would receive better land and guidance to help them "manage themselves to earn a reasonable and comfortable living."[12]

At the end of the grim summer of 1934, with some people leaving, most cattle going, and words like "submarginal" being bandied about, Francis Case came to Lemmon to campaign for Congress. He stood proudly against the tribulations of the day; his words echoed the pioneer faith: "The West River is a young country. Our best is yet to be. We have dreamed of opportunity for youth, of happiness of middle age and security for old age. That is our birthright and we will not sell it."[13]

The winter and spring of 1935 brought more troubles. The Rural Credits board began another round of farm foreclosures, and more families moved west, including some of "the most thrifty and successful" pioneers who had "built up . . . the most attractive places." In April the dust began to blow. After two weeks of wind the River Park correspondent described the misery simply: "Don't you still taste the dust in your mouth?" In mid-May the Chance correspondent explained that "no one in this locality seems to be very enthusiastic about farming this spring, due to so much disagreeable, windy weather and lack of moisture."[14]

To keep hopes up and ambition alive, the *Dakota Farmer* sponsored "My Plans for 1935," a contest in which Dakota farm families could share their plans with readers and win prizes awarded by the editors. A Perkins County woman said her family "planned to go on with their work so that we can get the most out of little things." A Fall River County woman, whose farm lay in the submarginal buy-out district, told the *Dakota Farmer* that she and her family "still had faith in South Dakota. . . . [We] are going right ahead and put in our regular crop. . . . We will do our part and trust to the Lord for the harvest." A Harding County man, who reported that he had put up enough Russian thistles to save his entire herd of cattle in 1934, told *Dakota Farmer* readers that he planned "to do better in 1935." One way he hoped to do so was to let "excess acreage go back to native wheat grass. . . . There is no better and surer hay crop." Theo Gerard of Lyman County wrote that he believed "in planning ahead. . . . Careful planning has made it possible for us to weather — unassisted — the great drought, depression and grasshopper plague." His plans included general principles rather than specific steps; Gerard told readers that storing surpluses, for example, had "kept the wolf from our door. . . . (Joseph filled the storehouse and so should we.)" "Sticktoitiveness" was another entrant. "Never give up," he wrote, "look for the silver lining."[15]

The children of a submarginal farmer, Pennington County, 1936.
Library of Congress, courtesy of the South Dakota Archives.

The faith of the *Dakota Farmer* planners was rewarded to a degree in 1935. Early summer rains fell in abundance. The River Park correspondent exulted at the lush wildflowers abundant on the prairies, while the South Coal Springs notes rejoiced over "crisp juicy onions and radishes. . . . We had almost forgotten how good homegrown fresh vegetables could taste." Later in the season the dry weather returned, but some people raised crops, and there was hay for the stock. It was not enough to halt the sense of regional decline, however. When the Kadoka Kola Club sponsored their annual Free Day celebration in September, the *Press*'s editor explained that, while "far off it may look like a feeble attempt to celebrate, . . . right here it means more than that" — it meant survival in the face of crisis. "Fine families" continued to leave the area in troubling numbers. Relief work still provided most of the income in the area. Yet 1935 gave people hope that normal times could return.[16]

It was, of course, a false hope, at least for the immediate future. The winter provided the warning. By late January 1936 the high temperatures frequently remained below zero, and constant winds moved the snow ceaselessly across the prairie. By February travel was almost impossible. The *Bison Courier* reported serious frostbite injuries for two teachers traveling home from country schools. Supplies of coal and other fuels ran low, and impassable roads prevented resupply. One day in February the temperature rose only to −21 degrees. The mail into Bison arrived a week late, and rural mail carriers were frequently stranded in the snow and cold. For thirty-five days in January and February 1936 the temperature did not rise above zero. The March 5 issue of the *Courier* included the first correspondence from the Date area since the beginning of the year, reported Meadow's first church service in six weeks, and carried the River Park correspondent's mention of the hand shoveling being done by farmers in her area to open the road to Bison. Even in March some areas of Perkins County remained impassable. The Johnson school correspondent told of mail being received on March 3, the first mail since January 28. The carrier in that area was still unable to reach some patrons due to impassable roads.[17]

George Reeves, a rancher in Meade County, remembered that terrific winter. In those days, every morning at 9 A.M. the telephone operator gave a general ring to all patrons on the phone line and provided a weather report for the day. One day in January 1936 she relayed the news of an approaching storm and urged all to protect their stock. The day was warm and the ground bare. "That night," Reeves recounted, "the snow came in on a high wind. It roared past our windows in a steady sweep. . . . It was thirty below." Blizzards continued for six weeks, and at one point the thermometer hit −52 degrees. Reeves observed the pattern. "Mornings when the sun came up, the earth might be as still as death, and from sky line to sky line there would be nothing to see but white. . . . Then the wind would come up, slowly gathering might." Soon a ground blizzard would be raging as the snow began to move. "A white haze would march across the glistening land . . . then plumes would grow to clouds, the light of sun would disappear, the air would be full of flying snow." The wind changed direction frequently, one day blowing from the north and the next day from the south, quickly filling any paths or trails. The cold remained intense. On the Reeves ranch, "we did our chores at a high run, handling forks and scoops whose handles seared the hands like hot coals. At short intervals we galloped for the house to thaw out frozen members." When not at work outdoors, Reeves and his family clung to the "red-hot stoves."[18]

The severe cold and penetrating winds sorely tested the spirits of west river people. Most people heated their homes with stoves, and the rooms away from the heat source could be arctic. In times of severe cold, even rooms nearer a stove could be frigid. One family with a "good" home in eastern Pennington County decided to test the temperature in the upstairs bedroom and in the downstairs rooms closer to the stove. In both cases the thermometer read −18 degrees. People went without food, fuel, or mail and were shut off from friends and neighbors for days or weeks. The telephone provided a lifeline for those lucky enough to have one. George Reeves recalled the custom of listening in on others' conversations in the multiple party lines typical of the era, which provided amusement, and of the importance of the line in emergencies. In one case a man lay ill twenty-eight miles from town and desperately needed medical care. His wife tried to get a plane to fly him to help, but the storm was too fierce. After several days of trying to get assistance, the family finally loaded the sick man into a truck filled with loose hay and, with neighbors and others alerted by the telephone line, hand shoveled the road to town.[19]

The harshness of the winter, paradoxically, gave west river farmers new hope. The snow that had fallen, they believed, would prepare the seedbed for a bountiful crop. They were wrong. By mid-March "black wind clouds" hung over the region. At the end of May the *Bison Courier* reported the "general feeling" that if no rain fell within two weeks the crops for the year would be lost. In June the situation became critical. Farmers tried to cut any remaining grain for hay or turned their stock into the fields to provide some feed before the drought dried it up completely. Dams, water holes, and creeks began to dry up again. One farmer told the *Courier* that he would have to dig up the potatoes he had planted and eat them if it didn't rain soon.[20]

T. E. Hayes, a Perkins County farmer, provided an overview of the discouraging 1936 crop season in the *Dakota Farmer*. "With the spring of 1936, after the snow had melted," he wrote, "farmers as optimistic as ever went to work in the fields to put in the new crop, and although many fence rows were piled high with the drifted soil, conditions seemed and weather prophets told us we had reached the end of the drouth." Unfortunately, that was not true. "Before the end of May," Hayes recounted, "the grain was dying off and the pastures were brown, grasshoppers and all kinds of bugs were busy cleaning up everything green in fields and gardens." "After completing that job," he continued, "they took to the trees we have been trying for years to grow. By the end of June the trees looked like they do in December—absolutely bare of leaves." All across the west river country the color green disappeared in drought. One man in Haakon County had no hay fever that year—because there was no "hay"—the only year in his life until he reached old age that he avoided the summer misery.[21]

Precipitation totals for the year 1936 fell to record lows, although they varied dramatically from place to place. The northwestern corner of the state received the least precipitation. Bison in Perkins County, for example, received only 4.91 inches of precipitation for the entire year. Camp Crook in Harding County received just 4.33 inches. Farther south the totals were not much better. Ottumwa in Haakon County received 6.21 inches of precipitation, while Cottonwood in Jackson County received 7.13 inches. In Gregory and Tripp counties precipitation totals were quite a bit higher at two reporting stations, Gregory and Winner. Gregory recorded 15.81 inches of precipitation; Winner received 14.42 inches. Both stations, however, were below their typical averages of 17.13 and 18.22 inches, respectively. By June the old-timers began to declare 1936 worse than 1911. The *Bison Courier* and the *Buffalo Times-Herald* both reported the reflections of local pioneers to that effect. The *Kadoka Press* noted that the White River was dry for the first time in a quarter of a century—since 1911.[22]

The incredible summer heat in 1936 added to the growing disaster. Temperature records were broken day after day. In June the *Kadoka Press* reported a new all-time high for the town at 114 degrees. By the first week in July the temperature had reached 119 degrees at Kennebec in Lyman County. McIntosh in Corson County, which had recorded the state low temperature of −58 degrees on February 17, on July 6 recorded a temperature of 114 degrees. In the days before air conditioning there was little way to find refuge from the intense and prolonged heat. The *Courier*'s editor noted that people were sleeping on their porches or in their basements to escape the heat. One family in Meade County slept outdoors in their hay wagon, high off the ground to escape rattlesnakes. During the day, families also tried to hide from the heat. In September, after the heat had subsided, the South Coal

Springs correspondent commented, "It is quite a relief to be able to live in our houses again since the cooler weather came, instead of spending the largest part of the day in cellars or caves as we did during the hot weather."[23]

The drought and heat forced farmers and ranchers to move their stock to better pastures or to sell what remained of their herds. Even the Russian thistles, until then a reliable feed source, had failed to grow. The *Courier's* editor remarked in July that "all one hears these days is that someone just left with their stock for the eastern part of this state or adjoining states, seeking pasture or range lands." The South Coal Springs correspondent reported that the only callers in her neighborhood had been cattle and sheep buyers. "There's not much left here for them to buy," she commented. "Most people are keeping only a few milk cows and others a few sheep — just enough for a [new] start." As the year progressed, hope seemed to wane. As winter approached, many lost the will to farm in such a barren land. Dust storms struck in November and December, and people worried that the ground was too dry to freeze. The South Creek correspondent to the *Kadoka Press* noted in December that a neighbor was sowing rye. "As far as we know," she wrote, "this is the only fall grain sown in this vicinity. Here's hoping the harvest will be bountiful."[24]

With no hope of sustenance from nature and relief the only apparent option, the trickle of west river departures became a flood. The August 13, 1936, issue of the *Kadoka Press* reported three departures; the next week there were five. In July the *Bison Courier* reported that "a few of the local county people have loaded their household and personal goods and moved out of the state and many do not intend to come back." The July 30 edition mentioned three families leaving for California; on August 20 the editor told of farewells for two families, each with twenty-five years in the county. The September 17 issue listed six families with plans to move, five to the west, one to Wisconsin. In October the Perkins County auditor abruptly resigned his position and headed to Oregon. The same issue reported the closing of the Imogene post office because it had lost so many patrons in the past year. The Antelope Community Club stopped meeting because its leaders had all moved away, although the correspondent noted that their absence was for the winter only.[25]

It was federal relief and agricultural programs that saved the west river country. In December 1934 South Dakota had a greater percentage of its people on relief than any other state. Fully 39 percent of South Dakotans needed relief to survive; over 50 percent of farm families were on relief. It was impossible to avoid the omnipresent relief apparatus, whether individuals needed relief themselves or not. The local papers carried lengthy stories about federal programs in virtually every issue. The social notes reported who was working on which project and noted injuries or interesting experiences, just as they did for people working at home on their farms. Community leaders campaigned for Civil Works Administration and Works Projects Administration projects to keep local people working and to improve the quality of life in the region. In a profound irony, given the usual allegiance paid to rugged individualism and self-help, relief projects provided the amenities (and sometimes the basics) of life — roads, dams, sewer systems, playgrounds, and community buildings — that west river people had never been able to afford themselves, even in the best of times.[26]

Relief appeared in many forms. Some relief projects were temporary, such as the provision of a county nurse as part of a project to help unemployed nurses and provide nurses to marginal areas. Others were permanent, such as roads and sewer systems. There was some discussion about which projects were most vital. Isolated rural residents urged the building of roads. The River Park correspondent in Perkins County interrupted her reporting on the drought and forced sale of cattle to remark with joy about "the hum of the road caterpillar" which was "sweet music to those who have waited so many years." The Bison Courier's editor pushed for dam construction on every creek or draw, anywhere where runoff water might be contained. Dams, he argued, were more important than roads. "Dry years will break the country," he explained, "and we'll not need roads." After another epistle on the need for many small dams, he concluded, "more power to the WPA and to the men who will build them."[27]

Towns with effective organizations fought to get all kinds of projects. The Philip Pioneer-Review's editor expressed a common attitude. He was generally opposed to the New Deal relief programs, but since they were in place, "each community [should] try to line up something that will bring in some returns." He urged the building of large dams on major rivers for irrigation purposes as a means of saving the west river country for farmers.[28]

Kadoka, through its Kola Club, developed an effective lobbying group that brought home a number of federally funded projects and helped raise local matching funds. The Kola Club lobbied for money for a sewer system but suffered delays in receiving it, campaigned for a relief canning plant for the town and saw it developed, and pressured state relief directors for dams for the area and got those as well. The Kola Club also graveled the road between the town of Interior and the Badlands to enable the state to advertise an all-gravel route across the state to the Black Hills and built a telephone line from Kadoka to Wanblee as a relief project, in part with subscription money raised in both towns. (The source of the financing for the Badlands road was not specified.)[29]

Besides these projects, in the 1934–1936 time period the federal government operated a sewing room in Kadoka to provide work for women on relief; it held a relief sewing room style show for the community in June 1936 with clothes modeled by the women and children of the community, built a number of tourist cabins at the town's park, helped gravel the streets of Kadoka, provided aid for dormitories for high school students from the county (1934 only), and paid relief workers to grade township and county roads in the area and build dams. At the end of 1936 the town planned to ask for cement sidewalks leading to the school and for a new fire house, although it was willing to subordinate those requests to the need for a better water system, a plan pending at the time.[30]

Such relief work, combined with the government agricultural program payments put into effect in 1933, helped many individuals to survive and aided businesses because their patrons had a bit of money. In Jackson County, for example, the amount of relief that poured into the county from all sources between July 1933 and December 1935 was $158 per capita, or approximately $416,488. The government agricultural programs instituted under the Agricultural Adjustment Act (AAA) and the emergency cattle buying program brought in $425,269 between January 1, 1934, and December 31, 1935. For Perkins County the relief figure was $74 per capita, or $645,058 for relief, and $249,655 in AAA programs by December 1935; the emergency cattle purchase payments brought in $376,376 by October 1934, and the county agent estimated a total of $400,000 by the time all cattle were purchased. The county agents recorded the appreciation of area farmers in their reports to their superiors in Washington, D.C. In one report the Perkins County agent quoted a farmer who called the AAA payments "a Godsend." In his 1936 report the agent wrote that "the money received by the producers was a life saver. . . . Many farmers have advised this office that had it not been for the benefit payments, they did not know really what they would have done."[31]

The impact of relief and agricultural programs was profound. The Wanblee correspondent described the change in her town when relief money began to flow into the area: "The Relief Work in its different forms has made a great difference in Wanblee — people are busy and happy. That old hopeless worried look is gone, business is good, there are no empty houses of any kind and it seems like old times. . . ." When the U.S. Supreme Court declared the first Agricultural Adjustment Act (of 1933) unconstitutional in January 1936, the *Bison Courier* agreed that the justices might have been correct in their legal interpretations but stated unequivocally that "the AAA saved the west river country farmer."[32]

The relief applications completed by individuals provide an enlightening portrait of the depth of the need for relief. In the spring of 1935 the federal government established new relief guidelines, generated standardized forms for applications, and required all on relief to reapply. This created for the first time a consistent set of questions for relief clients to answer. From a sample of 244 people on relief in one west river county, 157 completed the standardized form in May, June, or July of 1935. Of that number, 143 were men and 14 were women. The great majority of men, 92 percent, were married; of the women, thirteen were widowed, and one was single. People of all ages applied for relief. For men, thirty-one were under thirty; thirty were in their thirties; thirty-four were in their forties; thirty-five were in their fifties; thirteen were over sixty. For women, three were under thirty; one was in her thirties; four were in their forties; the remaining six were in their fifties.

The pioneers, people who arrived in the county before 1911, were well represented in the relief rolls in 1935. Of the 157 applicants, fifty men and eight women, or 37 percent, had been in the west river country since 1911 or earlier. Thirty-five of the pioneers had come as adults,

The son of a Pennington County Rural Rehabilitation client does the chicken chores, 1936.
Library of Congress.

while seventeen migrated as children. Six had been born west of the river. Twenty percent of the applicants had come to the west river country after the first big drought in 1911 but before the crash of 1921. Another 22 percent had established homes in the county in the 1922– 1930 time period. A final group of 17 percent had come during the Depression and dust bowl years.[33]

Most of the applicants who applied for relief in 1935 were farmers — 120 of the 154 that listed their occupations, or 78 percent. For the men who did not farm, the largest single category of work was "odd jobs," ten of thirty-four workers. These men often had more substantial work prior to the Depression but had been laid off and were willing to try any kind of work to support themselves. One man, for example, had worked for the state highway department but had lost that job because of cutbacks; another had farmed until losing his place and "now does any kind of work he can get." Others had always been on the periphery of stable employment. Case 79, for example, had "always done whatever work was available." The caseworker listed his main problems as "no skills and poor education." Case 185 had worked through "a long list of odd jobs." The other male workers were divided among ten different occupations, including bridge builder, mechanic, stock buyer/auctioneer, and railroad employee.[34]

The women applicants illustrated the hardships of widowhood in an agricultural community. While women were important economic producers on the farm, when they were left alone there was no one to do the heaviest labor. Four of the relief applicants were farm or ranch women with adult sons who helped with the work, but when the crops failed, it was unclear who should support whom. Relief workers generally expected adult sons to provide for their mothers: if the sons could get some kind of work, the mother was then taken off relief. In one case, the sons of a ranch family did not wish to declare their cattle as part of the property available to support their mother; the mother was denied relief as a result of her sons' property. Four of the women had managed to keep farms operating for several years with the help of younger children or neighbors but could not cope with the crisis of the thirties and had to ask for aid. One of them had been widowed in 1924 but had managed to keep her family together and in school. She told the caseworker she would "be able to hold the farm for only one more year" but was grateful for the aid.[35]

Town widows suffered from the lack of work available for women. One with two small children reportedly was eager for "any honest work to make a living." Another, who had left her farm in 1932, did housework, cared for the sick, and tended mothers and babies after childbirth to support her family. A third town widow "worked at anything" to support her two children. These women were candidates for the county mother's pension program, although several west river counties ran out of funds for their welfare program in the thirties. The women worked in the sewing room once it opened.[36]

Most of the applications reflect real hardship. Several of the applicants who had come to the west river country as pioneers (before the first crisis in 1911) had lost their places to depression and drought in the twenties or early thirties. Some of the younger men who had come with their parents to homestead had been left rootless when their parents lost their farms just as the young men reached adulthood. They married and tried to get a start but often moved from place to place in search of a living. Only a lucky few now farmed their parents' original claim. The applications make clear the damage drought caused. With no crop and no pasture, families had to sell their livestock, their one means of accumulating wealth. For indebted owners or itinerant renters, the loss of stock meant financial disaster.[37]

The standard relief application forms included a space for the clients to explain why they needed help. Some of the answers were short and to the point. "I am out of money," one man wrote. "To keep myself and wife from starving," wrote another. "So I can buy the daily bread," explained a third. Other clients provided more details. Case 148 explained that he "had no crop, was compelled to sell my chickens and horses in order to live during the past four years." He concluded, "Am at the end of my resources now." Another applicant expressed his anger. He needed aid "because we have had a total crop failure for three years and we had to sell our cattle and chickens till we have no income." His family had tried to avoid relief. "We haven't drove a car for five years trying to get along," he wrote, "we have also worked hard while about 50% of our neighbors spent their relief checks for whiskey and good times." "So," he stated, "I think we deserve a little help."[38]

The caseworkers made clear that most people in the relief system were there through no fault of their own. It was the "conditions of the country" that created the misery. Only a few were labeled poor managers barely able to get by in the best of times. As the crisis dragged on, a larger number would look to relief as the solution to all of their problems; an entitlement mentality began to develop among a hapless few. In the mid-thirties, however, the caseworkers more frequently had to ferret out the deserving and force them to take aid in spite of their pride. And when they checked the references applicants were asked to supply, again and again the answer came: "He is a good man and a hard worker. He would not ask for aid unless he really needed it."[39]

The years 1934–1936 threatened not only the livelihoods of west river residents but the very faith upon which their society was founded. In Genesis, God had promised the faithful that "while the earth remains, seedtime and harvest . . . shall not cease," yet for several years all of the plagues of Egypt and more had befallen the land. As 1936 drew to a close, even the relief structure (which could be accommodated, if somewhat uneasily, as necessary help to a people doing good work) was threatened. Rumors flew that the Works Progress Administration would no longer accept farmers for work relief; local newspaper editors tried to stop the panic with reassurances that the region, with its heavy caseload of distressed farm families, could not, would not, be forgotten. In December 1936 the federal government published *The Future of the Great Plains*, the report of the Great Plains Committee, a presidential committee appointed to develop long-term solutions for the publicly labeled "marginal area." It seemed to imply that there was no future for the region unless the people there gave up their most prized values: individualism, self-determination, and their pioneer faith in limitless growth and development. The drought would wear on for five more difficult years, although it was never again as pervasive or intense as it was in 1936. The ideological and philosophical battles over the future of the west river country continued as well. The belief in the pioneer as builder collided head-on with the New Dealers' image of the pioneer as destroyer. Neither side would win a clear victory.[40]

8

The Plainsman Cannot Assume . . .

Farms go back to grass. Men seed crested wheatgrass in Stanley County, 1938 or 1939.

The Plainsman cannot assume that whatever is for his immediate good is also good for everybody—only of his long-run good is this true, and in the short run there must often be sacrifices; he cannot assume the right always to do with his own property as he likes—he may ruin another man's property if he does; he cannot assume that the individual action he can take on his own land will be sufficient, even for the conservation and best use of that land. He must realize that he cannot "conquer Nature"—he must live with her on her own terms, making use of and conserving resources, which can no longer be considered inexhaustible.

—Great Plains Committee, *The Future of the Great Plains*, December 1936

If farmers will quit listening to political demagogues, attend to their own business, use common sense and a workable system, they will eventually make a good living, and more, on this great "desert." It is promised in the Bible that such places shall be made to blossom as a rose. The farmers who stick are going to more than see that prophecy come true. . . . For one, I am going to stay with the "desert." . . . Like the Swede, "we ain't afraid for scare."

—E. H. Klock, Fall River County, *Dakota Farmer*, November 7, 1936

IN LATER YEARS, when west river people wrote of the hard times and blowing dust of the thirties, the years after 1936 received short shrift. The reminiscences tell of the tragic grasshopper years, the extremes of heat and cold, the bitter gall of forced cattle sales, and the salvation provided by the Works Progress Administration (WPA) and other relief programs. The years after 1936, however, are telescoped together with simple descriptions: "After 1936," they wrote, "things got better." The reminiscences are not wrong—things did get better, but very slowly and in the face of tremendous challenges from nature and from the social and economic forces set in motion by the crisis. Relief records show that federal direct relief and work relief programs remained a powerful and necessary presence in the region until the plentiful rains and war returned in 1942, creating a vast new source of demand for labor and agricultural commodities. Although some people avoided relief completely and others moved in and out of the system as needed, a third group had been so devastated both economically and psychologically by the Depression and dust of the thirties that relief had become a way of life. Dependency had never been part of the west river 165 dream, but it became institutionalized for some in the years between 1937 and 1942.

The relief records of the late Depression era document in some detail the ongoing struggle of many area residents for mere survival. Of the sample 244 relief cases from one west river county, 121 remained in the relief system after 1936. (Thirteen were still involved in 1942, when the program shut down.) This number does not include those farm families whose Farm Security Administration (FSA) loans and grants were sufficient to support them; FSA clients appeared in the records in the later Depression years only if they could not get by on the FSA plan alone. Those families then came to the relief office and applied for surplus commodities, sewing room clothing, or, when government regulations allowed it, work relief through the WPA. One farmer, on his own place since 1903, moved to town in 1937 because "he lost all hopes of being able to pay off the mortgages and various encumbrances on his place." A son helped support the family with work on WPA projects. An elderly couple, also pioneers in the region, had once been "in fairly good circumstances financially . . . but lost practically all they had accumulated." They lived on direct relief until they departed for Oregon with their adult children. A divorced man had lost most of his assets through foreclosure in 1937 and had "sold his cows and eaten his chickens." All he had left was five horses, "one very old." He became a WPA worker. A family of five whose goal was "to go somewhere where there was steady work and good schools" instead "squatted" in a shack along a creek to avoid paying rents, which they could not afford. "Existence is their immediate problem," the caseworker noted. The FSA would not take them because they were not really farmers. The WPA became the solution, although the paperwork took time and the man of the family felt "cheated" by the delays. Other caseworkers noted toothless women and "listless and sickly" children. But most aid clients kept up the struggle. Families "forced off the farm practically destitute" tried hard to "get a new start in life." In spite of their efforts, relief remained the only viable option for many until the war and plentiful rainfall helped the west river country as a whole get a new start.[1]

Even though the gradual return of better weather in the years after 1936 augured the gradual demise of federal relief programs, the federal presence was becoming institutionalized in other less visible but more profound ways. The federal government during these years became part of the very warp and woof of the economic fabric of west river life. Even as direct relief gradually diminished, federal regulation and policy-making designed to alter the region's economy in fundamental ways proliferated. As better weather and gradually improved conditions moved into the west river country, and direct threats to basic physical survival receded, the perennial fight over the potential of the west river country re-emerged, configured differently in this round because of the presence of the federal government. In the years 1937–1942, the battle for the hearts and minds of west river residents resumed. Would they keep their faith in the country or lose it? Would they flee the struggle or embrace it? Were the policies and tools offered by the federal govern-ment an opportunity or a death knell for the west river country? If west river residents were, as one county agent wrote, "taking stock of their life work," what did they find? The stalwarts of the "next year country" faith interpreted the gradual return of better weather and somewhat improved economic conditions as a sorely belated vindication of their faith in the potential of the country; the county agents and other ad-vocates of New Deal programs, on the other hand, saw the return of better weather as only a respite and a possible danger—the danger being that west river residents would relapse into "next yearism" and halt the process of adaptation to the climatic and agricultural limits of the region. For those who stayed in the west river country, the final five years of dust and depression was a time to come to terms with their re-ordered world.

WEATHER AND CROP reports were not matters of detached moni-toring for the people in the countryside, whose livelihood depended di-rectly on rainfall and crop conditions. West river residents believed, as many county agents did not, that the west river climate, when normal, would provide a comfortable sustenance. They watched the skies and rejoiced in the rains, taking each as a sign that climatic normalcy had returned. In the five difficult years before 1942, the rural correspondents charted every rain and every dust storm, every step toward and every step back from the regular rhythms of rural life they knew would return.

As 1937 opened, the Lyman County agent reported the "attitude, or outlook, held by farmers" to be "the lowest in years." The seemingly endless drought, its accompanying pests and dust storms, and the grinding poverty that afflicted so many had taken a serious toll. Many looked to signs and portents, trying to divine just when normal conditions might return, but as the River Park correspondent once reminded her readers, "all signs fail in dry weather." The year, however, while not normal by any means, was considerably better than 1936 had been.[2]

The Jackson County agent noted that 1937 "was infinitely better than 1936," although wheat yielded only five bushels an acre and the corn was "very poor." Lyman County also experienced conditions "considerably improved" with "plenty of rough feed" and "a partial small grain crop." The Perkins County agent was less optimistic, terming 1937 "another year of set-back," although it was better than the year before. According to his observations, the improvements in the year could not make up for the "lessening of reserves" that had accrued annually since the Depression started. Still, Perkins County feed crops had done well, and pastures were at 50 percent of their normal growth; the agent hoped for winter snows to "lodge in the rank growth of weeds" that infested the prairie and to help provide the moisture that might bring the grass back. The Tripp County agent called the outlook "much brighter," with farmers having some feed on hand, which would help them avoid more feed loans. Rural correspondents told of neighbors so heartened by spring rains that they rushed outdoors to plant gardens while the rain still fell. A Pennington County woman described her family's joy over a steady Sunday rain to the *Dakota Farmer*. Her son had used the time indoors to pen a letter to an absent brother: "Mom just breaks out singing, 'Praise God from whom all blessings flow' every time it rains extra hard," he wrote. But just a month later the South Creek correspondent announced that "the dread and ravenous beetles have arrived." Perkins County recorded numerous pests infesting the prairie, including "large green worms." A federal agriculture report released at the time listed 6,500 kinds of grasshoppers alone. "So," the *Courier's* editor commented, "we still have a few new faces to see." As the disappointing year drew to a close, the Potato Creek correspondent to the *Kadoka Press* wished readers what they all hoped fervently to have for

1938: "a joyous and prosperous yearful of days, with seedtime and harvest and rain in due season."[3]

The next year saw great improvement in Lyman County, where the agent rated "grazing and feed conditions very good," which had encouraged "a return to normal livestock production: hogs, poultry and milk cows." Tripp County also enjoyed the benefits of a good growing year in 1938, which produced "one of the heaviest forage crops in the history of the county." The agent bemoaned the lack of livestock, because of the cutbacks of the drought years, to eat it all. Both Jackson and Perkins counties, however, struggled. In Jackson County, the cash grain crop was cut by half due to untimely rains, but forage did well late in the season, when the much needed moisture finally fell. Perkins County, according to the agent, had "again been subject to the stress of very unfavorable conditions." Perkins County had enjoyed a reasonable rainfall, but "the worst grasshopper outbreak in memory of the old-timers" had destroyed crops and forage alike. As a result of the disaster, "more than 800 farm and ranch homes were receiving direct [FSA] grants. . . ." "When people are disappointed again," the agent concluded, "when a gain means everything, they lose spirit."[4]

The newspapers again charted the halting steps forward and the disappointing setbacks. The Potato Creek writer reported in April that farmers there were "enjoying the rain and painting the clouds with rainbows." In June the South Creek correspondent described "prairie flowers in all their glory, the yard around our little church and cemetery [where two of her children were buried] was beautiful on Memorial Day." Later that month an infestation of grasshoppers and then Mormon crickets afflicted the country. The Ada correspondent to the *Bison Courier* reported the disaster: "Grasshoppers by the millions are in full swing." The next week her column began "Hoppers! Hoppers!" At the end of the month when the Mormon crickets appeared, several correspondents used the same language in their columns: "What next?" The hoppers left in August after "eating the best of everything." At the end of the year, National Youth Administration workers cut down the landmark trees at the Perkins County courthouse that had "been planted in the early days of Bison . . . but fell victim to drought and insect pests." Christmas Day brought a dust storm mixed with sleet. The South

Creek correspondent's final column of 1938 reported a "high cold wind" that "rolled in from the northwest, carrying clouds of loose real estate before it." One step forward, two steps back.[5]

Nineteen thirty-nine began inauspiciously. The winter and spring were harsh. Dust storms came frequently. A River Park correspondent reported neighbors trying to read signs in the moon, hoping for an indication of better weather. The South Creek correspondent wrote of "roaring dust storms" and storms "so dense it made it dark in the house." For Perkins County, however, June brought relief. The *Courier*'s editor celebrated the rain: "It's a different West than a few days ago. . . . One good rain brightened the brown prairies and thirsty fields." The editor and his correspondents alike remarked on "the soft carpet of young green grass, the beds of pale prairie roses. . . ." The new agent in Jackson County, William Woods, did not provide the usual overview but alluded to rainfall approximately two inches below normal for the growing season. For Lyman County, the report was above-average rains, with a surplus of feed grain, forage, and pasture; Tripp County also received above-average rainfall, which produced "one of the heaviest small grain crops in the history of the county." Even benighted Perkins County reported more moisture and no grasshopper infestations. The cultivated crops had suffered from drought, but grass and hay crops had done well. Farther south, 1939 remained a year of struggle. In Jackson County, the South Creek correspondent knew of only one successful vegetable garden in her neighborhood and only one with flowers. Only three farmers sowed winter grains in September, but in October rain turned more farmers' thoughts to planting. The *Kadoka Press* published a notice that Lyman County had surplus feed and pasture and would board cows for its stricken neighbors. When a heavy snow finally fell in December in Jackson County, it broke a four-month drought.[6]

The early 1940s brought an end to sustained widespread drought in the region. In 1940 some west river residents began to notice changes that reminded them of the climate of the old days before the drought. In March the South Creek correspondent remarked that the weather patterns had begun to seem "the way it used to be in the years we had good crops." In April the *Bison Courier* reported "one of the largest flights of ducks, crows and hawks that have been observed in this country for a number of years. . . ." "More indications," the editor hoped, "that the drouth period is perhaps broken at last." Housewives who worried about dust now fretted about mud, according to the paper, and the rural correspondents rejoiced that wet fields were delaying farm work. By May the tractors could be heard day and night. Again, Perkins County had better luck in 1940 than Jackson and Washabaugh counties had, but improvement seemed to be the order of the day in most areas. Although 1940 brought disappointment to many of those outside Perkins County, 1941 and 1942 were excellent crop years throughout the region. Heavy rains and less insect damage helped provide substantial farm income for the first time in at least twelve years, especially in Tripp and Lyman counties. As the Lyman County agent put it, "Lyman County farmers made money." By 1943 he noted "an air of prosperity" in the region. The Tripp County agent in 1944 noted that farm income there was "the highest since 1920." (Both Perkins and Jackson counties discontinued their support of the county agent program in the early forties; with the return of a modicum of prosperity, the more marginal counties refused to bear the expense.) As the county agents' reports indicated, consistently good weather did not return to all west river counties until 1941, and the apparatus of relief did not disappear until a year after that, but the war clouds looming on distant horizons helped divert attention from the presence or absence of rain clouds.[7]

The five-year road back to a semblance of normalcy was a time of challenges and adjustments that ultimately made the west river country a different place. The population decline that had begun in 1934 accelerated. The departures further undermined the already shaky social institutions of the west river country. To the west river residents — most of whom were first or second generation settlers — the mark of success and development was increasing population; decreasing population signified regression into an earlier historical epoch, when vast stretches supported tiny numbers of Indians and ranchers. In contrast, many of the federal policies for the region contemplated the partial depopulation of the region, either directly (for example, the resettlement and the grasslands programs) or indirectly (by conversion from tillage to ranching); for the federal policymakers and bureaucrats, population loss represented progress in adapting to the uses of the land and moving people into more productive areas. Thus, what the residents viewed as progress was considered irrational nostalgia by the planners, while the planners'

A "submarginal" farm targeted for federal buy out, Pennington County, 1936. Library of Congress, courtesy of the South Dakota Archives.

vision was seen by the residents as a giant leap backward into the region's past. The federal government's efforts to get the region on a sounder economic footing helped depopulate parts of it as massive land purchases and resettlement programs decimated neighborhoods; relief workers, paid by the government, then tore the abandoned buildings down as well. This "unsettling" of the prairie had a profound impact on those who chose to stay, resulting in a deep-seated ambivalence about the benefits of federal assistance. The scale of the migration, and the predominance of California and Oregon as destination points, led to a rivalrous dialogue between "stickers" — to use Wallace Stegner's term — and those who had emigrated over the wisdom of their respective decisions. The struggle between the old ideas and new, between the agents of change and the stalwarts of tradition, as well as the "stickers'" own ambivalence, helped flavor the era.

The rock bottom year of 1936 prompted a spate of departures in 1937. The *Bison Courier*'s editor tried to put the brakes on what he feared might be a mass movement. "Let us not act too hastily in condemning it [the west river country] as a place unsuitable in which to make a living. . . . The wheel of fortune, we are sure, will someday shower us with all the good things of life." The Cash Literary Society debated the topic "Why Perkins County is better to live in than elsewhere"; the affirmative won, but notices of departures filled the columns of the papers. In April Charley Settle in Perkins County sold out "the best place in the county" to move to California. The Kadoka paper recorded farewell after farewell, including one for a businessman in town for twenty-five years. When it rained so promisingly in June of 1937, the *Courier's* editor wrote a celebratory editorial about his convictions that the refugees would return with the rainfall. "We'll be glad to see them," he wrote, "and we know they'll be glad to be home." With more wistfulness than confidence, the Cole correspondent hoped "the rains will continue so more of our friends and neighbors will come back."[8]

Departures continued, however. The *Gregory Times-Advocate* noted at the end of 1937 that "many of the boosters have gone." Two months later the *Winner Advocate* recorded ten farm sales in a week's time. One of the most haunting chronicles of a community's dismantling appeared in the *Bison Courier* in 1939. The River Park community was purchased, virtually in its entirety, by the federal government under the Land Utilization program. Lena Jennewein, the River Park correspondent, recorded the death of the neighborhood that had been hers for thirty years. In March 1939 she told of the departure of the Olien family. "Our community is fast dwindling away." Four families had left in the fall of 1938, and others would go by the end of 1939. "Soon River Park will be nothing but a memory." In September 1939 she wrote of the farewells for the Sam Wentzel family. "The Wentzels have spent all their married life here and Sam a few years before that. The children were born and raised here and they have built up a fine ranch and home." That there was more pain to come was explained in the concluding lines: "They were among those who sold to the government, the rest of whom will soon be leaving." In November Jennewein told of another loss. "River Park has again lost some of its good citizens. . . . Mr. and Mrs. Carl Bakke moved to their new home. . . . The Bakkes homesteaded here and are among the first settlers." Two weeks later the Timber Draw school, which served the River Park community, was put on the auction block. The *Courier* explained that, after the government buy out, there would be only one or at most two families in the area, no children to attend the school, and no remaining school board members.

By the end of the year the River Park correspondent complained that "the inhabitants of River Park are getting to be so few and far between" that she could not write any local news without treading on another correspondent's territory. The same issue informed readers that the Jenneweins themselves would retire from their ranch into a "one room apartment" in Bison. In 1941 the Marshfield correspondent began to cover the remnants of River Park. The new correspondent reported the removal of a barn from an abandoned farm place and commented, "We, the people of Marshfield, regret seeing these buildings moved away or wrecked."[9]

Other correspondents felt the same way as the countryside became emptier and emptier. The Fairview correspondent to the *Kadoka Press* remarked on the changes in her community as WPA workers tore down the buildings sold to the government. "Last week the Tom Blair place was torn down and destroyed," she noted. "One by one the farm buildings are disappearing." In Perkins County, an abandoned house became a death trap for some yearling cattle, who had wandered into the farmhouse to seek shade. The door shut behind them, and four starved to death before their owner discovered them. The Cash Budget reporter called it a "terrible tragedy" for the family who owned the cattle, but also for the poor cattle. When WPA workers tore down such empty buildings, local farm families got to keep the wood, which provided them with a ready fuel source. For one family in the Oelrichs area, it meant the end of cow-chip fires. Still, it was unsettling to see the work of a lifetime disappear. When Henry Miller wrote his memoirs of life on a Perkins County homestead, he told of his parents' decision to sell to the government in 1939 and retire. The farm had encompassed ten sections of land and had supported a family of fourteen for thirty years, but "nothing at all remained. There is not even a windmill tower to mark where the homestead once was."[10]

The population dropped in every west river plains county except Pennington, where the substantial growth of Rapid City boosted the overall population figures. Twelve of the eighteen counties lost 20 percent or more of their people between 1930 and 1940, following even greater losses between 1910 and 1915. Three of the twelve counties, Corson, Jackson, and Ziebach, lost more than 25 percent of their population. The farmlands were especially empty; many towns in counties that lost population overall actually gained in population themselves. Kadoka in Jackson County, for example, gained seventy-nine residents, for a population increase of more than 20 percent, although Jackson County as a whole was one of the biggest losers at almost 26 percent. (That loss occurred, according to the *Press*'s editor, "due to the many disasters that have been felt here.") Many west river towns grew at the expense of the surrounding countryside, as families gave up on farming in such a dry and difficult place. The spaces between towns thus became emptier and emptier.[11]

The crisis of the thirties accelerated a process that had begun with the wide use of the automobile twenty years earlier. Cars and trucks allowed farm families to travel long distances relatively quickly; they could then bypass the tiny neighborhood stores, which, along with the rural post offices and schools, had been centers of rural community organizations. When the stores lost their trade, they shut down, and community boundaries began to change. Towns began to be more important as the centers of rural communities, at least economically. After 1930, towns also began to be centers of social interaction for farm people. The advantages of town schools, with their higher standards, seemed important to many, and the recreational opportunities in towns seemed richer as well. Even churches began to leave the rural areas for locations in villages and towns. With the large-scale depopulation in west river rural areas in the thirties, these tendencies toward change became necessities; there were simply too few people left in many farm areas to maintain any kind of community life. Federal programs, such as the removal of farmers from submarginal land and even the WPA, which after 1936 was available, with only a few exceptions, to town residents, exacerbated the process. A letter to the *Dakota Farmer* written in 1945 explains the impact of this change in very human terms. "Long, wintry evenings are here again," the woman wrote, "and although we have plenty of work to do, I do find it rather lonely here in our ranch home in western Stanley County. There are only two farm dwellings occupied on the roadway between our place and town, a distance of 35 miles."[12]

The impact of depopulation was especially notable in the schools. West river school districts generally encompassed one township or more, but by 1940 many could not "maintain even one satisfactory sized school" in the district. During the 1941–1942 school year, ten west river counties were maintaining less than half the number of schools they had supported in their very best year; three counties had one fourth the schools they had maintained in better times. According to a South Dakota Agricultural Experiment Station study, on average only 1.47 farm people per square mile populated the west river country, far too few to support rural school districts, even those of thirty-six square miles (a township) or more. The old school districts remained, but typically they used their administrative and taxation powers to send local pupils as tuition students to other districts still operating schools. Tuition and even transportation costs were less expensive than maintaining a building and paying a teacher. By the end of the 1942–1943 school year, some west river districts began to close their small high schools. Nineteen such high schools closed their doors in 1943. Under a state law passed in 1943, the districts that closed their schools were obligated to pay the transportation costs to "the nearest accredited high school" for those students who wished to attend. The report on high schools attributed the closing of high schools to several factors, including the migration of many families out of the state to work in war industries. While the Depression and the dust of the thirties had acted as "push factors" propelling people out of the state, the lure of good war industry jobs in the forties was a "pull factor" that enticed more away. Paradoxically, the prosperity of the forties did not check the forces of depopulation that had been set loose by the Depression.[13]

Churches were affected as well. The breakdown of the rural neighborhood and the consequent focus on town churches helped undermine the open-country church, as did the poverty of the thirties. Between 1926 and 1936, the rural areas of the state as a whole lost 318 churches. This process continued over the years. The South Creek Lutheran Church in Jackson County, for example, began with sixteen families; by 1937 only seven remained. In 1953, "due to population changes," the congregation built a new church in Kadoka and changed the name to Faith Lutheran. Christ Evangelical Lutheran Church in Bison resulted from the joining of the Meadow and Bison Lutheran congregations in 1938. Consolidation and centralization shaped church life west of the river.[14]

Flora Evans and child, from Perkins County, photographed in Montana en route to Oregon, 1936. Library of Congress, courtesy of the South Dakota Archives.

People who left did not always do so willingly or without second thoughts. And, because they sometimes left family and certainly friends behind, they remained in contact with the region they had abandoned. This established interesting and often competitive links between the old home and the new.

Departed residents sometimes wrote to the local paper to tell of their journey and their new home. The Crow family moved to northern Minnesota in an open Model T Ford in February. "It was a rather cold trip," Mr. Crow wrote, "but we are tough." He explained both the relief and the sadness the family felt. "It seems so good not to see the dust blowing all the time," but "it was tough to leave our little place we had built up." He provided careful directions to their new home and added, "Our latch string will always be out." The family hoped that Perkins County friends would write and visit. Allen English told the homefolks in detail about the wonders of southern California and about his family's circumstances. "We are not farming," he explained, "but I have a steady job at the Lemon By-Products Plant . . . and we have a garden where we can make it rain anytime we wish for a dollar." He concluded with an explanation of the three stages a migrant to California passed through: "At first he is a knocker, then he is a booster and then he is a liar." English hoped to "miss the third stage." He signed off, "We wish you all plenty of rain."[15]

Others corresponded with the rural reporters who then duly communicated the news to their readers. Some liked their new homes, others were not yet sure. Several made comparisons with South Dakota. The Hemmingsons wrote back from Michigan that the wind blew there, too, but they had "an abundance of fruit and vegetables and it rains almost every day." The son of Katie Renning, the South Creek correspondent, moved to California but reported wind there, too. "South Dakota is not the only windy place," she concluded.[16]

The correspondents also knew that many refugees still subscribed to the local paper. They frequently challenged the migrants to California to match a particularly nice Dakota day. Or, on a hard day—for example, a −34 degree day in January—they might comment, "Do you California people realize how well off you are?"[17]

That there was ambiguity about the meaning of migration is clear. Migration could be seen as a failure to maintain the good fight, or it could be interpreted as a logical response to the crisis of the thirties. When one of the pioneers died a year after he moved to California, a letter to the *Courier* listed all of his accomplishments in Perkins County, and asked, "Who could blame them for moving to California?" T. E. Hayes, visiting a gathering of Dakotans in Oregon, reported that many of the migrants "felt rather hurt because some of the papers referred to them as quitters because they had moved out west." He explained that the people attending had relocated because their "load of debt was so heavy"; many planned to return to South Dakota once conditions improved. They maintained their fighting spirit even in exile. Hayes quoted "one fine old lady" who said, "Give us in Dakota half the rain they get in Oregon, and we would surprise the world."[18]

Sometimes migration was seen as "answering opportunity's call." It could be celebrated as an adventure or as part of an ongoing process of frontiering. When a group of Perkins County women held a shower for a new bride, for example, all of the gifts were loaded into a covered wagon labeled "Going West"; the young couple planned to relocate shortly after the party. In either case, the absent ones were frequently remembered and greatly missed.[19]

Those who moved to California or the Pacific Northwest found themselves part of a mass movement. South Dakota picnics in the West were frequent and well attended. Migrants reported to their former newspapers that they had met many from their particular county or community at the gathering. In one case, a fairly large picnic in Oregon was comprised of people who had nearly all belonged to the same church, the Presbyterian church in Kadoka. Inevitably those attending relayed the message that they still thought of South Dakota, that they admired those still willing to face the struggle there, and that they hoped for rainfall and good crops for everyone left behind. Mr. and Mrs. A. D. Burns, formerly of Corson County, for example, wrote the *Dakota Farmer* about their new circumstances in the Yakima Valley in Washington. "We enjoy the mild climate, also the many fruits and vegetables, and beautiful scenery," they explained, but they often thought of home and of "those faithful relatives and friends who are still hanging on . . . always hoping for better luck next year." When their new neighbors argued that "anyone is a fool to stick in that dried-up desert," they retorted with some pride, "No, they aren't — they are the best people that ever lived, the biggest-hearted, cleanest-minded people in the world, and if they could only get the water that is going to waste here, this Yakima Valley wouldn't be in it at all." They closed with a promise: "If it's ever possible for us to return to our old home, we won't be from South Dakota anymore."[20]

Sometimes when the refugees came home to visit, they took a bit of South Dakota back with them. The Rabbit Creek correspondent told readers that when Rod Wiedenbaugh returned to California, "he took a sprig of sage with him to look at and smell when he gets lonesome for this country."[21]

While those settlers who stayed and those who fled felt emotional attachments to the region, the county agents who implemented federal policies were decidedly unsentimental in their perspective. The county agents were at the heart of the battle for local allegiance to the new ideas about conservation and land use. They had come to the region during years of intense crisis with a reform mission: they were to save farm families from themselves and as much as possible convert them into ranchers and their fields of grain and corn to grass. This was, of course, controversial. Successful implementation of their plans meant fewer families in the west river country as individual units grew larger. Fewer families meant fewer schools, less business for small towns, fewer taxpayers to support other institutions, and less opportunity for social interaction.

The government's plans and programs smacked of the deepest betrayal. County agents in the teens and twenties had encouraged farmers in the belief that proper methods would lead to agricultural success on the plains. Mechanization, consolidation of farms, adapted crops, purebred stock, and the right system, the agents had said then, would bring west river farmers returns comparable to those in humid regions. Now the agents (some of them the same men) told the same audience that they had been fools all along. As one farmer who had actively cooperated with the extension agents in the twenties saw it, the extension service, "more than any other thing, had led us along the way of producing two blades of grass where one had grown before. . . . [Now] they have the nerve to tell us it is all wrong; that this land should be let go back to prairie . . . and it should be parceled out in big ranches." Adding to the insult, the agents also said that the presence of farm families was putting "additional burdens upon those people who use the land for the purpose for which it is best adapted (meaning big ranches)." Farm families should, therefore, give up their homes to those who would be better for the land. "One would think the extension service would feel pretty small," the farmer wrote, for abandoning its constituents "because some fellows back east had a sort of fool brain wave." [22]

The county agents' reports and newspaper columns reveal some of the struggles they engaged in to alter the goals, ambitions, and techniques of their clients in the later years of the Depression. The most outspoken and acerbic of the agents was William Woods, who came to Jackson County in February 1939. His column, "Brass Tacks," in the *Kadoka Press* occasionally communicated some of his impatience with the local ethos. In June 1940 he told his readers that Land Utilization Program investigations had shown that "cash grain farming in the area brought bent backs and tears" even before the drought hit. Later in the year he provided an overview of the rocky history of agriculture in the region and reminded his readers that "we never go back to old times." By June 1941 he had lost patience with the need to explain and educate. "The county agent certainly does not intend to enter into a toilsome discussion of the value of the protection of crops from 'hoppers,'" he wrote, "or of protecting poultry from coyotes, or of protecting grass from overgrazing." His conclusion was quite definite: "There just simply isn't anything to argue about in either case."[23]

Woods's reports to his superiors in Washington were even more blunt. In 1939 he described the people of Jackson County as "burdened by debt and despair and confronted by problems of adjustment for which they were utterly unprepared." Government money they received had been spent on "living expenses and seed in the hope that an extraordinary favorable 'next year' would trip the jackpot." He tallied the government money that had come into his county in 1938–1939 ($461,172), listed what it had purchased (including 182 stock water dams, seventy-six farm reservoirs, two school buildings, and much more), and concluded that it had also convinced "94% of farm operators" of one of two things, that "something is wrong with their system of operation" or "that the climate has changed." He alluded to his past experience in the county teaching "short courses" (agricultural education workshops) twenty-five years earlier; at that time, he stated, "no hall was big enough to hold the crowds." But in 1939 in the west river country, federal farm program elections were "attended by only 10% of the beneficiaries of the program."

In 1940 Woods's report was even sharper. He told his supervisors that he had hung a sign in his office for all to see. It said, "88% OF THIS COUNTY IS IN NATIVE GRASS. LIVESTOCK EATS GRASS." The "outlook" section laid out what he believed to be the dynamics of the county. The "old-timers" were engaged in a "wishful hope that 'next year' may be like the wet years" and bring a big crop of wheat at a high price. Their children, Woods believed, had seen their parents' "crushed fortunes and hopeless accumulations of seed and feed loans" and were "carefully considering Land Use Adjustments that will let them take over the old home place under a new name" and "begin livestock production." Under the heading "HOPE SPRINGS ETERNAL," he laid out the role of the Extension Service: "teaching those who will study the climate," with the end result of "better livestock, better reared, by better informed operators." His report concluded, "THIS IS A STOCK COUNTRY."[24]

William Woods may have expressed himself more forcefully than most, but his attitudes were typical of those charged with implementing federal policies in the face of an ambivalent audience. Woods and others struggled with what they viewed as the regressive and nostalgic attitudes that inhibited progressive change. From the bureaucrats' standpoint, farmers took government assistance when physical necessity compelled it but viewed the controls that inevitably accompanied it as interference and oppression by outsiders who did not know what the country was about. Imbued as farmers were with the ethos of struggle and given their commitment to build up, not tear down; to order and control nature, not subject themselves to nature's limitations; to domesticate the grass, rather than see it return on its own terms, the full implications of the agents' plans were unthinkable. Farmers could adjust and adapt by degrees, but they resisted a full scale surrender to the forces of nature and government policies. Woods remarked in one column that he was getting "all kinds of questions" about a new planning group; he tried to reassure readers that there was "nothing mysterious about the function of the Planning Committee." (His insistence on calling every Jackson County agriculturalist a "rancher" probably did not reassure his readers, however.) The *Bison Courier*'s editor received a letter that spelled out local fears about the effort to hire a county planning manager. "The rumor is that this is a man who will be subservient to big land interests," the concerned citizen wrote. What was needed, he argued, was someone "who will give small operators a break."[25]

Regardless of sentiment, for the "stickers," federal agricultural programs were both a lifeline and a challenge. The federal government had been an active participant in regional agriculture since the creation of the Agricultural Adjustment Act (AAA) in 1933; although that particular program had been declared unconstitutional in 1936, other programs had proliferated. State planning boards, charged with the task of studying institutions, agricultural conditions, and any other relevant subject with an eye toward planning for further development, began their work in 1935; county planning boards were in place by 1938. The Soil Conser-

Abandoned hotel in Batesland in Fall River County, 1940.
Library of Congress.

vation Service (SCS) programs, designed to encourage the planting of soil-building crops and the conservation of soil through proper techniques, replaced the original AAA programs in 1936 as an important source of government payments to farmers who cooperated. Land purchase programs provided funds to buy out farmers on the most marginal lands, with the goal of a complete return to grasslands, which in turn could be part of new, group-controlled grazing districts. These programs worked hand in hand with the rehabilitation efforts of the FSA (formerly the Resettlement Administration), which educated its clients in modern and progressive agricultural methods, while helping them become self-supporting. Such federal monitoring and group planning had not been part of the pioneer dream, but in the years after 1936, it was rapidly becoming institutionalized.

In a campaign designed to sell the new ideas to wary residents, federal officials visited with local residents who had successfully implemented the planners' suggestions; the tour was duly reported in the

Bison Courier. A large group of state and federal officials toured Perkins County to observe progress made under the Water Facilities program jointly administered by the SCS, the FSA, and the Bureau of Agricultural Economics. The tour included visits to ranchers and farmers who had built water conservation or irrigation systems. The first rancher, Harold F. Thompson, had used a $200 FSA loan to build a diversion dam with accompanying ditches and dikes, which allowed him to irrigate 125 acres of feed crops, which in turn supported "his fine herd of white face cattle." His "headquarters ranch" was located in the midst of lands purchased by the government under the Land Utilization program; his neighbors' removal provided Thompson "with a large acreage of good grazing and pasture land for summer range."[26]

The second stop on the tour was the Walter Reinochls farm on Rabbit Creek. Here, FSA assistance provided an irrigation pump for the family; they used a Fordson tractor to lift water from the creek onto nine acres of bottomland, where they grew a large garden (Mrs. Reinochls had canned 700 quarts of produce) and feed crops for their livestock. When the touring government officers arrived, Mr. Reinochls was ambitiously at work creating a system of ditches to irrigate sixty-five acres of alfalfa.[27]

In another case, the *Courier* published a story about Virgil Veal of the Chance community, who had been a sheep rancher for fifteen years, although "the drouth years of 1934 and 1936 [had] been too much for even a veteran rancher" like him. Veal owned 480 acres and leased another 3,500 acres for his operation; in 1939 he took an FSA loan to purchase sheep and cattle to restock his range. "This gave him a new start and with his knowledge of sheep raising and pasture conservation he was soon able to get his enterprise back on a profitable basis." He and his family followed "the farm and home management program of Farm Security." This meant that they planted a large, irrigated garden and canned the produce for winter use. (In 1940 Mrs. Veal had canned 1,000 quarts of vegetables plus meat and poultry.) Their small herd of cows furnished dairy products for the table, and they sold the surplus for cash. The Veals also raised chickens and turkeys "in keeping with the family's policies of home production of foodstuffs." Their house was "modern," and their outbuilding "adequate." In 1940 the Veals had won the sweepstakes competition for lambs at the Faith sheep show, which demonstrated the effectiveness of Virgil's emphasis on excellent breeding stock and pasture conservation. The story, which had no by-line, has the sound of a government press release intended to show what could be done with proper techniques and a commitment to the wise management of the government agencies.[28]

By 1941 the *Courier* asserted that Perkins County residents had become more conservation minded and reprinted the winning entry in a contest run by the *Oklahoma Farmer-Stockman* entitled "Maybe the Indian Was Right After All," whose very title suggested the traditionalists' greatest fear. The journal had published two photos, "one of a dilapidated house and the other of an eroded field," and the contestants were to explain the meaning of the photos. The winner, in a tribute to federal policies if not to Indians or to poetry, had written: "Both pictures show white man crazy. Make big tepee. Plow hill. Water wash. Wind blow soil. Grass gone, land gone, door gone, window gone; whole place gone to hell." The Indians, according to the winner, had a better idea. "No plow land. Keep grass. Buffalo eat. Indian eat buffalo . . . no ask relief."[29]

The rural correspondents reported the large numbers from their communities who had signed up for soil conservation benefits or other programs or who had attended grazing district meetings. Such activities had become social events incorporated into the rhythms of community life. In the late thirties and early forties residents in agricultural areas even held annual banquets to commemorate the passage of the first AAA legislation in 1933; good food and radio messages from President Roosevelt and his agriculture secretary were the highlights of the events. The county agents, however, warned that the high percentage of participants in federal programs did not mean that west river people had become converts to the land-use doctrines prevalent in Washington. As one put it, "In emergencies desperate men grasp at straws. Under drought conditions and economic maladjustments, any man will comply with any sort of regulation if he is paid to do so." When normal conditions returned, he implied, cooperation might vanish.[30]

The newspaper editors, like their readers, wanted to build up their communities and act as advocates of progressive agriculture at the same time; the dilemma of the late Depression years was that doing one seemed to preclude the other. The *Courier's* editor tried to find a middle ground. "Western South Dakota is not wholly a farm country nor is it wholly a range country," he wrote; "they go hand in hand." This was an answer that satisfied very few partisans in the debate, but it was the best that could be had at the time and for many years thereafter.[31]

9

Outside the Shelterbelt

Mellette County farm, 1940.
Library of Congress.

Under this set-up [federal agricultural programs] the farmer living in the corn states has been persuaded to plant more wheat, flax, soybeans, tobacco and other crops new to him; wheat farmers have been encouraged to try corn, peanuts, cotton and sunflowers . . . while the farmer in the Dust Bowl District has been informed that from now on the wind will forever blow, grasshoppers and dust forever fly, and rain cease to come again, unless he turns his land back to the Indians, the government or to the big ranchers.
—J. R. Hartz, Jones County, *Dakota Farmer*, October 22, 1938

The farmer on marginal land is somewhat different from the farmer in the other states. He came here with nothing but a will to work and make a home. . . . The farmer on the marginal land feels that this is really his home; he has taken the virgin prairie and made it into a home. . . . They are not just hayseeds but men. . . . Also our women are not just bridge players. . . . These people have fought drouth, hail, rust, grasshoppers in the summer and blizzards in the winter to establish a home for themselves and families. Do we wonder if they stand with their backs to the wall and fight to defend these homes?
—T. E. Hayes, Perkins County, *Dakota Farmer*, June 10, 1933

THE GREAT DEPRESSION, and the dark years of dust and insects that accompanied it, brought the third great test of west river faith and endurance. While the people had faced drought before, it had never been so extreme. The voracious hordes of insects and clouds of blowing dust brought levels of suffering they had never before experienced. Many former believers "voted with their feet" and departed to more developed areas. Nearly 22,000 people, or 14 percent of the 1930 west river population, were gone when the census takers made their rounds in 1940.

The Depression represented the most extreme climatic and financial conditions that had afflicted the plains since the time of initial white settlement. Because no greater calamities have struck the northern plains since then, the adaptations enforced by the rigors of the Depression have, by and large, continued to the present. The process of that adaptation was difficult, even brutal. In the end, the west river people emerged with a fundamentally altered ideological and physical "work-scape": different concepts and attitudes, different expectations and hopes, different dimensions to their operations, different mixes and proportions of crops and livestock. The old ways, the old beliefs, and the old dreams died hard, clamoring to the west river people not to abandon the faith that had brought them there. But finally, even the pioneer stalwarts had to choose between departing the region or parting with their old dreams. Those who stayed — those whom Wallace Stegner has immortalized as the "stickers" — had at least partially to transmogrify themselves into something they had long reviled — the rancher — and to embrace their lives without the ambition of being either a young Chicago or a young Iowa. Instead, they had to satisfy themselves with the ambition of being a people as unique as the region itself. In the process of this change, the west river folk ironically enshrined as changeless virtues the pioneer traits that the pioneers themselves had seen as a temporary stage before "civilization" would come to the west river country. "Civilization" never came, but the west river people stayed anyway.

PERHAPS THE MOST conclusive proof of the failure of the pioneers' original vision of a new Iowa on the Plains was the nature of their salvation in the 1930s. The west river country had weathered major crises in previous periods without succumbing to the ultimate and undeniable sign of failure: federal relief. Federal relief during the Depression was a massive, open, and visible wound, a sure sign of a body in extremis. The west river people throughout the thirties struggled with drought, insect plagues, blistering summers, arctic winters, low prices, and other evidences of having made a historical mistake. In addition, however, their dependence upon government assistance of one kind or another for much of the decade mocked their most treasured illusion, that of independence and self-sufficiency. And, even as the federal government saved the region from a pell-mell plunge into oblivion, west river people perceived, accurately in some cases, that the federal government's preferred alternative was simply a more structured and orderly establishment of oblivion on the plains. Thus arose the curious attitude of west river residents toward the federal government that has frequently been commented upon, that of a willingness to accept aid combined with a thoroughgoing contempt for and distrust of the federal government.[1]

During the crises of the thirties, brain trusters and bureaucrats toured the region; their reports helped shape controversial New Deal policies. For example, Lorena Hickok, chief investigator for Harry Hopkins, FDR's confidante and head of the Federal Emergency Relief Administration, wrote detailed letters about Depression conditions. While visiting South Dakota in November 1933, Hickok wrote to Hopkins that Roosevelt could have his own Siberia in South Dakota, should he ever decide to become a dictator. "He can label this country out here 'Siberia' and send all of his exiles here. . . . A more hopeless place I never saw." A few days later she wrote to her close friend Eleanor Roosevelt of "Russian thistles rolling across the roads. Unpainted buildings, all going to seed. . . . Now and then a shabby little town. . . . What a country — to keep out of." After Hickok toured the Rosebud country, she wrote to Mrs. Roosevelt that it "used to be a grand grazing country, and it probably never should have been used for anything else." She labeled the three west river towns she visited "horrid" and pitied "these poor, confused people, living their dreary little lives." Hickok's attitudes were not atypical among New Dealers, who regarded the people of the Great Plains as the lineal descendants of historical mistakes. Locals resented the New Dealers even as the New Deal saved their lives. T. E. Hayes commented that "a number of young men, mostly students from the eastern states, were sent out to look over the situation. . . . It is strange to the people living here, that people coming here for a few days or weeks, know so much better what is the matter" than those who, like him, had been in the west river country twenty-five years or more. Nor did it help that some of the experts who joined in the New Deal chorus had sung a different tune about the country during the teens and twenties.[2]

The New Deal programs for resettlement of the plains population and the construction of a vast shelterbelt of trees challenged the very legitimacy of west river settlement. The government labeled hundreds of thousands of acres "submarginal" and planned to move farm families out. The shelterbelt program, developed in 1934 at the special behest of Franklin Roosevelt, "an ardent tree planter" himself, was to plant thick stands of trees at approximately the 99th meridian from Canada to Texas. The idea came from the Ukraine, where the Russians in the 1880s had had some success with it. Its proponents hoped the trees would halt the spread eastward of the growing desert on the plains, would eventually permanently alter the climate, and would provide a forest haven in an otherwise sparse landscape.[3]

Congress doubted the efficacy of the shelterbelt concept and never provided adequate funding for the program. The symbolic implications of the plan, however, were well understood in western South Dakota, located as it was on the windy and sunny side of the shelterbelt. Those on the east side would be protected from hot winds, blowing dust, and blizzards, and perhaps as well from the sight of failure to the west. West river residents, outside of the shelterbelt by a decision of their own government, would stand unprotected. It was seen as another example of the New Deal's seeming commitment to dismantling everything the pioneers had so painfully built up. In the government's view, the pioneers were not builders, as they saw themselves, but destroyers; not the final chapter of manifest destiny, but a manifest failure; not heroic pioneers, but foolish hangers-on.

It was only natural that some of those hanging on in the west river country came to similar conclusions themselves. Harry Putnam, born on Plum Creek near Wendte in Stanley County, left the country in the thirties. He acknowledged his rejection of the west river faith in a poem.

> Depression, drought assailed us, summer's heat and winter's cold
> Wreaked their worst upon us, yet we were always told
> That next year would be better, and when my youth was past
> I learned the promised next year was no better than the last.

Philip Beck of Dewey County wrote the *Dakota Farmer* to complain about the prevailing beliefs in the country and in "next year."

> Who can call a country like this a farm country, where you can not raise more than one crop in three? . . . And that crop is not a big crop. . . . In the first place we have no soil to farm; on the other hand we have not the climate. . . . I never did see anything grow on a hot stove, even if it had moisture. . . . And yet, some will holler and say we have just as good a country as anywhere else.

Harry Hibner of Perkins County delivered an even harsher verdict on the country. In response to a "next year" optimist's hopeful letter to the *Dakota Farmer*, Hibner argued:

> This west river country is not a newly settled country; it is no frontier. It is a bankrupt, desolated, poverty-stricken, over-populated, over-grazed semi-desert. . . . The picture [the optimist] draws of subduing the earth, of green fields, and bursting granaries and schools and a house on every section of land is very fine indeed; but how does he propose to supply sufficient rainfall, or if he could, then how to prevent this thin, poor soil from leaching? What about the poor, broken poverty-stricken ones who have tried to live on a couple of quarters of this land?

Hibner insisted that the prevailing faith and efforts were wrong. He condemned the optimists: "It is people like you who are trying to make of this country something that it was never intended for. It can't be done. If it could it would have been done many years ago. It has been tried for 25 years and it can't be done."[4]

Others wondered whether it might be best to abandon the land to the Sioux. Such an admission indicated the depths of despair (and the impact of government policies and publications) in the region. There had always been a link between wilderness and Indian peoples in the minds of west river agriculturalists. Indian peoples, in this sense, represented unfettered, unconquered nature. To give the land back to them was to reverse history and unsettle the plains. In 1936 the *Bison Courier*'s editor reflected on the possibility. "They say we ought to try to give this country back to the Indians," he wrote. "We fought them to get it and would probably have to fight them again to get them to take it back." He was not sure returning the land was a good idea, but he recognized that some changes had to be made. "Anyway," he concluded, "we should at least try and not waste it."[5]

Another west river resident wrote a poem on the subject, in response to his grandmother's bitter remark, "We should have given this land back to the Indians long ago." He called his poem "Dakota Land." It went, in part:

The weather's been the driest the world has ever seen
And those runty little pines are all we have that's green
The crickets got the pastures, and the hoppers got the grain
And half the old men on the place have never seen it rain

Uncle Sam, he dug a well, but that's been dry for years
For the only subsoil moisture is the poor old settlers' tears
The settlers quit their crying and stop no more to think
They just can't spare the water from what is left to drink

After years and years of farming and fighting drought and pest
We have come to the conclusion that the Indian way was best
So come back, old Crazy Horse, bring all your Indian band
Come back and set your tepee on this great South Dakota Land.[6]

Even the pioneer stalwart T. E. Hayes on one occasion allowed that the Indians might have been right, although he was not willing to undo what the settlers had done. "The farmer on marginal land feels that this is really his home," he noted, but "often I have thought of the old Indians who used to shake their heads when we broke up the virgin sod. . . . Perhaps they were right, but the thing is done, the old buffalo grass is plowed under . . . and people are living here." Of course, those people would now defend their homes, even if they were "farming land that should not be farmed at present."[7]

Other doubters challenged the shibboleth of "freedom" that west river partisans defended. A few people argued that the freedom claimed by the faithful was not true freedom and was, in fact, detrimental to west river life. R. Jones of Lyman County defended New Deal efforts to take chances and try new solutions to stubborn problems. The person he targeted for criticism was T. E. Hayes, the standard-bearer for the west river faith.

Those who sit in the scorner's seats advocate our return to the old policy of blind drifting and inaction . . . they talk of losses of freedom, of independence. What do they mean? Freedom to go wherever you please when your farm is foreclosed? . . . That we are not dependent on Minneapolis, Pittsburgh, Birmingham, and Tulsa for fuel, textiles, and markets?

Jones pointed to the interdependence of all aspects of the national economy and argued that some liberties had to be given up so that people could prosper. He chose as one example "the right of individual farmers to use, for costly grain production, land better suited for grazing, forest, or golf courses." In a second letter in the same issue of the *Dakota Farmer*, Jones expanded upon his theme. "There is no such thing as absolute 'freedom.' Even the sturdy individualist in the gone but not forgotten (unfortunately) pioneer days, did not have complete liberty." It was necessary for some "liberties" to disappear so that planning might take place that would promote the general welfare. It was a new world, Jones maintained, and people would have to recognize the need to experiment and would have to accept change.[8]

The voice of the faithful in the west river country through much of the Depression was T. E. Hayes. Hayes was an Englishman who had migrated to Aberdeen, in the eastern part of South Dakota, in 1904, where he managed a brickyard for four years. In 1908 he joined the homesteaders in the west river country, settling on a claim in Perkins County. He ran a diverse operation that included dairy cattle and sheep, and he sold cream to a local cooperative. He was the head of the Fairview Community Club for many years and was a regular contributor of letters, editorials, and egregious doggerel to the *Dakota Farmer* and other regional publications. He served two terms in the state legislature and held many other offices. In 1934 he was selected as one of the state's "Eminent Farmers" by the South Dakota State College. Hayes's writings and arguments were popular, and he continued to hold the faith through the worst years of the Depression.[9]

Hayes expressed the conviction from the beginning that all would turn out well for those who had patience and faith, and he noted every reason why that would be so. In 1931 he wrote about the Depression using the theme "Things at their worst will mend or end." He told about the taxing drought in the summer of 1930 and how it had ended, "and although too late for the grain, alfalfa and sweet clover soon responded to these refreshing rains, late flax fields began to bloom and inside of two weeks we appeared to be living in a new world." "The old book has promised," he noted, "that seedtime and harvest shall not fail; it might also add, the law of supply and demand shall not fail." In response to his neighbors' oft-asked question, "What are we going to do?," Hayes

Houses at the outskirts of Martin in Bennett County, 1940.
Library of Congress, courtesy of the South Dakota Archives.

reaffirmed his creed. "Personally," he wrote in 1934, "I am not afraid of the future. I for one cannot believe God has forgotten us. . . . I believe His promise that seedtime and harvest, summer and winter, shall not fail while the earth remains." He believed that the prairie would come back, that rains would fall and crops would grow. "What are we going to do?" he asked. "That to a great extent depends on the individual who is willing to join with his hopeful neighbors whose great hope is in God and freedom."[10]

As the New Deal developed its programs of relief and production control for agriculture, Hayes queried whether the loss of independence that government presence entailed was not a greater long-term threat than the temporary vicissitudes of the Depression. The deliberate destruction of excess crops and stock struck him and others as an abomination, and they worried that God would find ways of retribution; some concluded that God had exacted retribution with the drought and with the dust. Hayes, along with his friends and neighbors, rejected the bureaucrats' conclusion that they had hitched their wagons to a falling star. Hayes argued that west river "people have and are still going through a process of adjusting themselves to conditions as they find them. If left alone [they] will find the way out without advice of eastern profs." He was defiant in defense of his region. "No," he wrote in 1935, "even if they build a shelterbelt and leave us on the outside, we will still plant a few trees of our own; still plow and sow and reap if we get a little moisture." He concluded, "We have reclaimed this country and in spite of all the ballyhoo, we shall stay here and keep the home fires burning . . . and anyone or combination that tries to move us out will be up against the old pioneer spirit that knows no defeat." His doggerel on the shelterbelt plan bespoke defiance:

> The folks who live east of that belt will be protected then
> Their troubles will be over, they will soon all be rich men.
> No more to buck the blizzard when it's raging way out west;
> No more to suffer dust storms, their country will be blest.

The west river experience would be different.

> But we who farm west of that belt will all be moved away,
> Because they do not need our help to feed the world today. . . .
> We've made no plans for moving; no plans for changing gear,
> Although outside that tree belt, we figure to stay here. . . .
> We have won this country and here we mean to stay;
> In spite of all the brain trusts, or — there'll be hell to pay.[11]

A Hayes supporter, Butte County's William Greenberg, argued in the *Dakota Farmer* in 1935: "Western South Dakota is still a poor man's country — the land of promise to him who has the pioneering spirit." While times were hard, he went on, the problems could be surmounted: "The end can never be doubted, we are engaged in our old set task of subduing the earth, and the men on the ground can be trusted to do it successfully, if the federal government does not step in to remove the opportunity." In 1939 the Sorum correspondent to the *Bison Courier* rejoiced over a wet snowfall and told of her faith. Most of her neighbors "were sure this year would be a 'wet' one. In spite of grasshoppers, drouth and mortgage, South Dakotans still have faith in the sunshine state." A Jackson County woman told *Dakota Farmer* readers her vision of her neighbors: "Personally, I think the people in South Dakota are exceptionally courageous. It takes so much to really down them. Their faith — like strong rubber bands — can be stretched and stretched (by 'hoppers, dust, hail, drouth and blister beetles); then, given a few nice spring rains, and back it springs, — good as ever!" A Jones County man, J. B. Hartz, wrote to the *Dakota Farmer* to encourage his friends and neighbors to keep the faith. "Let us do the very best we know how and leave results to Him who knows our hearts and sees our every effort and will reward us accordingly in due season." [12]

That they were better people because of their faith and their struggle was an important part of their daily sustenance. As in the response to previous crises, the west river folk made a virtue of necessity. The editor of the *Bison Courier* wrote: "We are rising from the defeat of the past years, stronger, wiser, less arrogant and conceited of our own ability and more trustful of superior powers and more thankful for the advantages we enjoy." "The RAIN," he concluded, "has made all things grow; let us be thankful. The DROUGHT made us stronger men; let us be thankful." [13]

The leading part played by T. E. Hayes in the debate over the future of the region, and his enhanced standing as one who had stuck through the drought of 1910–1911 and on through the Depression, made it an especially discouraging blow when he departed for Oregon in late 1936, finally broken by the Depression. He worked as a carpenter there the rest of his life. The departure of a pioneer stalwart like Hayes was a sure sign that faith in the country was not enough and that fundamental changes were required if the west river country was to survive as anything other than a historical monument to the perils of optimism. [14]

The adaptation process, of course, had been ongoing since the early days of settlement. Various regimes of dry farming, livestock breeding, and livestock-crop mixes were tried in succession. As wave after wave of pioneers abandoned the plains — the speculative homesteaders, who had taken land only as an investment without intending to stick with the country, the inexperienced urbanites, who found farming harder than they thought, those driven out in the great exodus following the 1910–1911 drought, those driven out by the Depression, and those, throughout the period of settlement, who had simply failed for the myriad reasons people have failed anywhere — and were not replaced, the land holdings of those who stayed increased. This process reached its apotheosis in the Depression, as the pioneer generation was reaching old age and, having stuck with the country for three or four decades, now took stock of it. Jud Pepper, who had homesteaded near Kadoka in 1907, wrote in rhyme of his move to his claim, of his neighbors, and of the anger of the ranchers when "we stopped the ranching business, when we started building fence." After "over thirty years" he had learned a lesson.

> But in the time I've been here, I can see our big mistake
> That the stockman knew his business, but it is too late.
> For it is a real cow country and no better can be found
> But you've got to leave it grass side up and never turn it down.
> But now the homestead days are over, and the soddies are gone away;
> And the ones of us that are still here, I think are here to stay.[15]

Given the historic hostility of the farmers to the ranchers, whose land-use regimes and accompanying social structures were antithetical to those of traditional agriculture, it was a considerable adjustment to embrace ranching as at least a partial feature of the permanent landscape of the west river country. Ranching was viewed as little different from the Indians' use of the land: extremely large amounts of land to support minuscule populations and primitive social institutions imposed by the low population densities. The return of ranching meant to many a reversion to primitive conditions, an abandonment not just of farming practices but also social institutions and ways of life: towns, neighborhoods, schools, churches. The process of abandoning the vision of traditional agriculture in the west river country as a result came grudgingly but inevitably in the blast furnace conditions of the Depression. The fact that the federal government promoted a process that many in the west river country saw as social regression, and accepted only as a last resort, insured a residual layer of hostility toward the federal government.

In *A Man from South Dakota* (1950), George Reeves recounted his experiences in the west river country during the 1920s and 1930s. Reeves began farming on his own in 1926. As a "reasoning," college-educated person, he initially believed he could bend the forces of nature to his will. But when he watched his wheat and flax die and saw a tantalizing cloud slip away without giving rain,

I cursed the enemy wind, I cursed the cloud, I cursed the goddam country that I had chosen for a place to live. When my rage had worn itself out, I was disturbed. My voice hadn't been that of a reasoning educated man. It had been the hoarse, irrational bellowing of a wounded caveman. . . . It was irrational but I couldn't escape the feeling that somehow I could bend this force to do my will. The caveman was slow to learn that he could only duck.[16]

The battle became very personal in the 1930s: Reeves versus tricky, vicious, and unpredictable "Dakota." Reeves worked to develop techniques and strategies to outwit Dakota, but he needed money to finance his ideas. Money was extremely scarce, and the federal government had become the only source of cash for farm operators. But Reeves viewed the government with contempt. Government officials, he said, "lined up facts in perpendicular columns and life didn't come that way." The requirements they forced him to meet and the time it took for them to fill his requests for cash got in the way of his very personal struggle with Dakota. Even before the New Deal, Reeves proclaimed, "I hate government." After Roosevelt took office, his scorn grew. Reeves believed that he could beat Dakota — that was his faith — but he "was afraid of governments, for they had eyes, and with them they could make themselves brutal tyrants." He refused a neighbor's request to participate in the corn/hog allotment program, stating, "This is my land, and I'll put a hole through the first guy that tries to tell me what to do." He had seen both famine and surplus, and he doubted if government policymakers had personally confronted those conditions. Until they did, they had no right to solve the Dakotans' problems.[17]

As the drought deepened, Reeves's cattle began to suffer, and he was forced by necessity to participate in the government's cattle buy-up program. It was a shotgun wedding, and Reeves adopted a cynical strategy of bilking the government as a sort of revenge for his dependency. "There was nothing in my rule book that prevented me from taking this sucker's money," he said. Dakota was his adversary and an admirable foe, "an opponent who would never tire, who always offered something new to imperil — and improve — the flavor of next year." Government officials, planners, and anyone else who had never "looked up from his work with his eyes full of grit and dust to see the Devil standing there

spraddle legged above the black clouds of a dust-storm" and yet had refused to give up were not worthy of Reeves's respect. Reeves's brand of
west river ideology was tough and hard, self-righteous and stubborn,
and guided by uncompromising self-interest. He shared none of the
faith in the promise that helped many west river people stay afloat during hard times. The force he fought was blind and unfeeling; God may
have been a source of consolation for Reeves, but the Devil was running
the show.[18]

Reeves, like most of the "stickers" who made it through the Depression, accepted federal help, eventually developed a successful ranching
operation, and continued to rail against the federal government. Many
others feared, like Reeves, that the federal government would become
the managing rather than the silent partner in the enterprise. In a culture that prized independence and self-reliance above all, the dependence on government "partnership" was a family secret best forgotten
or at the least bowdlerized. In a 1977 survey of South Dakotans (not
just in the west river country) who had lived through the Depression,
Inda Avery found that many believed that the government had helped
others but, as to their own families, they recalled toughing it out on
their own.[19]

WHILE THE west river people deeply resented and feared the federal
government's agenda for depopulating the west river country, in the
end it was not government policy but the rigors of the Depression itself
that put an end, even in west river minds, to dreams of a new Iowa on
the plains. The towns and densely populated rural areas that the pioneers had envisioned were now a repressed memory—like government, something to be forgotten out of a sense of decorum; a lingering
defensiveness, reflecting a knowledge that outsiders viewed the country
much as Lorena Hickok did, is the regional Freudian slip.

Farmers in the west river country adapted, in the years following the
Depression, to a combined livestock and crop system of agriculture that
bore a family resemblance more to the ranching regime that had pre-
ceded them than to traditional agriculture; one of the primary legacies
of the traditional agriculture period, however, was the relatively even
distribution of land—there are no King ranches in South Dakota—

The Dewey County courthouse, Timber Lake, 1942.
Library of Congress.

and family ownership and operation. The process of adapting agriculture to the region has generally been successful since the recovery from
the Depression. The high prices and strong demand for such crops as
wheat during the World War II and Korean War eras and the generally
good climatic conditions in western South Dakota encouraged crop
production, although livestock sales remained the predominant source
of cash income on west river farms. The result of this process was the
emergence of a specific type of agriculture characterized by family ownership and operation of farms that were very large by midwestern and
eastern standards, the use of portions of the land for grazing, the growing of crops related to livestock production, and a variety of mechanical
and technical adaptations that allowed individual farm families to operate vast tracts efficiently. Farmers and ranchers worked to conserve the
environment with proper tillage techniques, shelterbelts, and pasture
management; county histories written since the sixties often include
sections on the Soil Conservation District and its functions, as well as

photographs of elaborate shelterbelts planted around farmsteads. The volumes express considerable pride in the efforts to coexist wisely with the land.

In 1920 there were 18,017 farms in the west river country; their average size was 806 acres. By 1930, despite the prolonged stagnation in farm prices, the availability of cheap farmland in the region had led to an increase in the number of farms to 21,129, each averaging 716 acres. But after ten years of depression, the number of farms in the west river country in 1940 had dropped to 15,371, and their average size had increased dramatically to 1,174 acres, with most commercially viable farms substantially larger than that; between 1935 and 1940 alone, the number of farms 1,000 acres or more in size increased by 25 percent. In the 1940s 20 percent of west river farms were abandoned, a rate much higher than that in the rest of the state and the nation at the time; in the next decade another 20 percent of west river farms were abandoned, although this was lower than the national abandonment average of 31 percent for the decade.[20]

These trends have continued to the present. By 1992 the west river country had only 8,040 farms — a little more than a third of the Depression-era numbers — while the average size had more than quadrupled in the same period, to 3,010 acres. The crops changed as well. Although corn had been the most commonly grown crop in the mid-twenties, by 1992 only 19 percent of west river farms grew corn. Less than a third (30.4 percent) still grew wheat in the nineties. Hay continued to be a vital crop, with 67 percent growing hay crops in 1982. Milo, sorgum, and other forage crops are also important, indicating the predominance of livestock in modern west river farming. The west river rural population has stagnated since the Depression. Although Rapid City and Sturgis on the edge of the Black Hills have grown steadily since 1940, spurred by defense spending and tourism, when those two cities are removed from the population figures, the outlying areas have experienced little population change. In 1930 the west river plains population (without Rapid City and Sturgis) was 140,366. By 1940 it had dropped to 114,416. As of 1990, the population of the west river plains country (minus Rapid City and Sturgis) was little changed at 115,002, of whom only 14,693 live on farms. As in the rest of the nation, even the rural population has mostly moved to small towns.[21]

In a development that surely would have astonished Lorena Hickok, millions of Americans now drive annually through the west river country, Hickok's nominee as the American Siberia, headed for the tourist attractions of the Black Hills, Mt. Rushmore, and the Badlands. On their way to these famous attractions, tourists from the east travel through the west river country on Interstate 90, built along the long since abandoned Milwaukee and Chicago Northwestern roads. Tourists recite the trials of driving through such empty country and wonder what manner of people live there, and why anybody had ever come to settle it.

THE DROUGHT and dust and the arrival of the bureaucrats in the 1930s generated debate among west river pioneers about their legacy as pioneers. If we reap what we sow, they wondered, what will our harvest be? West river residents had always paid homage to the first generation of the eastern Dakota pioneers, the settlers of the 1870s and 1880s; they used the hardships of the earlier group to push themselves onward through their own tests and trials. They knew that they, too, were pioneers. They had worn the mantle proudly, but under the press of drought and doubt they, too, grew defensive. "Will somebody please write something nice about us," one editor implored, instead of the ". . . unpainted, treeless, dry, dusty, starvation view." With outsiders so willing to lament their bad fortune or foolishness, west river people wrote their own analysis of their character and legacy. Pioneers, they believed, were people of thrift and ingenuity who were able to dig in and endure extreme hardship without flinching. "They fatten on privation," one man wrote in 1936, and "bare their teeth at the wolf." Although their government might indict them (one government pamphlet said, "The years of land settlement have given us countless brave stories about the race of pioneers. . . . Many of us would like to forget that they were also years of fraud, greed and costly blunders"), the west river pioneers knew that they had been engaged in a good work.[22]

During the decade of the thirties, many of the original west river pioneers died. Their passing (or sometimes their migration) provided an opportunity for reflections on their contributions. What had they done? As the survivors—the "stickers"—saw it, they had built something where there had been nothing but raw, untamed nature. They cherished signs of human habitation; they loved nature but in their own way. An ordered and domesticated nature was good; it fulfilled God's promises and commands.

The tributes paid to the dying pioneers in the 1930s reflected this pioneer heritage. When Albert McKinstry died in 1937, the minister's sermon was addressed to "The Pioneer Builder." When May Witcher died in 1938, the obituary lauded her efforts to build a ranch and social institutions in her neighborhood. She "assumed responsibilities in community affairs and was a leader in all that was good for her neighbors." Witcher routinely rode eight miles on horseback every Sunday in the early days to lead a Sunday school. Widowed at a young age with five small children to raise, she became a respected rancher of "strong character and high courage" whose "faith in this wide area of the western country never failed." When Charles Settle died, also in 1938, a neighbor wrote that the Settle family's "light in the window was a beacon to many travelers; often has this good man gone as guide to pilot those who were less familiar with the trackless prairies, leading them in safety to their shacks and homes." The Settle home was a haven of safety for anyone caught by bad weather — "never was their home too full not to house more till the storms passed." One pioneer always did "her share in meeting the problems of earning a livelihood in their new prairie home"; she had been a "substantial and worthwhile builder." Another had been "instrumental in the building up of the country" and a "good friend" to all. In the fall of 1938 three pioneer men died within a few weeks of each other. The Lemmon paper memorialized them as "men of vision and purpose" whose "contributions to pioneer life and to progress" had done "so much to encourage faltering souls and to soften the effects of severe natural handicaps."[23]

In 1936 Thomas Gerard of Lyman County wrote an essay on west river life for the *Dakota Farmer*. "With a view to cheering my friends," he described what he believed the west river legacy to be. "The Pioneer spirit is indefatigable. It never gives up and if it grows weary it keeps forging ahead. Its faith is something marvelous. It is indestructible — you can bend it but it will not break; crush it and it will rise again. Its slogan is, 'Tomorrow or next year, I will find the solution to the problem. . . .'" After noting numerous examples of this spirit from history, Gerard concluded that "none of these manifest a greater degree of patience, courage and perseverance than does the west river pioneer." In a new world of limits, for their refusal to admit defeat "they stand as beacons of hope for generations unborn."[24]

The pioneer generation's vision of a thickly populated plains, with all the proper appointments, blew away in the dust storms of the Depression; the pioneers' bequest to their successors was not success but a regional character shaped by eternal struggle and persistence through years of defeat. Even as the west river Depression generation buried the pioneer generation and its dreams, they eulogized the pioneer generation's virtues — risk-taking, independence, self-reliance, and hard, hard work — as permanent values, eternal verities of life on the high, dry plains of the west river country.

Notes

1. In this book the terms "plains" and "prairie" are used interchangeably. Technically, the area west of the 98th meridian is the Great Plains, characterized by its short grasses. Iowa, western Minnesota, eastern Nebraska, and eastern Kansas are prairies, characterized by their long grasses. In common usage and by dictionary definition, however, "prairie" refers to any rolling grassland; west river people used "prairie" to describe their homeland more frequently than they used "plains." They also used "prairie" to name places, churches, and groups, such as the Prairie Home Ladies Aid in Draper and the Our Lady of the Prairie Catholic Church near Reva. I have utilized the common usage rather than the scientific definition.

INTRODUCTION: AFTER THE WEST WAS WON

1. To "prove up" meant to win the title to the homesteaded land. Settlers proved up by maintaining the required residence time on their claims and meeting the other stipulations set by the government for size of the residence, amount of land in cultivation, and a water source.
2. The *Madison Daily Leader* for November 28, 1924, carried the most complete story of Sharon's death. (Madison was the nearest larger community to Wentworth, the site of the suicide.) The *Kadoka Press* of December 5, 1924, told of the death, speculated about Sharon's motives, and included the obituary. Otto Sharon was born in Missouri but moved to east river South Dakota at age ten. He lived in Tyndall and Armour before his move to the Kadoka area. He was buried in Armour next to his first wife.
3. The history of the Dakotas is sometimes described as "boom and bust." The first Dakota boom occurred with the discovery of gold in the Black Hills in 1874 and the ensuing rush. The second, or "great," Dakota boom occurred between 1878 and 1887, when 250,000 settlers rushed into the eastern halves of what became North and South Dakota in 1889. West river settlement came after 1900 in the third great promotional boom.
4. There are many books and articles about Lakota culture and history. Richard White, "The Winning of the West: The Expansion of the Western Sioux in the 18th and 19th Centuries," *Journal of American History* 65

(September 1978): 319–343, explains the Lakota's rise to dominance on the Northern Plains. Royal Hassrick, *The Sioux: Life and Customs of a Warrior Society* (Norman, Okla., 1964), provides important cultural perspectives. Robert F. Utley, *The Last Days of the Sioux Nation* (New Haven, 1963), describes the final defeat of the Sioux. His biography of Sitting Bull, *The Lance and the Shield: The Life of Sitting Bull* (New York, 1993), examines the life of this important Sioux leader.

5. Utley, *Last Days of the Sioux Nation*, 40–59, explains the impact of the 1889 agreement on the Lakota people. Herbert Schell, *History of South Dakota*, 3d ed. (Lincoln, Nebr., 1975), 242–247, describes the Dakotans' effort to open the reservation to general settlement.

6. Walter Prescott Webb's classic work, *The Great Plains* (Boston 1931), spells out the fundamental differences between the plains and humid America. John Wesley Powell's ideas are included in his *Report on the Lands of the Arid Regions of the United States* (Washington, D.C., 1878). Schell, *History of South Dakota*, 4–8, describes the topography of western South Dakota.

7. Charles Lowell Green, "The Administration of the Public Domain in South Dakota," *South Dakota Historical Collections* 20 (1940): 7–280, provides a careful explanation of federal policies as they applied to South Dakota. Schell, *History of South Dakota*, 170–174, explains the Homestead Act and other nineteenth-century land acts; Schell discusses the Enlarged Homestead Act on page 349. For the *Dakota Farmer's* view of the new boom, see the issue of July 15, 1906, p. 10.

8. The quote about cactus appears in the *Dakota Farmer*, August 15, 1906, pp. 3–4. Mary W. M. Hargreaves, *Dry Farming in the Northern Great Plains, 1900–1925* (Cambridge, 1957), 8–10, analyzes the importance of precipitation and climatic variables. Semiarid lands are those receiving 10–20 inches of rain per year.

9. Hargreaves, *Dry Farming in the Northern Great Plains, 1900–1925*, 8–10.

10. Paula M. Nelson, *After the West Was Won: Homesteaders and Town-Builders in Western South Dakota, 1900–1917* (Iowa City, 1986), tells the story of the west river boom and bust.

11. Ibid., 14–23, 42–50.

12. Ibid., 32–33.

13. Ibid., 33–40.

14. Ibid., 82–99.

15. Ibid., 62–80, 102–118.

16. Ibid., 120–141; the population figures come from Doane Robinson, *Doane Robinson's Encyclopedia of South Dakota* (Pierre, 1925), 990.

17. Nelson, *After the West Was Won*, 144–154.

18. Ibid., 156–177.

I. ROOM AT THE BOTTOM

1. The title for this chapter comes from Lois Phillips Hudson's book of essays, *Reapers of the Dust: A Prairie Chronicle* (Boston, 1964). In it she tells the story of her family's displacement from North Dakota to Washington state in the 1930s, where they became transient farm workers. She comments: "Once I had believed what everybody told me: that there was always room at the top. (Nobody had told me that there was always room at the bottom: people don't say things like that to children.) But now I understood that the room at the top had disappeared along with the good bottomland."

2. *Timber Lake Topic*, January 10, April 25, August 15, 1919.

3. Ibid., July 2, August 20, 1920.

4. *Kadoka Press*, January 13, 1919.

5. Ibid., May 19, 1918, for ranch price; January 17, July 11, June 13, 1919, for price of cows and amount of land; February 13, 1920, for sale of bull. The January 14, 1919, issue discusses the home loan plans; for discussion of building, see issues of February 14, 28, May 2, 9, June 27, July 25, 1919, and February 6, 1920. The school building endorsement appears in the April 11, 1919, issue, and the temporary building is described in the November 7, 1919, edition. Graduation is covered in the May 14, 1920, issue. Utilities are discussed in the September 19, 1919, and February 2, 1920, issues. It is impossible to determine the exact date of the petition, but it occurred between July 25 and August 15, 1919.

6. Ibid., September 12, 1919; July 23, March 5, 1920.

7. Interpretive information comes from Chester C. Davis, "The Development of Agricultural Policy since the End of the World War," in U.S. Department of Agriculture, *Yearbook of Agriculture, 1940* (Washington, D.C., 1940), 298–299; prices come from Owen L. Dawson, *South Dakota Farm Production and Prices*, South Dakota Agricultural Experiment Station Bulletin 225 (Brookings, 1927), 56, 61, 82, 85, 88, 86, 98, 96.

8. Gilbert S. Fite, "The History of South Dakota's Rural Credit System," *South Dakota Historical Collections* 24 (1949): 220–225, 229, 231, 233–234.

9. *Kadoka Press*, October 8, 1920. The lists of mortgage foreclosures in the paper grew noticeably in the 1921–1925 era. The Rural Credits foreclosures were especially high in 1925.

10. For farm foreclosure statistics, see Harry A. Steele, *Farm Mortgage Foreclosures in South Dakota 1921–1932*, Agricultural Economics Department, South Dakota Agricultural Experiment Station Circular 17 (Brookings, 1934), 8 and Appendix Table I; Gabriel Lundy, *Farm Mortgage Foreclosures in South Dakota 1933–34–35–36–37* (Supplement 1 to Circular 17), Agricultural Economics Department, South Dakota Agricultural Experiment

Station (Brookings, 1938), 4; and Gabriel Lundy, *Farm Mortgage Foreclo-sures in South Dakota 1934–1938* (Supplement 2 to Circular 17), Agricul-tural Economics Department, South Dakota Agricultural Experiment Station (Brookings, 1939), 4–7, 14.

11. *Kadoka Press*, November 26, 1920; November 23, 1921.

12. *Dakota Farmer*, September 1, 1923, p. 771.

13. Ibid., July 1, 1923, p. 613; April 15, 1923, p. 404; *Bison Courier*, March 2, 1922; *Kadoka Press*, February 17, 1922.

14. *Dakota Farmer*, May 15, 1922, pp. 402, 403; January 1, 1922, p. 17; Febru-ary 15, 1922, pp. 140, 141, 142; July 15, 1923, p. 660; January 15, 1922, p. 55; February 1, 1922, pp. 93, 94.

15. *Kadoka Press*, October 15, November 26, 1920; January 6, 1922; for water bonds see the May 21, 1920, issue; banking hours appear in the February 18, 1922, issue. See *Timber Lake Topic*, December 16, 30, 1921, for notices about reservation land payments. The chiding editorial appears in the *Kadoka Press*, August 15, 1922.

16. *Kadoka Press*, September 22, 1922; January 25, February 8, 1924; November 18, 1926; November 21, 1924; April 28, 1927. The information about Ka-doka's banking future comes from *Kadoka Press*, 75th Anniversary Edition, June 18, 1981.

17. *Bison Courier*, March 9, 16, 30, 1922.

18. Ibid., July 5, 1923.

19. *Kadoka Press*, December 9, 1921; January 13, February 24, 1922; March 7, 1924. For information on the agricultural agent, see *Bison Courier*, April 6, 1922, and *Kadoka Press*, November 10, 1922.

20. Dawson, *South Dakota Farm Production*, 56, 88; *Fourteenth Census of the United States, 1920: Agriculture*, vol. 6, Part I: 654–660; *U.S. Census of Agri-culture, 1925: Reports for States*, Part I: 1064–1075; *U.S. Census of Agriculture, 1935*, Part I: 306–311; Steele, *Farm Mortgage Foreclosures*, Appendix Table I.

21. *Kadoka Press*, April 26, May 17, 1928; January 31, March 28, 1929.

22. Ibid., July 2, 1926; June 7, 1934; November 27, 1925; May 6, 1927.

23. Ibid., December 29, 1922.

2. THE COW, THE SOW, AND THE HEN

1. Harry C. McDean, "Social Scientists and Farm Poverty on the North American Plains, 1933–1940," *Great Plains Quarterly* 3 (Winter 1983): 18–21, explains the origin of New Deal plains policies in the work done there in the twenties.

2. The Smith-Lever Act of 1914 provided partial federal funding for the county agent system. States and counties who wanted agents were re-

quired to provide the remaining funding. The U.S. Department of Agriculture in Washington, D.C., and the land-grant colleges in the various states operated the system. In the early years the Farm Bureau, a private farm organization which represented the commercial farming industry, often acted as the impetus for spreading the county agent system. Typically, interested farmers in a county organized a Farm Bureau unit and then lobbied state and county authorities to fund an agent. The county agent system's ties with the Farm Bureau were controversial and alienated some other farm groups, who resisted the extension system; additionally, poorer counties, which perhaps needed agents the most, simply could not afford them.

The recollections of T. E. Hayes appeared in the *Dakota Farmer*, April 13, 1935, p. 141. The South Dakota county agents' annual reports are on microfilm as *Extension Service Annual Reports: South Dakota, 1913–1944*, at the National Archives, Microcopy T-888. I have used the reports from Jackson, Lyman, Tripp, and Perkins counties, which for the twenties appear on Reels 5, 6, 8, 10, 11, 13, 15, and 17. Not all west river counties had agents in the twenties. In 1920 only six of the twenty-one west river counties had agents. In 1924 thirteen west river counties employed agents, the high figure for the decade. By the end of the decade, the number of counties with agents had dropped to eight. The names of the agents were published in the *Official Directory: County Agricultural Agents, Farm Bureaus, and Boys and Girls Clubs in the United States*, published annually by Wm. Grant Wilson Publishers in Cambridge, Massachusetts.

3. The experimental farm yields appear in such publications as A. N. Hume, *A Decade of Crop Yields from Vivian Farm*, South Dakota Agricultural Experiment Station Bulletin 253 (Brookings, 1930), and A. N. Hume, Edgar Jay, and Clifford Franzke, *Twenty-One Years of Crop Yields from Cottonwood Experiment Farm*, South Dakota Agricultural Experiment Station Bulletin 312 (Brookings, 1937). The dry land bulletin is discussed in the *Dakota Farmer*, December 15, 1920, p. 2019.

4. *Dakota Farmer*, December 15, 1920, p. 2019. A lister planted corn in a deep furrow cut by the moldboard plow attached to the front of the implement. Great Plains farmers believed that the deep furrow protected the plants from drought and hot winds. See R. Douglas Hurt, *American Farm Tools: From Hand-Power to Steam-Power* (Manhattan, Kans., 1982), 33–34, for photographs of the equipment and an explanation of its use. Much of the general information in this chapter comes from agricultural reference works available in the 1920s. See especially Liberty Hyde Bailey, *Cyclopedia of American Agriculture*, 4th ed., 4 vols. (New York, 1912), and E. L. D. Seymour, *Farm Knowledge*, 4 vols. (New York, 1918), (published for Sears Roebuck). The Wiley Agricultural Engineering series published in the

twenties and thirties was also very helpful. See especially J. Brownlee Davidson, *Agricultural Machinery* (New York, 1931), and W. A. Foster and Deane G. Carter, *Farm Buildings*, 1st ed. (New York, 1922; 2d ed., 1928).

5. *Dakota Farmer*, December 15, 1920, p. 2019.

6. The statistical data come from the *Census of Agriculture, 1925*, 1055–1118. In the 1930s the South Dakota Agricultural Experiment Station published *A Graphic Summary of the Relief Situation in South Dakota*, Bulletin 310 (Brookings, 1937) by W. F. Kumlien. It identifies the place of origin of South Dakotans; Iowa exported the most people to the state, followed by Minnesota, Nebraska, Wisconsin, and Illinois. The *Dakota Farmer* frequently promoted the silo. See the issues of March 15, 1921, and March 15, 1922, for examples. A west river man wrote at length on the uselessness of silos in a dry country in the *Dakota Farmer*, April 15, 1921, p. 478. County agents urged farmers to construct trench silos (rectangular pits dug in the ground) as a cheap means of storing silage. The *Dakota Farmer* reported that, when a North Dakota farmer built one with his county agent's help, his neighbors laughed at him and called it "the county agent's grave." *Dakota Farmer*, July 15, 1925, p. 641.

7. See examples of advice given in the *Kadoka Press*, April 2, 16, 1926. See the *Census of Agriculture, 1925*, 1076–1085, for livestock and poultry figures and 1065–1075 for tractor ownership.

8. See *Census of Agriculture, 1925*, 1056–1064, for farm size and 1086–1095 for crops grown. R. H. Rogers and F. F. Elliott, *Types of Farming in South Dakota*, South Dakota Agricultural Experiment Station Bulletin 238 (Brookings, 1929), 51–53, made a special tabulation of the 1925 census data to illustrate the variety of farming types in the state. They developed six separate types for the west river region and further subdivided each type according to the sizes of farms typically found within each. Area VIII, for example, included "Haakon, Stanley, Jones, Lyman, Mellette, the northern part of Todd and Tripp counties and part of Jackson County." Within that, the authors found these typical farm sizes: 160 acres, 320 acres, and 480 acres. The most common farm organization for 160 acres included "40 acres of corn, 30 acres of hay and 85 acres of pasture and other land." For those with 320 acres, two types existed in equal numbers. One grew "30 acres of corn, 0–30 acres of wheat and 60 acres of hay"; the other had "65 acres of corn, no wheat, and 40 acres of hay." Farmers with 480 acres again followed two main types of organization. The first grew "40 acres of corn, 40 acres of hay and 350 acres of pasture"; the second plan provided for "80 acres of corn, 100 acres of hay and 280 acres in pasture." The larger farms tended to have a greater number of cows. By the end of the decade, wheat had become a more important crop. Ten counties grew more acres of wheat than of corn; twelve counties still grew more acres of corn. The

1929 agricultural census recorded 10,112 west river farms that planted wheat. In that same year 15,941 farms grew corn. *Census of Agriculture, 1935,* 316–321.

9. *Dakota Farmer,* August 25, 1922, p. 592. Virtually every issue carried tractor advertisements in the 1920s.

10. Ibid., July 1, 1920, pp. 1268, 1276, 1277.

11. Ibid., August 1, 1922, p. 559, gives the price of the Moline tractor. The Sears prices come from a reprint of the *Sears Roebuck Catalogue for 1927* (New York, 1970), 1061. The *Census of Agriculture, 1925,* 1065–1075, includes the number of tractors in use.

12. The *Dakota Farmer* carried articles about the importance of seed corn selection every year. See the September 1, 1920, issue, pp. 1496, 1498, and 1500, for examples. Carl Hamilton, *In No Time at All* (Ames, Iowa, 1974), 68–69, explains the system. The story of hybrid seed corn is told in Merle T. Jenkins, "Corn Improvement," in U.S. Department of Agriculture, *Yearbook of Agriculture, 1936* (Washington, D.C., 1936), 455–522.

13. *Dakota Farmer,* October 15, 1920, p. 1781. The information on walking mileage is from Robert C. Williams, *Fordson, Farmall and Poppin' Johnny: A History of the Farm Tractor and Its Impact on America* (Urbana, Ill., 1987), 131.

14. Hamilton, *In No Time at All,* 70–74.

15. Gladys Leffler Gist, *Chasing Rainbows: A Recollection of the Great Plains* (Ames, Iowa, 1993), 45. Hurt, *American Farm Tools,* 30–34, illustrates the types and use of corn machinery. Auction notices appear in the *Bison Courier,* September 20, 1923; May 8, 1924; *Kadoka Press,* August 22, September 5, November 24, 1924; August 28, September 25, December 11, 1925.

16. *Dakota Farmer,* July 1, 1925, p. 616; Davidson, *Agricultural Machinery,* 146–147.

17. *Dakota Farmer,* September 1, 1920, p. 1498. Hurt, *American Farm Tools,* 38–39, tells of the importance of the cultivator versus the hoe in allowing the production of larger crops.

18. See examples in *Dakota Farmer,* September 1, 1920, pp. 1496–1498; *Extension Service Annual Reports,* Reel 13; *Dakota Farmer,* July 1, 1920, pp. 1276, 1277.

19. *Dakota Farmer,* January 1, 1924, pp. 18, 21, for mill ads; *Extension Service Annual Reports,* Reel 13. The Lyman County agent reported in some frustration that he had tried to get area farmers to go together to buy a "small disc separator" to remove weed seeds from grain but had failed.

20. *Dakota Farmer,* January 1, 1924, p. 23.

21. Ibid., November 1, 1921, p. 903; November 15, 1921, p. 930; December 1, 1921, p. 996; May 1, 1922, p. 352. Virtually every issue has some information on alfalfa, in which there was considerable interest.

22. See note 15 for auction bill dates in the *Kadoka Press* and *Bison Courier*; Hamilton, *In No Time at All*, 91–94. Hurt, *American Farm Tools*, 87–95, illustrates the equipment, as does Davidson, *Agricultural Machinery*, 216–237.

23. Faith Historical Committee, *Faith Country Heritage* (Pierre, 1985), 811 (hereafter cited as *Faith County Heritage*).

24. Henry Miller, et. al., *From a Soddy* (n.p., n.d.), 143; Hurt, *American Farm Tools*, 49–51, illustrates their use.

25. Thomas D. Isern, *Bull-Threshers and Bindlestiffs: Harvesting and Threshing on the Northern Great Plains* (Lawrence, Kans., 1990), 76. See the rural correspondents' notes in the newspapers in the fall months. For example, the South Creek correspondent in the *Kadoka Press* on October 3, 1941, reported who was helping whom cook for threshers that season.

26. Iola M. Anderson, *The Singing Hills: A Story of Life on the Prairies of South Dakota* (Stickney, S. Dak., 1977), 102–103. The *Kadoka Press* reported in its August 16, 1928, issue that only one team and wagon waited at the elevator to unload grain. The rest came in trucks.

27. *Dakota Farmer*, November 1, 1924, p. 872.

28. Ibid., September 15, 1925, p. 828.

29. Hamilton, *In No Time at All*, 69; *Dakota Farmer*, September 1, 1920, pp. 1496, 1498, 1500.

30. Kenneth Hassebrock, *Rural Reminiscences: The Agony of Survival* (Ames, Iowa, 1990), 107–108; Miller, *From a Soddy*, 143; Anderson, *Singing Hills*, 108.

31. Gist, *Chasing Rainbows*, illustrates the care and concern often shown for horses, as does Anderson, *Singing Hills*. Hassebrock, *Rural Reminiscences*, 117–123, is more negative about the horse-human relationship. *Dakota Farmer*, July 1, 1920, p. 1302.

32. Seymour, *Farm Knowledge*, vol. 1: 49–58, explains dairying. *Census of Agriculture, 1925*, 1076–1084, provides the statistics on milk marketing.

33. South Dakota Department of Agriculture, *Report of the Commissioner for the Period Ending June 30, 1927* (Pierre, 1927), 23–24.

34. *Dakota Farmer*, July 15, 1923, p. 666, includes a letter discussing the creamery butter versus home-produced butter issue. *Census of Agriculture, 1925*, 1076–1084.

35. William L. Cavert, "The Technological Revolution in Agriculture, 1910–1956," *Agricultural History* 30 (January 1956): 24, explains the link between surplus skim milk and hogs.

36. Hassebrock, *Rural Reminiscences*, 65–69.

37. Ibid., 69–70.

38. *Extension Service Annual Reports*, Reel 6. In 1920 the *Dakota Farmer* explained why some west river farmers opposed the use of manure on their

fields. They had to spread it by hand, and it lay too thickly on top of the soil, twenty to twenty-five tons per acre. This type of application loosened the soil and caused it to dry. The solution was lighter application — six to eight tons per acre. See issue of October 15, 1920, p. 1781. The information on flies comes from J. W. Rockey and S. S. DeForest, "Engineering the Farmstead," in U.S. Department of Agriculture, *Yearbook of Agriculture, 1960* (Washington, D.C., 1960), 265.

39. *Dakota Farmer*, April 15, 1923, pp. 397, 410.
40. Hassebrock, *Rural Reminiscences*, 128–131; *Dakota Farmer*, May 1, 1924, p. 501.
41. *Dakota Farmer*, May 1, 1924, pp. 467–468.
42. *Extension Service Annual Reports*, Reels 13 and 18; *Dakota Farmer*, January 1, 1928, p. 4; *Extension Service Annual Reports*, Reel 13.
43. Wayne D. Rassmussen, *Taking the University to the People: Seventy-Five Years of Cooperative Extension* (Ames, Iowa, 1989), 85; *Census of Agriculture, 1925*, 1076–1085.
44. Anderson, *Singing Hills*, 104, 107, 121.

3. IF A WOMAN IS A TRUE COMPANION

1. W. F. Kumlien, Charles P. Loomis, et. al., *The Standard of Living of Farm and Village Families in Six South Dakota Counties, 1935*, South Dakota Agricultural Experiment Station Bulletin 320 (Brookings, 1938), 32, 33, 34.
2. Ziebach County Historical Society, *South Dakota's Ziebach County: History of the Prairie* (Pierre, 1982), 257, 280.
3. Federal relief records for persons receiving relief from a variety of agencies during the 1930s are available at the South Dakota State Archives in Pierre, organized by county. I have referenced the records in a way to preclude individual identification. I chose, at random, an unscientific sample of 244 records from one unspecified west river county. I assigned my own numbers to the case files; the records I consulted and a key that correlates my arbitrary case number to actual file numbers are available to researchers at the State Archives. The figures referenced in the text were compiled from these records, hereafter cited as Relief Records.
4. Relief Records, Cases 12 and 93. The direct quotes came from specific applications.
5. Reprints of catalogs with ready-to-order homes are available today from Dover Publications. Gordon–Van Tine Company, *117 House Designs of the Twenties* (Davenport, Iowa, 1923; reprint, New York, 1992). Sears, Roebuck and Company, *Sears Roebuck Catalogue of Houses, 1926* (New York, 1991) is a reprint of the Sears *Honor Built Modern Homes* catalog of 1926.

6. Gordon–Van Tine, *117 House Designs*, 17, 21, 26, 27, 40, 45, 47, 80.

7. *Dakota Farmer*, June 15, 1922, p. 459; January 25, 1923, p. 57.

8. Ibid., May 15, 1929, p. 576; March 1, 1923, p. 240; March 1, 1922, p. 163.

9. Ibid., February 1, 1923, pp. 118, 119.

10. Ibid., May 1, 1923, p. 475. Letters in response to Haas, other letters directed to the "Home Department" of the *Dakota Farmer*, and memoirs written about the period provide a detailed look at women's work on the farm in the twenties.

11. Ibid., March 13, 1937, p. 134; Anderson, *Singing Hills*, 35–36, 62–64; American Legion Auxiliary, *Eastern Pennington County Memories* (Wall, S. Dak., 1966), 360 (hereafter cited as *Eastern Pennington County*). The "Help One Another" column began in 1918 and included several recipes in every issue of the *Dakota Farmer*.

12. Susan Strasser, *Never Done: A History of American Housework* (New York, 1982), 22–23, 26–28, explains the history of canning; *Dakota Farmer*, May 1, 1923, p. 474.

13. *Dakota Farmer*, March 15, 1922, p. 237.

14. Ibid., September 15, 1922, p. 811.

15. Ibid., January 1, 1932, p. 18; April 15, 1922, p. 231; January 1, 1923, p. 23.

16. Strasser, *Never Done*, 32–49; see the *Dakota Farmer* "Home" pages in virtually every issue in the 1920s for advertisements for kitchen stoves.

17. *Dakota Farmer*, January 15, 1922, p. 37. C. Larson, *Ice on the Farm*, South Dakota Agricultural Experiment Station Bulletin 185 (Brookings, 1919), explains how to build and maintain an ice house. South Dakota Department of Agriculture, *Report of the Commissioner for the Period Ending June 30, 1929* (Pierre, 1929), 5, notes that a study done to discover how much electricity refrigerators used in the farm home had compared the temperature of the old-fashioned icebox with that of the new electric marvel. Ice boxes averaged 52.5 degrees, compared to 42.5 degrees for electric refrigerators.

18. *Faith Country Heritage*, 593; *Dakota Farmer*, January 15, 1922, p. 35; January 1, 1923, p. 20; March 15, 1921, p. 397.

19. *Dakota Farmer*, June 15, 1918, pp. 823–824.

20. Ibid., p. 825.

21. Ibid., pp. 822, 824–825.

22. Ibid., February 1, 1923, p. 119; September 15, 1923, pp. 807–809; September 1, 1923, p. 763.

23. Ibid., May 1, 1923, p. 474.

24. Ibid., March 15, 1923, p. 508; March 15, 1922, p. 236; Esther Marousek Letellier, *The Man Who Works* (Pierre, 1984), 92.

25. *Dakota Farmer*, January 1, 1923, pp. 20, 21; January 15, 1923, p. 66. The South Dakota Agricultural Experiment Station surveyed the use of time

by rural housewives. The results indicated an average workweek of sixty-six hours and ten minutes; fifty-four hours and thirteen minutes were spent in homemaking activities. Eleven hours and fifteen minutes, on average, were spent on farm (or outdoor) work. Nearly half of the homemaking time was spent on food production. Grace E. Wassen, *Use of Time by South Dakota Farm Homemakers*, South Dakota Agricultural Experiment·Station Bulletin 247 (Brookings, 1930).

26. *Dakota Farmer*, September 15, 1923, p. 808; February 1, 1922, p. 83; *Faith Country Heritage*, 356.

27. *Dakota Farmer*, April 1, 1929, p. 421; May 15, 1929, p. 591.

28. Ibid., September 26, 1936, p. 480; January 15, 1922, p. 64.

29. Ibid., February 1, 1922, pp. 102–103; March 15, 1922, p. 216; January 15, 1922, p. 64.

30. Anderson, *Singing Hills*, 94–95.

31. Ibid.

32. Letellier, *The Man Who Works*, 91, 99, 103, 104, 106.

33. *Dakota Farmer*, April 1, 1929, p. 421; September 1, 1931, p. 618; October 31, 1931, p. 722; September 15, 1923, p. 810; May 13, 1933, p. 151; for other examples not quoted see *Dakota Farmer*, January 16, 1937, p. 40; May 19, 1932, pp. 256–257; February 6, 1932, p. 67; August 1, 1930, p. 769.

34. Ibid., January 16, 1937, p. 40; April 30, 1932, p. 226.

35. Ibid., December 1, 1930, p. 1054; Letellier, *The Man Who Works*, 92, 97, 99–100.

36. Steven Mintz and Susan Kellogg, *Domestic Revolutions: A Social History of American Family Life* (New York, 1988), 120–123; Barbara Ehrenreich and Deirdre English, *For Her Own Good: 150 Years of the Experts' Advice to Women* (New York, 1978), 183–210.

4. NOT A YOUNG CHICAGO

1. See Nelson, *After the West Was Won*, chapter 7, for a description of Kadoka in 1910. The statistics in this chapter come from the *Fourteenth Census of the United States, 1920, Manuscript Census of Population*.

2. In 1920 there were thirty-eight incorporated west river towns outside of the Black Hills. Only one had reached a population of 2,000; Winner in Tripp County had exactly 2,000 people. Only four had attained populations of 1,000 or more: Belle Fourche, Edgemont, Gregory, and Lemmon. Fifteen towns were smaller than Kadoka, which in 1920 had a population of 341; twenty-three were larger. Robinson, *Doane Robinson's Encyclopedia*, 991–994. For discussion of the bank failures, see chapter 2. The drugstore failure is recorded in the *Kadoka Press*, April 3, 1925.

3. *Kadoka Press*, 75th Anniversary Edition, June 18, 1981, p. 10.

4. Ibid., January 6, April 17, 1927; October 18, November 1, 1928.

5. Ibid., 75th Anniversary Edition, June 18, 1981, p. 10; August 24, 1923; June 19, 1930. The notices regarding stock appeared in the May 20, 1921, and May 5, 1927, issues; for the new cattle guard at the tourist park, see the issue of June 8, 1923. The outdoor plumbing comment came late—July 19, 1934.

6. Ibid., October 19, 1923; June 7, 1928; June 14, 1934; October 8, 1920; April 17, March 20, 1925; March 17, 1927.

7. Strasser, *Never Done*, 72–74, 81–82; Ruth Cowan, *More Work for Mother: The Ironies of Household Technology from the Open Hearth to the Microwave* (New York, 1983), 93–94.

8. Background on R. N. Rounds comes from the *Kadoka Press*, December 26, 1919, and September 2, 1926. The electrification story is told in the *Kadoka Press*, May 30, June 6, 27, September 19, November 29, 1919; March 5, July 16, 1920.

9. Ibid., January 19, 1923.

10. Ibid., February 9, 1923.

11. Ibid., February 9, 16, August 3, 1923; the angry comment from the editor appears in the September 21, 1923, issue. The remark about the car appears in the September 28, 1923, issue.

12. Ibid., February 22, 1924.

13. Ibid., February 29, March 7, April 11, May 16, 23, 1924.

14. Ibid., October 14, November 18, 1926; September 15, 1927.

15. Ibid., June 14, 1928; June 20, 1929; April 20, 1930; the quote from the editor is in the August 7, 1930, issue.

16. Ibid., December 14, 1933.

17. Strasser, *Never Done*, 93–103; Cowan, *More Work for Mother*, 86–89; *Kadoka Press*, March 18, April 1, 1921; August 17, 1923.

18. Water system history is reported in the *Kadoka Press*, February 6, March 19, May 21, 1920; July 29, 1921.

19. Ibid., June 6, 1922; the October 13, 1922, issue reported that the cost of bonds was $32,239.54; July 20, August 17, 24, September 21, October 5, 1923.

20. Ibid., January 18, February 22, 1924.

21. Ibid., November 20, 1925; May 7, June 22, November 11, 18, 1926.

22. Ibid., May 5, 1927; August 9, 1928; March 7, 1929; May 24, 1934; 75th Anniversary Edition, June 18, 1981, tells of the later history of water in Kadoka.

23. Ibid., September 5, 1924; September 4, 1925; August 7, 1930; November 8, 1928; July 25, 1929; October 18, 1928. Frieda Tupper, *Down in Bull Creek* (Clark, S. Dak., n.d.), 30, tells of her mother doing laundry on their

homestead for town women from nearby Wasta, "which finally was responsible for us getting a better education and no doubt going to school better clothed."

24. *Kadoka Press*, April 17, 1925; *Dakota Farmer*, April 1, 1923, p. 368; April 15, 1923, pp. 425–426; September 1, 1923, p. 762.

25. *Kadoka Press*, May 2, 1929; January 2, 1925; *Fourteenth Census of the United States, 1920, Manuscript Census*.

26. *Fourteenth Census of the United States, 1920, Manuscript Census*; Rose Van Schaak, *A Time Remembered: Memoirs of a Prairie Wife* (Mesa, Ariz., 1987), 60–63, explains the old-style telephone system. She was an operator at age seventeen; she and her new husband lived in the telephone office for the first months of their marriage.

27. *Kadoka Press*, August 11, 1922; June 15, September 3, 1923. Jackson-Washabaugh County Historical Society, *Jackson-Washabaugh Counties, 1915–1965* (Pierre, 1965) (hereafter cited as *Jackson-Washabaugh Counties, 1915–1965*), tells of Mrs. Steele's editorship. (There is no microfilm available for her tenure at the helm of the *Press*. The files of the paper end in April 1942 and resume in August 1946.) Contrary to the oft-stated myth that married women could not teach, Kadoka and the rural schools around the town frequently employed married women in the twenties and thirties. This was true in the Bison area as well. See teacher lists in the *Kadoka Press*, September 2, 1921; September 7, 1923; September 4, 1925; August 29, 1929. The *Bison Courier* usually carried a list of every teacher in the county each year during the first week in September.

28. *Kadoka Press*, May 9, 1924; February 6, 20, October 9, 1925; August 18, 1927; March 6, 1930; *Fourteenth Census of the United States, 1920, Manuscript Census*, lists the hired girl and boarders, and various issues of the *Kadoka Press* tell of the hired girl on vacation and of the new teachers boarding at the Fryberger home (May 24, 1928 and April 3, 1930, issues). Other examples include Mrs. Schimke's management of the Variety store while her husband worked in Rapid City (July 5, 1928, issue); Mrs. Brucher's work in the office at the grain elevator, where her husband was the manager (June 12, 1930, issue); and Mrs. Schmidt's absence from her husband's dental office, which necessitated the hiring of a replacement (August 27, 1931, issue).

29. *Kadoka Press*, February 2, 1925; October 10, November 21, 1924; May 21, 1926; October 3, 1929; Mrs. Coye's millinery is mentioned in the February 13, 1925, and June 18, 1926, issues.

30. Ibid., October 7, 1926, carried a lengthy article on the sale of Martinsky's store to the Margulies families. Martinsky was a fixture in Kadoka for many years. She always closed her store for the Jewish holidays in September and in 1919 was in charge of fund-raising locally for Jewish relief. The

July 18, 1919, issue explains the fund-raising. For the Margulies hired girl, see issue of May 2, 1929. The *Kadoka Press* noted the departure of the Sam Margulies family in the July 11, 1929, issue; the Dave Margulies family left in August (see the August 8, 1929, issue). On October 3, 1929, "the first chain store to open" in town planned a grand opening in the Martinsky/ Margulies store. Martinsky would host the event, although the two male managers were new to the town. (Three local married women were to clerk.) By the thirties she and her daughter were clearly back in charge. She permanently sold out in June 1940 and died in Des Moines, Iowa, her former home, in December 1940. *Kadoka Press*, June 27, December 5, 1940.

31. Ibid., August 18, 1922; May 28, 1931; July 7, 1927.
32. *Fourteenth Census of the United States, 1920, Manuscript Census.*
33. Ibid.
34. *Kadoka Press*, May 2, 1929; April 10, 1930; November 7, 1924; April 16, 1926; November 8, 1928; November 6, 1930.
35. Ibid., September 14, 1923; May 21, 1926; May 7, 1929; July 3, 1930.
36. *Fourteenth Census of the United States, 1920, Manuscript Census; Thirteenth Census of the United States, 1910, Manuscript Census of Population; Kadoka Press*, May 28, 1926.
37. *Fourteenth Census of the United States, 1920, Manuscript Census.*
38. Ibid.
39. *Kadoka Press*, September 2, 1926.
40. Ibid.; *Thirteenth Census of the United States, 1910; Fourteenth Census of the United States, 1920, Manuscript Census.*
41. The February 20, 1925, issue of the *Kadoka Press* explains the Kadoka hours: the businesses closed at 7:00 P.M. every night except Wednesday and Saturday, when they would remain open their "regular hours," although the announcement did not explain what those hours were. The stores would also now be closed Sunday afternoons. The September 30, 1926, issue of the *Press* reported a robbery at the bakery, which had been open Sunday morning but had closed for the afternoon, with the money left in the till. In 1929 the local stores had agreed to close during some much anticipated boxing matches. The doors would be locked from 8:00 to 10:00 P.M. but would reopen for shopping after that time (December 26, 1929, issue). The *Press* social notes on May 5, 1922, recorded the travels of the local band, some high school students, and the "town boosters" to promote the oratorical and athletic day program. The Custer Battlefield Highway Association needed delegates for the convention and annual parade. The issues of August 26, 1921, August 4, 1922, September 21, 1923, and August 8, 1924, include discussion of the plans and delegates. Business improvements were always noted and praised. J. H. Fryberger came in for special acclaim when he modernized his store, removed the old-fashioned ladder designed

for clerks to reach the stacked goods, and rearranged the products for better customer access. *Kadoka Press*, March 28, 1929.

42. For the Lutherans, see *Kadoka Press*, November 18, 1921; October 17, November 7, 18, December 26, 1924; February 7, 1925.

43. Father Daley was only twenty-six years old when the 1920 census was taken. *Jackson-Washabaugh Counties, 1915–1965*, p. 150, comments that Daley was newly ordained when assigned to Kadoka; being from New York, he had a difficult time adjusting but eventually became a fixture. Father Daley stayed in Kadoka for forty years. In 1928 one of the Margulies families entertained Father Daley at dinner; that same year the *Kadoka Press* noted that Father Daley would give his "cash prize scholarship" again. *Kadoka Press*, May 17, March 8, 1928.

44. *Kadoka Press*, January 5, 1923; December 17, 1920; November 25, 1926. Examples of activities listed in the *Kadoka Press*: card party and basket supper, March 25, 1921; card party, midnight brunch, and dancing, February 17, 1922; sale and election day lunch, November 3, 1922; baked goods sale, March 30, 1923; box social and dance, "want to duplicate the old days social," March 1, 1928. Every issue includes several activities. The identification of active members comes from a cross-listing of the census and the *Press* social notes, as well as an intensive reading of the *Press*. Quote appears in the November 25, 1926, issue; the February 27, 1925, issue includes a list of prizewinners.

45. Ibid., April 25, 1924, explains the financing history.

46. Ibid., May 19, November 10, March 31, 1922; July 18, 1924; June 5, 1925.

47. Ibid., November 16, 1923; June 11, 1926.

48. The *Kadoka Press* carried at least 173 separate Ladies Aid and Missionary Society notes from 1919 through 1930. (There may have been more than the 173 events that happened to be noted in the *Press*.) Typical notes: forty attend regular meeting, February 13, 1920; food sale and bazaar, December 10, 1920; made sixty dollars from lunch, July 1, 1921; gave a recital, October 21, 1921; spent the afternoon quilting, February 15, 1924; met in the country at Schnee's, sixty attended, June 20, 1924; to progressive dinner, each stop a different ethnic food, February 5, 1926. The repair of the basement was reported in the April 11, 1929, issue; the reshingling and redecorating were reported in the June 12, 1930, issue.

49. The Missionary Society was also well documented in the *Kadoka Press*.

50. *Kadoka Press*, September 15, 1922, includes the threat to the stray dogs; on January 27, 1922, the paper carried the story of the broken record. School news notes began in the January 21, 1921, issue. The board had at least two women by 1927. *Kadoka Press*, June 2, 1927.

51. Examples of activities listed in the *Kadoka Press*: sports teams coverage, December 26, 1919; January 30, March 19, 1920; senior class night

coverage, May 21, 1920; plays put on, December 10, 1920; May 13, 1921; March 3, 1922; PTA organizations, November 11, 1921; January 27, March 10, April 14, 1922 (200 attended); October 24, 1924; December 12, 1929.

52. Ibid., February 9, 1928; December 11, 1925. When the druggist had a stroke or heart attack and died at age forty-three, his obituary listed memberships in four lodges. *Kadoka Press*, February 24, 1927.

53. Like other organized groups, the lodges' news was widely covered in the *Kadoka Press*: the Cinosam Club held dances in 1919 and 1920 (December 26, 1919, and September 10, 1920, issues); the Woodmen and Royal Neighbors had a big picnic in the early summer of 1921, besides their regular meetings (June 10, 1921, issue); the Odd Fellows and Rebeccahs held a social meeting and "good feed" in September 1925 (September 25, 1925, issue).

54. Ibid., September 29, 1922; September 12, 1924; July 15, 1926.

55. Ibid., June 27, 1919; March 4, 1921; February 13, 1920; March 28, July 11, May 16, 1924; June 11, December 30, 1926.

56. Ibid., January 13, 1927. The occupations come from a close reading of several years of the *Press*. For examples of activities, see the issues of February 3, April 7, September 8, November 24, 1927, and February 2, 1928. See chapter 6 for a discussion of the Legion and Auxiliary relief activities.

57. See chapter 4 for a more complete discussion of radio in the west river country.

58. *Kadoka Press*, April 25, 1919; December 17, 1920; Robert Sklar, *Movie Made America: A Cultural History of American Movies* (New York, 1975), 144–149, explains the block-booking process.

59. *Kadoka Press*, February 5, 1926, tells of Mrs. Hafner's party at the Hotel Dacotah, which she and her husband owned. She introduced Mah-Jongg to Kadoka. The Triple H Whist Club was named for the three member couples whose names started with H — the Hafners, Hulls, and Hunts. They met regularly in the mid-twenties. Examples appear in the July 18, 1924, April 24, December 11, 1925, and February 5, 1926, issues. Women's card parties were a regular part of Kadoka social life (May 1 and September 4, 1925, issues). Dances also appear frequently. The old-time dance series is featured in the October 21, 1926, issue. R. N. Rounds's Roof Garden opened in June 1925 and featured many traveling bands (June 26, 1925, and August 26, 1926, issues). The golf course is mentioned in the April 26, 1928, issue. For hair bobbing, see the July 28, 1922, issue. For youth problems see the August 30, September 27, October 11, November 1, and November 22, 1928, issues. For alcohol deaths see the December 1, 1927, issue. There were several local cases in May 1922 (May 5 and May 12, 1922, issues).

60. Ibid., January 16, 1925, reports the presence of a KKK speaker in town. The editor ridiculed the credentials of the speaker and sarcastically urged locals "to clean up" Jackson County under cover of darkness.

61. Charles Ranbow, "The Ku Klux Klan in the 1920s: A Concentration in the Black Hills," in James A. Wright and Sarah Z. Rosenberg, eds., *The Great Plains Experience: Readings in the History of a Region* (Lincoln, Nebr., 1978), 357–362, explains Klan activity in the Black Hills, west of Kadoka. The story of the Klan robes converted into band uniforms comes from Northeast Fall River County Historical Society, *Sunshine and Sagebrush: Oral and Smithwick History* (Pierre, 1976), 59–60.

5. THE SOCIAL COSTS OF SPACE

1. The title of this chapter comes from Carl Kraenzel, *The Social Cost of Space in the Yonland* (Bozeman, Mont., 1980).
2. *Census of Agriculture, 1925*, 1066–1075. East river roads were relatively better. There, 14 percent of farm families lived on gravel roads, and 55.3 percent resided along improved dirt roads; only 35 percent had to cope with unimproved dirt roads. *Extension Service Annual Reports*, Reel 27. Geography also played a role in communication problems. The Badlands posed a formidable barrier to travel; only three passes through them were useable.
3. Letellier, *The Man Who Works*, 88, 99.
4. *Dakota Farmer*, March 15, 1922, p. 236. The *Kadoka Press* and *Bison Courier* often carried social notes that recorded travel in search of medical care.
5. George W. Mills, *Fifty Years a Country Doctor in Western South Dakota* (Wall, S. Dak., 1972), 45–48, 53. Dr. Mills describes the difficulties of medical practice in the west river country. His patients were widely scattered. At one point he had as patients two families of Thompsons, one of which lived sixty-five miles northwest of Wall, the other forty miles southeast. He had to be very sure which family was calling him to avoid a one hundred–mile mistake. Another patient thirty-five miles southeast of Wall provided the following directions: "Come to the town of Conata, then east on highway 40 about eight miles to a gate on the right leading into a pasture. Then follow a trail southward and it will lead you to her house." Dr. Mills had to drive through the White River to get to her, a fact his caller had neglected to mention. Mills, *Fifty Years a Country Doctor*, 88.
6. *Kadoka Press*, February 3, 10, 1927.
7. Letellier, *The Man Who Works*, 70, 79, 85–86, 97, 99, 103, 107.
8. West river communities recognized the difficulties farm families faced with schooling, and they wanted their town enrollments to increase. Once the need for relief generally became apparent in the 1930s, the use of relief funds for the building, staffing, and maintenance of dormitories was widely discussed. Kadoka had a dormitory in 1934–1935 but had no funds

for one thereafter. The August 23, 1934, *Kadoka Press* announced the funding. The August 1, 1935, issue explains the lack of outside aid and the closing of the local dorm. State aid to schools helped provide money for maintenance, but that aid lasted for just one year. In later years, local people requested the construction of dorms as WPA projects. Bison build a dorm along with a school in 1939. *Bison Courier*, August 24, 1939. The Sorum district in Perkins County also maintained dorms for their rural district; the boys slept in sheep wagons while the dormitories were under construction. *Bison Courier*, May 18, 1939.

9. Letellier, *The Man Who Works*, 103, 105, 107.

10. Tupper, *Down in Bull Creek*, 79–80.

11. *Bison Courier*, September 18, 1930; *Kadoka Press*, May 22, 1925; May 31, 1928; May 22, 1930; *Bison Courier*, March 9, 1922. At the end of World War I, the Red Cross looked for domestic issues to which to apply its organizational skills and popular support. One project was a rural nurses program. The Perkins County Red Cross chapter took advantage of the program and employed a Red Cross nurse to help keep watch over children's health issues and aid the needy. *Bison Courier*, November 3, 1921. She arrived in Bison in the winter of 1921–1922 and quickly became controversial for her outspoken stand against alcohol (she claimed that "three of our tiny schoolgirls drink more or less of moonshine" and "four or five boys drink home brew to the degree of drunkenness" in just one rural school, listed other affronts, and condemned the sheriff for his lack of action). *Bison Courier*, May 4, October 19, December 22, 1922. For the Red Cross story see Foster Rhea Dulles, *The American Red Cross: A History* (Westport, Conn., 1971; reprint of 1950 edition), 214–225, 251–253.

12. *Kadoka Press*, March 6, 1925; February 5, 1926; *Timber Lake Topic*, March 17, 1919.

13. *Camp Crook Range-Gazette*, April 29, May 20, 1920.

14. Ibid., November 25, 1920.

15. *Dupree Leader*, September 5, 1912; January 1, 1914.

16. Ibid., January 20, February 3, 1916.

17. *Camp Crook Range-Gazette*, July 22, 1920.

18. *Kadoka Press*, April 27, 1923; January 11, March 21, 1924; September 25, 1925. The *Press*'s editor provided detailed coverage of the event in the October 2, 1925, issue. According to him, the Indians in the battle "were clumsy and ponderous for not having been in active practice for over a generation"; nevertheless, he found the spectacle impressive.

19. Ibid., July 4, February 7, 1919; December 9, 1921; January 13, 1922; July 27, 1923. The Rapid City comment was quoted in the August 1, 1924, issue; the story about the governor appears in the August 11, 1922, issue.

20. Ibid., April 17, 24, July 24, 1925.

21. Ibid., December 5, 1924.

22. James Cracco, "History of the South Dakota Highway Department, 1919–1941" (master's thesis, University of South Dakota, 1970), 22–69. On page 85, Cracco points out that the west river country was the only area in South Dakota that lacked natural supplies of gravel; this forced builders to haul it long distances and added to the cost.

23. *Kadoka Press*, June 11, 1920; August 31, 1923; May 6, 1921; June 11, 1920; August 31, 1923; December 8, 1922.

24. *Camp Crook Range-Gazette*, April 15, 29, May 20, 1920. The Buffalo paper was quoted in the *Range-Gazette*, July 15, 1920.

25. Phil Patten, *Open Road: A Celebration of the American Highway* (New York, 1986), 40–42, 43.

26. *Lyman County Herald*, July 15, 1926.

27. *Kadoka Press*, March 5, 1920. The Custer Battlefield Highway began at Omaha, crossed over the Missouri River to Council Bluffs, thence to Sioux City before turning west to Sioux Falls. From Sioux Falls it traveled to Mitchell, Chamberlain, Kadoka, the Black Hills, Sheridan (Wyoming), the Custer Battlefield in Montana, and then to Yellowstone and Glacier National Parks. Local funds were used to mark the route and promote it to eastern tourists.

28. *Kadoka Press*, March 28, 1924, tells how the Custer Battlefield Highway representative failed to meet her $200 fund-raising goal in Kadoka. The July 20, 1923, issue explains the Rainbow Trail and Atlantic Yellowstone Pacific routes. The June 16, 1927, issue mentions the Badlands route.

29. Ibid., January 29, 1926; October 1, 1929.

30. The *Kadoka Press* noted the first and last tourists of the year, the size of the tourist trade, and auto accidents caused by the heavier traffic and drivers unfamiliar with local roads. In 1926 the editor applauded Peter Simon's plan to build a tourist camp. Forty-five thousand tourists had come through the previous summer, and Kadoka might get more business. *Kadoka Press*, May 28, 1926.

31. Ibid., August 17, November 2, January 27, 1923.

32. Ibid., March 28, 1924; May 12, January 29, 1927.

33. J. Fred MacDonald, *Don't Touch that Dial: Radio Programming in American Life, 1920–1960* (Chicago, 1979), 1–90.

34. *Kadoka Press*, July 28, 1922; March 9, 30, June 28, 1923.

35. Ibid., November 14, December 12, April 18, 1924.

36. *Bison Courier*, December 7, 1922; *Kadoka Press*, March 14, 1924; *Dakota Farmer*, October 15, 1922, p. 758.

37. *Kadoka Press*, January 30, 1925; March 21, 1924; Book and Thimble Club, *Proving Up: Jones County History* (Murdo, S. Dak., 1969), 182–183; *Dakota Farmer*, December 15, 1922, p. 909; March 1, 1923, p. 211.

38. *Kadoka Press*, January 1, 1926; February 1, 1924; *Dakota Farmer*, June 15, 1922, p. 450.
39. Reynold M. Wik, "The Radio in Rural America during the 1920s," *Agricultural History* 55 (October 1981): 339–350, explains the use and impact of radio. The columns of the local papers make clear its importance, especially for health-related and weather-related messages.
40. *Kadoka Press*, March 14, 1924; Richard Schickel, *Intimate Strangers: The Culture of Celebrity* (New York, 1986), 85–86.

6. SEEDTIME AND HARVEST SHALL NOT CEASE

1. *Bison Courier*, June 6, 1929.
2. Ibid., August 8, 19, September 19, October 17, December 26, 1929.
3. *Kadoka Press*, June 12, July 10, 24, August 7, 21, October 16, 1930; *Bison Courier*, December 11, 1930.
4. *Winner Advocate*, May 28, 1931; *Bison Courier*, June 11, 1931; Gist, *Chasing Rainbows*, 50–51.
5. Gist, *Chasing Rainbows*, 50; *Winner Advocate*, October 29, 1931; *Kadoka Press*, September 3, July 23, 1931; Gist, *Chasing Rainbows*, 51.
6. *Winner Advocate*, June 11, 1931; *Bison Courier*, July 2, 16, 30, 1931. The importance and the impact of Russian thistle are explained in James A. Young, "Tumbleweed," *Scientific American* 264 (March 1991): 82–87. Vera Hoffman, *Country Melody* (Stickney, S. Dak., 1974), 87; *Bison Courier*, July 30, 1931; *Dakota Farmer*, August 1, 1931, p. 550; *Kadoka Press*, July 30, August 20, 27, September 7, 1931; *Winner Advocate*, September 17, 1931; *Bison Courier*, November 5, 1931; *Kadoka Press*, December 3, 1931.
7. *Bison Courier*, February 25, 11, 18, March 10, 24, 1932.
8. *Extension Service Annual Reports*, Reel 26; *Winner Advocate*, July 28, 1932; *Bison Courier*, June 16, 1932; *Kadoka Press*, July 28, October 20, 1932.
9. *Bison Courier*, June 22, 1933; *Kadoka Press*, June 29, 1933; *Bison Courier*, July 6, 1933; *Kadoka Press*, June 29, July 6, 13, 1933; *Bison Courier*, August 3, 24, 1933. In the *Kadoka Press*, July 20, 1933, the South Creek correspondent reported cattle being moved to find water; the *Bison Courier*, August 24, 1933, recorded 2¼ inches of rain, the first since July 6; *Kadoka Press*, September 14, 1933, notes budding trees.
10. *Winner Advocate*, November 16, 1933; *Kadoka Press*, November 16, 1933; *Winner Advocate*, November 16, 1933.
11. *Kadoka Press*, January 1, 15, October 22, December 17, 1931.
12. *Faith Country Heritage*, 596; *Eastern Pennington County*, 335; *Kadoka Press*, July 14, 1931; January 12, 1933; the 1926 prices are from Dawson, *South Dakota Farm Production and Prices*, 54, 56, 86, 98.

13. *Kadoka Press*, January 23, February 2, 1933; *Bison Courier*, December 1, July 28, 1932; the Faith item was reported in the *Bison Courier*, January 19, 1933; *Kadoka Press*, October 12, 1933.

14. Oelrichs Historical Society, *Shadow of the Butte* (Pierre, 1984), 347; Van Schaak, *A Time Remembered*, 172. The relief records indicate a large number of unpaid store and doctor's bills. Dr. George Mills of Wall recounts his receipt of two spotted ponies on one occasion, a load of corn on another, and half of a hog on another, in payment of bills. In Wall, a local woman who ran the phone office took stock in lieu of wages until she ended up owning the phone company. She refused to remove "the last phone in any locality" even if the bills had not been paid. She wanted isolated farm neighborhoods to have some link to town. Mills, *Fifty Years a Country Doctor*, 94–95, 81.

15. *Kadoka Press*, October 8, 1931; April 27, 1933; Dallas Historical Society, *Dallas, South Dakota: The End of the Line* (Dallas, S. Dak., 1971), 54 (hereafter cited as *Dallas, South Dakota*).

16. *Kadoka Press*, November 19, 1931.

17. *Bison Courier*, December 1, 11, 1932.

18. *Kadoka Press*, November 24, July 13, 1932.

19. Ibid., June 7, 1934. Nowhere in the laudatory *Press* article does it mention that the church was merely a covered basement. A photo in *Jackson-Washington Counties, 1915–1965*, 150, shows the building as it looked in the fifties.

20. See chapter 1 at notes 17–18 for discussion of school taxes.

21. *Kadoka Press*, August 20, 1931; February 25, 1932; Ruth Morgan, ed., *Memoirs of South Dakota Retired Teachers* (Stickney, S. Dak., 1976), 123. This Cottonwood teacher paid one couple four dollars a month for his room and another sixteen dollars a month for board, "the best of whatever Mr. Morgan could scrounge." Morgan, *Memoirs*, 124. *Kadoka Press*, July 21, 1932.

22. *Kadoka Press*, March 16, 1933.

23. The Murdo editor is quoted in the *Kadoka Press*, January 16, 1933; June 30, 1932; *Bison Courier*, August 11, 1932.

24. Van Schaak, *A Time Remembered*, 173–174.

25. *Kadoka Press*, February 5, 1931; May 7, 1932; August 20, 1931; *Bison Courier*, December 31, 1931; June 2, 1932; *Kadoka Press*, June 23, 1932.

26. *Dakota Farmer*, December 24, 1932, p. 593; April 2, 1932, p. 168.

27. For more information on the county consolidation fight see *Kadoka Press*, May 5, 26, June 2, 9, 16, October 20, 27, November 3, 1932. The quote from Gordon Stout appeared in the October 27, 1932, issue, as did the editor's remarks on the effort's impact on Kadoka.

28. *Bison Courier*, August 13, 27, 1931; *Kadoka Press*, November 2, 23, 1933.

29. *Bison Courier*, August 13, 27, 1931; *Kadoka Press*, November 2, 23, 1933.

30. Van Schaak, *A Time Remembered*, 169–170.

31. Ibid., 170-171.
32. Bennett County Historical Society, *70 Years in Bennett County* (Pierre, 1981), 348.
33. *Kadoka Press*, September 24, October 29, 1931; *Bison Courier*, August 13, November 19, 1931.
34. *Kadoka Press*, December 3, November 5, 1931; January 21, March 3, 1932; January 21, 1931; March 17, 1932.
35. Ibid., March 17, April 7, November 17, 1932.
36. Ibid., March 17, November 13, 1932.
37. Gist, *Chasing Rainbows*, 82.
38. *Kadoka Press*, March 17, November 17, 1932; Mary W. M. Hargreaves, *Dry Farming in the Northern Great Plains, 1920-1970* (Lawrence, Kans., 1993), 88-89; Relief Records, Case 66.
39. *Kadoka Press*, January 5, 1933; *Bison Courier*, October 27, 1932; *Kadoka Press*, October 17, 1932.
40. Paul A. O'Rourke, "South Dakota Politics during the New Deal Years," *South Dakota History* 1 (Summer 1971): 231-271, explains the political climate and the mixed feelings about relief.
41. *Kadoka Press*, August 10, September 21, October 26, 1933; *Extension Service Annual Reports*, Reel 28.
42. *Extension Service Annual Reports*, Reel 27; *Kadoka Press*, November 9, 1933.
43. *Kadoka Press*, September 7, 1933.
44. Ibid.; *Winner Advocate*, October 19, 1933; *Kadoka Press*, September 7, 1933. The FERA program provided direct relief to individuals in distress. Local governments established the committees and organization to manage the work and distribute the federal funds and state matching funds. The original intent was to provide work relief rather than direct payments, but as Jerome Tweton has explained, "Direct relief accounted for the lion's share of funding during 1933 because of the urgency of the situation." D. Jerome Tweton, *The New Deal at the Grass Roots: Programs for the People in Otter Tail County, Minnesota* (St. Paul, 1988), 42-43.
45. *Kadoka Press*, November 2, 1933.
46. Relief Records.
47. Ibid., Case 50.
48. Ibid., Cases 91, 77.
49. *Kadoka Press*, November 30, December 28, 1933.

7. IN THE LAST DAYS, PERILOUS TIMES SHALL COME

1. Agnes Whiting of Tripp County is an example of a person unwilling to describe the hardships in any detail. She told part of the story and then

concluded, "The resulting hard winter and food shortage is one I'd rather not talk about." *Dallas, South Dakota*, 137.

2. *Bison Courier*, February 8, 1934; *Kadoka Press*, March 22, 1934.

3. *Kadoka Press*, April 26, 1934; *Bison Courier*, April 19, 1934; *Kadoka Press*, May 10, 17, 24, June 7, 1934.

4. Gist, *Chasing Rainbows*, 56, 51.

5. Van Schaak, *A Time Remembered*, 196, 195, 199–200, 202. The federal government established the WPA in 1935 to replace the FERA program, which fell into disrepute because of its direct payments without requiring work from recipients. The federal government administered the WPA program itself and provided money for work projects developed by political subdivisions (states, counties, and towns); these subdivisions assumed responsibility for those who were unable to work and thus ineligible for WPA relief. Tweton, *The New Deal*, 55, 63, 70–77.

6. Van Schaak, *A Time Remembered*, 203.

7. *Kadoka Press*, September 6, 20, October 4, 1934; January 10, 1935; *Bison Courier*, September 13, October 4, 1934; March 21, 1935. Van Schaak, *A Time Remembered*, 221, 237.

8. *Dallas, South Dakota*, 137; *Bison Courier*, August 23, 1934.

9. *Kadoka Press*, July 26, August 2, 16, December 13, 1934; *Bison Courier*, October 4, August 30, 1934. The cattle buy out was an emergency relief program limited to areas that had sustained extreme drought damage in 1934. The buy out was conducted by the Drought Relief Service established by the AAA; the cattle buy out began in May 1934, and by the end of the year the federal government had spent $111 million and purchased more than 8.3 million cattle. Sheep were added to the program in September 1934. Hargreaves, *Dry Farming in the Northern Great Plains, 1920–1990*, 99.

10. *Kadoka Press*, July 26, August 9, September 6, 1934; *Bison Courier*, September 20, 1934.

11. *Kadoka Press*, August 9, 16, 1934; *Bison Courier*, August 2, 1934; the *Philip Pioneer-Review* was quoted in the same issue of the *Courier*. The idea that some lands under cultivation were submarginal and incapable of supporting farm families was not new. In the 1920s agricultural economists had begun to develop schemes of land classification according to productivity and had urged the abandonment of lands classified as marginally productive. Portions of the Great Plains had been identified as "problem" areas in need of federal intervention. In 1932 both Democrats and Republicans had included the regulation and classification of agricultural land as part of their platforms. The emergence of the New Deal, and the extreme drought of the thirties, provided the opportunity and impetus for agricultural experts to implement their ideas about land use. Hargreaves, *Dry Farming in the Northern Great Plains, 1920–1990*, 108–115.

12. *Kadoka Press*, December 20, 1934.

13. Ibid., September 27, 1934. Francis Case, a Republican, lost in 1934 but won a rematch in 1936. Republicans did not do well in South Dakota in 1932 or 1934 but came back in 1936.

14. Ibid., January 10, February 28, 21, 1935; *Bison Courier*, April 11, May 16, 1935.

15. *Dakota Farmer*, March 16, 1935, p. 95; March 30, 1935, p. 116; April 13, 1935, p. 133; March 30, 1935, p. 116.

16. *Bison Courier*, June 13, 20, 1935; *Kadoka Press*, August 29, 1935.

17. *Bison Courier*, January 30, February 6, 13, 20, 27, March 5, 1936.

18. George Reeves, *Man from South Dakota* (New York, 1950), 162–163.

19. *Eastern Pennington County*, 360; Reeves, *Man from South Dakota*, 167.

20. *Kadoka Press*, March 26, 1936; *Bison Courier*, March 19, May 28, June 18, 25, 4, 1936.

21. *Dakota Farmer*, August 29, 1936, title page; Irene Caldwell, ed., *Bad River (Wakpa Sica), Ripples, Rages, and Residents* (Fort Pierre, S. Dak., 1983), 181.

22. U.S. Department of Agriculture, Weather Bureau, *Climatological Data, South Dakota Section*, vol. 31, no. 13 (Annual Report, October 1934) (Washington, D.C., 1937) (hereafter cited as *Climatological Data*); *Bison Courier*, June 18, 1936; the *Buffalo Times-Herald* was quoted in the *Bison Courier*, July 9, 1936; *Kadoka Press*, July 16, 1936.

23. *Kadoka Press*, June 18, 1936; *Climatological Data*; *Bison Courier*, July 9, 1936; *Faith Country Heritage*, 810; *Bison Courier*, September 3, 1937.

24. *Bison Courier*, July 9, 16, September 3, 1936; *Kadoka Press*, November 26, December 3, 1936.

25. *Kadoka Press*, August 13, 1936; *Bison Courier*, July 16, 30, August 20, September 17, October 15, November 5, 1936.

26. Schell, *History of South Dakota*, 292, provides the relief figures.

27. *Bison Courier*, September 20, 1934; September 17, July 9, 1936.

28. Ibid., December 20, 1934.

29. *Kadoka Press*, February 8, April 5, May 24, June 21, 28, July 19, 1934. The May 15, 1933, issue explains the reorganization of the club to replace the moribund Commercial Club.

30. Ibid., June 14, 1934; June 18, 1936; August 23, 1934; November 12, 1936.

31. W. F. Kumlien, *A Graphic Summary of the Relief Situation in South Dakota, 1930–1935*, South Dakota Agricultural Experiment Station Bulletin 310 (Brookings, 1937); *Extension Service Annual Reports*, Reels 36, 33, 30, 36, 33.

32. *Kadoka Press*, January 18, 1934; *Bison Courier*, January 16, 1936.

33. 1935 standardized applications in the Relief Records. Four percent did not indicate how long they had been in the area.

34. Relief Records, Cases 30, 150, 79, 185.

35. Ibid., Cases 15, 85, 238, 224, 182, 176, 125.

36. Ibid., Cases 222, 224, 158.

37. Ibid., Cases 33, 41. One hundred eighty-nine were pioneers who had lost their places. Cases 20, 16, 116, 127, 180, and 182 explain circumstances of younger pioneers.

38. Ibid., Cases 58, 88, 170, 148, 96.

39. The phrase "conditions of the country" or a similar phrase explaining the need for relief appears frequently in the caseworkers' reports. See Relief Records, Cases 12, 19, 20, 22, and 198, for examples. A number of people were so demoralized by the conditions that they were never again able to support themselves. This was especially true for the elderly. Case 148 is an example. He had "lost practically all of his resources, including land," and could not do the demanding physical labor required on the WPA projects. He owed debts for groceries and could not get more credit; his neighbors gave him food and told the investigator "that at times he goes hungry." Cases 21, 127, 152, and 207 are examples of people who were in very bad shape by the time they applied for relief. Cases 13 and 116 were people who refused to ask for help. Case 116 especially "tries very hard to be self-supporting and will go without essentials rather than ask." His children had almost no underwear, the younger ones had no everyday clothes at all and only one "best" dress. The school-age girls had one "worn silk dress" and "one much worn wool dress" apiece. Several people were accused of concealing assets to get more relief; see Cases 182, 207, and 230. Some were better off than most but wanted more and were critical of the way relief was provided; see Cases 24, 71, and 210. Other clients refused to plan for the future, and caseworkers feared they would become permanent charges; see Cases 16, 17, 45, 94, and 135.

40. *Kadoka Press*, November 26, 1936; the December 10, 1936, issue reported on the rumors and concluded that they were true, although the government promised to find different kinds of relief for farmers. Technically, the WPA had always been closed to farmers. But at least until December 1936, in areas of extreme duress, the government granted exceptions and allowed farmers to work on WPA projects. The Great Plains Committee, *The Future of the Great Plains* (Washington, D.C., 1936), 63–70, deals with "Attitudes of Mind" that had to be changed.

8. THE PLAINSMAN CANNOT ASSUME . . .

1. Relief Records, Cases 43, 135, 93, 102, 104, 151. New Deal administrators were divided on the proper approach to rural poverty. Some argued that the AAA helped only commercial farmers and offered little to the large class of tenant farmers and sharecroppers, or, for that matter, small

owners. The Resettlement Administration, organized in 1935, was designed to rescue poverty stricken farm families trapped on submarginal lands; the agency taught farmers improved land-use techniques and tried to rehabilitate farm families on the farm, but it also explored the possibilities of massive resettlement. In 1937 the FSA replaced the Resettlement Administration. The FSA taught farm and stock improvement and better land use and provided loans, all in the effort to create the efficient family farm. Robert S. Kirkendall, "The New Deal and Agriculture," in John Braemer, Robert H. Braemer, and David Brody, eds., *The New Deal*, vol. 2, *The National Level* (Columbus, Ohio, 1975), 97–99.

2. *Extension Service Annual Reports*, Reels 39, 40; *Bison Courier*, February 2, 1939.

3. *Extension Service Annual Reports*, Reels 39, 40; *Kadoka Press*, May 6, 1937; *Dakota Farmer*, July 17, 1937, p. 404; *Kadoka Press*, July 15, 1937; *Bison Courier*, August 5, 1937; *Kadoka Press*, December 30, 1937.

4. *Extension Service Annual Reports*, Reels 43, 44.

5. *Kadoka Press*, April 28, June 2, 1938; *Bison Courier*, June 9, 16, 23, August 4, December 15, 29, 1938; *Kadoka Press*, December 29, 1938.

6. *Bison Courier*, February 2, 1939; *Kadoka Press*, May 11, 25, 1939; *Bison Courier*, June 15, 1939; *Extension Service Annual Reports*, Reels 47, 48. *Kadoka Press*, August 3, 24, September 30, October 12, December 28, 1939.

7. *Kadoka Press*, March 14, 1940; *Bison Courier*, April 4, 11, May 16, 1940; *Kadoka Press*, December 19, 1940; *Extension Service Annual Reports*, Reels 56, 57, 59, 60, 62, 63, 65.

8. *Bison Courier*, March 18, April 1, 22, 1937; *Kadoka Press*, July 29, 1937; *Bison Courier*, June 17, July 15, 1937.

9. *Bison Courier*, December 16, 1937; *Winner Advocate*, February 10, 1938; *Bison Courier*, March 16, September 28, November 9, 30, December 28, 1939; May 8, 1941.

10. *Kadoka Press*, May 13, 1937; *Bison Courier*, July 20, 1939; Oelrichs Historical Society, *Shadow of the Butte*, 437; Miller, *From a Soddy*, 150. Land sales were controversial and threatened the livelihood of many in the towns. People in one North Dakota town asked the federal government to buy it along with the farms in the area, if purchase plans went forward. Approximately 50 percent of the county population was on relief already. "If the government buys all the land it has optioned," they wrote, "our business and residence property will be practically valueless." *Bison Courier*, January 12, 1939.

11. *Fifteenth Census of the United States, 1940, Population*; *Kadoka Press*, May 16, 1940.

12. W. F. Kumlien, *Basic Trends of Social Change in South Dakota: III. Community Organization*, South Dakota Agricultural Experiment Station Bul-

letin 356 (Brookings, 1941). See the entire bulletin for an explanation of the process, with examples. The comment on the impact of the WPA appears on page 13. *Dakota Farmer*, February 17, 1945.

13. W. F. Kumlien, *Local School Units in South Dakota: I. School Districts*, South Dakota Agricultural Experiment Station, Rural Sociology Pamphlet 110 (Brookings, 1944), 3. See the entire pamphlet for a complete overview of this problem. For the high school situation see W. F. Kumlien, *Local School Units in South Dakota: III. Special Problems of the Small High School*, South Dakota Agricultural Experiment Station, Rural Sociology Pamphlet 111 (Brookings, 1944), 30–31. The change in the numbers of students in need of schooling in the west river counties is instructive. The South Dakota Agricultural Experiment Station, Department of Rural Sociology, published a series entitled *The Problems of Declining Enrollment in the Elementary Schools*, with separate pamphlets for each county. On the cover of each, the author provided the grim statistics. In Stanley County, for example, the number of pupils dropped 65 percent between 1920 and 1940; in Mellette County the decline was 58 percent between 1928 and 1940 (Pamphlets 85 and 90). Jackson County lost 77 percent of its students between 1920 and 1940 (Pamphlet 84).

14. W. F. Kumlien, *Basic Trends of Social Change in South Dakota: VIII. Religious Organization*, South Dakota Agricultural Experiment Station Bulletin 348 (Brookings, 1941), 6–7, 12; History Book Committee of the Kadoka Centennial Committee, *Jackson-Washabaugh County History 2* (Pierre, 1989), 272; Mrs. L. I. [Adria B.] Sudlow, *Homestead Years, 1908–1968* (Bison, S. Dak., 1968), 263, 264, 266. Kumlien lists other factors in church closings as "radio and the competition of commercial amusements." Kumlien, *Religious Organization*, 7.

15. *Bison Courier*, March 30, 1939; July 22, 1937.

16. *Kadoka Press*, September 30, 1937; January 18, 1940.

17. *Bison Courier*, January 25, 1940.

18. Ibid., November 10, 1938; April 27, 1939; *Dakota Farmer*, April 24, 1937, p. 239.

19. *Bison Courier*, July 22, 1937.

20. *Kadoka Press*, February 10, July 7, 1938; February 6, September 1, 1941; *Dakota Farmer*, March 12, 1938, p. 120.

21. *Bison Courier*, October 3, 1940.

22. *Dakota Farmer*, April 13, 1935, p. 141.

23. *Kadoka Press*, June 27, December 19, 1940; June 5, 1941.

24. *Extension Service Annual Reports*, Reels 47, 51.

25. *Kadoka Press*, January 16, 1941; *Bison Courier*, March 14, 1940.

26. *Bison Courier*, May 16, 1940.

27. Ibid.

28. Ibid., January 16, 1941.
29. Ibid., April 24, 1941.
30. *Kadoka Press*, March 2, 1939. The March 7, 1940, issue of the *Bison Courier* explained the program for the seventh anniversary and encouraged attendance. "We are all farmers" and "must all look to agriculture" for prosperity, the editor explained. *Extension Service Annual Reports*, Reel 47.
31. *Bison Courier*, July 13, 1939.

9. OUTSIDE THE SHELTERBELT

1. See Inda Avery, "Some South Dakotans' Opinions about the New Deal," *South Dakota History* 7 (Summer 1977): 309–324.
2. The Lorena Hickok material is from Richard Lowitt and Maurine Brady, eds., *One Third of a Nation: Lorena Hickok Reports on the Great Depression* (Urbana, Ill., 1981), 83, 85, 88, 90. The editors' introduction discusses Hickok's unhappy teen years in "the dingy village" of Bowdle, South Dakota. Hickok's mother died there when Lorena was fourteen, and Lorena was hired out by her father to nine families in two years, before going to live with a relative on her mother's side in Michigan. The T. E. Hayes quote appeared in the *Dakota Farmer*, February 16, 1935, p. 61. For discussion of South Dakotans' reaction to the visiting New Dealers see John E. Miller, "Two Visions of the Great Plains: *The Plow that Broke the Plains* and South Dakotans' Reactions to It," *Upper Midwest History* 2 (1982): 1–12; Avery, "Some South Dakotans' Opinions"; and O'Rourke, "South Dakota Politics," 231–271.
3. For information on the shelterbelt program see Donald Worster, *Dust Bowl: The Southern Plains in the 1930s* (New York 1979), 220–223.
4. Caldwell, *Bad River*, 182; *Dakota Farmer*, August 3, 1935, p. 285; July 6, 1935, p. 255.
5. *Bison Courier*, October 22, 1936.
6. Northeast Fall River County Historical Society, *Sunshine and Sagebrush*, 464.
7. *Dakota Farmer*, June 10, 1933, title page.
8. Ibid., September 1, 1934, pp. 372–373.
9. Ibid., February 17, 1934, p. 77.
10. Ibid., January 1, 1931, p. 10; July 7, 1934.
11. Ibid., February 16, 1935, p. 61; March 2, 1935, title page.
12. Ibid., May 11, 1935, p. 172; *Bison Courier*, March 28, 1939; *Dakota Farmer*, July 20, 1935, p. 274; February 10, 1940, pp. 50–51. People's ability to spring back with the slightest encouragement worried William Wood, the Jackson County agent, and some of the cattlemen he served. In his 1939 report

to Washington, he reported that "two wet years in succession would — in the opinion of most stockmen — 'ruin the country again.'" *Extension Service Annual Reports*, Reel 47.

13. *Bison Courier*, May 23, 1935.

14. Sudlow, *Homestead Years*, 215.

15. *Jackson-Washabaugh Counties, 1915–1965*, 166; *Kadoka Press*, February 20, 1941. Pepper's dance band, known as "the Paupers" in the late thirties, became "the Pioneers" in the forties when better times returned.

16. Reeves, *Man from South Dakota*, 117.

17. Ibid., 143, 146, 149.

18. Ibid., 156, 221, 244.

19. Avery, "Some South Dakotans' Opinions," 312.

20. Census data are from the 1920, 1930, 1935, and 1940 agricultural censuses. Abandonment rates for west river farms in the 1940s and 1950s are from Hargreaves, *Dry Farming in the Northern Great Plains, 1920–1990*, 188.

21. Census data are from the 1930, 1940, and 1990 population censuses and from the 1992 agricultural census.

22. Nelson, *After the West Was Won*, illustrates the homage paid to the Great Dakota Boom generation. The *Kadoka Press*, May 19, 1938, carried the South Creek news in which Katie Renning lauds the earlier pioneers after reading Rose Wilder Lane's *Free Land*. The Bison area put on a major celebration for the state's fiftieth anniversary in 1939, which included many speeches that lauded the earlier generations, plus a "Parade of Progress." *Bison Courier*, July 20, August 3, 10, 17, 1939; the editor's comment comes from the *Walworth County Record*, reprinted in the *Bison Courier*, April 28, 1938; *Dakota Farmer*, January 4, 1936, cover; *Bison Courier*, June 24, 1937.

23. *Bison Courier*, July 29, 1937; June 30, July 28, October 13, November 10, 1938.

24. *Dakota Farmer*, January 4, 1936, cover, page 5.

Bibliography

SOUTH DAKOTA NEWSPAPERS

Bison Courier   *Lyman County Herald* (Presho)
Camp Crook Range-Gazette   *Madison Daily Leader*
Dakota Farmer (Aberdeen)   *Timber Lake Topic*
Dupree Leader   *Winner Advocate*
Kadoka Press

ARTICLES

Avery, Inda. "Some South Dakotans' Opinions about the New Deal." *South Dakota History* 7 (Summer 1977): 309–324.

Cavert, William L. "The Technological Revolution in Agriculture, 1910–1956." *Agricultural History* 30 (January 1956): 18–27.

Fite, Gilbert S. "The History of South Dakota's Rural Credit System." *South Dakota Historical Collections* 24 (1949): 220–275.

Green, Charles Lowell. "The Administration of the Public Domain in South Dakota." *South Dakota Historical Collections* 20 (1940): 7–280.

Kirkendall, Robert S. "The New Deal and Agriculture." In *The New Deal*, edited by John Braemer, Robert H. Braemer, and David Brody. Vol. 2, *The National Level*. Columbus, Ohio, 1975.

McDean, Harry C. "Social Scientists and Farm Poverty on the North American Plains, 1933–1940." *Great Plains Quarterly* 3 (Winter 1983): 17–29.

Miller, John E. "Two Visions of the Great Plains: *The Plow that Broke the Plains* and South Dakotans' Reactions to It." *Upper Midwest History* 2 (1982): 1–12.

O'Rourke, Paul A. "South Dakota Politics during the New Deal Years." *South Dakota History* 1 (Summer 1971): 231–271.

Ranbow, Charles. "The Ku Klux Klan in the 1920s: A Concentration in the Black Hills." In *The Great Plains Experience: Readings in the History of a Region*, edited by James A. Wright and Sarah Z. Rosenberg. Lincoln, Nebr., 1978.

White, Richard. "The Winning of the West: The Expansion of the Western Sioux in the 18th and 19th Centuries." *Journal of American History* 65 (September 1978): 319–343.

Wik, Reynold M. "The Radio in Rural America during the 1920s."
    Agricultural History 55 (October 1981): 339–350.
Young, James A. "Tumbleweed." *Scientific American* 264 (March 1991): 82–87.

BOOKS AND THESES

American Legion Auxiliary, Carrol McDonald Unit. *Eastern Pennington
    County Memories.* Wall, S. Dak., 1966.
Anderson, Iola M. *The Singing Hills: A Story of Life on the Prairies of South
    Dakota.* Stickney, S. Dak., 1977.
Bailey, Liberty Hyde. *Cyclopedia of American Agriculture.* 4th ed. 4 vols. New
    York, 1912.
Bennett County Historical Society. *70 Years in Bennett County.* Pierre, 1981.
Book and Thimble Club. *Proving Up: Jones County History.* Murdo, S. Dak.,
    1969.
Caldwell, Irene, ed. *Bad River (Wakpa Sica), Ripples, Rages, and Residents.*
    Fort Pierre, S. Dak., 1983.
Cowan, Ruth. *More Work for Mother: The Ironies of Household Technology from
    the Open Hearth to the Microwave.* New York, 1983.
Cracco, James. "History of the South Dakota Highway Department,
    1919–1941." Master's thesis, University of South Dakota, 1970.
Dallas Historical Society. *Dallas, South Dakota: The End of the Line.* Dallas,
    S. Dak., 1971.
Davidson, J. Brownlee. *Agricultural Machinery.* New York, 1931.
Dulles, Foster Rhea. *The American Red Cross: A History.* Westport, Conn.,
    1971; reprint of 1950 edition.
Ehrenreich, Barbara, and Deirdre English. *For Her Own Good: 150 Years of the
    Experts' Advice to Women.* New York, 1978.
Faith Historical Committee. *Faith Country Heritage.* Pierre, 1985.
Foster, W. A., and Deane G. Carter. *Farm Buildings.* 1st ed. New York, 1922.
——. *Farm Buildings.* 2d. ed. New York, 1928.
Gist, Gladys Leffler. *Chasing Rainbows: A Recollection of the Great Plains.*
    Ames, Iowa, 1993.
Gordon–Van Tine Company. *117 House Designs of the Twenties.* Davenport,
    Iowa, 1923; reprint, New York, 1992.
Great Plains Committee. *The Future of the Great Plains.* Washington, D.C.,
    1936.
Hamilton, Carl. *In No Time at All.* Ames, Iowa, 1974.
Hargreaves, Mary W. M. *Dry Farming in the Northern Great Plains,
    1900–1925.* Cambridge, Mass., 1957.

―――. *Dry Farming in the Northern Great Plains, 1920–1970*. Lawrence, Kans., 1993.

Hassebrock, Kenneth. *Rural Reminiscences: The Agony of Survival*. Ames, Iowa, 1990.

Hassrick, Royal. *The Sioux: Life and Customs of a Warrior Society*. Norman, Okla., 1964.

History Book Committee of the Kadoka Centennial Committee, *Jackson-Washabaugh County History 2*. Pierre, 1989.

Hoffman, Vera. *Country Melody*. Stickney, S. Dak., 1974.

Hurt, R. Douglas. *American Farm Tools: From Hand-Power to Steam-Power*. Manhattan, Kans., 1982.

Isern, Thomas D. *Bull-Threshers and Bindlestiffs: Harvesting and Threshing on the Northern Great Plains*. Lawrence, Kans., 1990.

Jackson-Washabaugh County Historical Society. *Jackson-Washabaugh Counties, 1915–1965*. Pierre, 1965.

Letellier, Esther Marousek. *The Man Who Works*. Pierre, 1984.

Lowitt, Richard, and Maurine Brady, eds. *One Third of a Nation: Lorena Hickok Reports on the Great Depression*. Urbana, Ill., 1981.

MacDonald, J. Fred. *Don't Touch that Dial: Radio Programming in American Life, 1920–1960*. Chicago, 1979.

Miller, Henry et. al. *From a Soddy*. N.p., n.d.

Mills, George W. *Fifty Years a Country Doctor in Western South Dakota*. Wall, S. Dak., 1972.

Mintz, Steven, and Susan Kellogg. *Domestic Revolutions: A Social History of American Family Life*. New York, 1988.

Morgan, Ruth, ed. *Memoirs of South Dakota Retired Teachers*. Stickney, S. Dak., 1976.

Nelson, Paula M. *After the West Was Won: Homesteaders and Town-Builders in Western South Dakota, 1900–1917*. Iowa City, 1986.

Northeast Fall River County Historical Society. *Sunshine and Sagebrush: Oral and Smithwick History*. Pierre, 1976.

Oelrichs Historical Society. *Shadow of the Butte*. Pierre, 1984.

Patten, Phil. *Open Road: A Celebration of the American Highway*. New York, 1986.

Powell, John Wesley. *Report on the Lands of the Arid Regions of the United States*. Washington, D.C., 1878.

Rassmussen, Wayne D. *Taking the University to the People: Seventy-Five Years of Cooperative Extension*. Ames, Iowa, 1989.

Reeves, George. *Man from South Dakota*. New York, 1950.

Robinson, Doane. *Doane Robinson's Encyclopedia of South Dakota*. Pierre, 1925.

Schell, Herbert. *History of South Dakota*. 3d ed. Lincoln, Nebr., 1975.

Schickel, Richard. *Intimate Strangers: The Culture of Celebrity*. New York, 1986.

Sears, Roebuck and Company. *Sears Roebuck Catalogue for 1927*, reprint, New York, 1970.

———. *Sears Roebuck Catalogue of Houses, 1926*, reprint, New York, 1991.

Seymour, E. L. D. *Farm Knowledge.* 4 vols. New York, 1918.

Sklar, Robert. *Movie Made America: A Cultural History of American Movies.* New York, 1975.

Strasser, Susan. *Never Done: A History of American Housework.* New York, 1982.

Sudlow, L. I., Mrs. [Adria B.]. *Homestead Years, 1908–1968.* Bison, S. Dak., 1968.

Tupper, Frieda. *Down in Bull Creek.* Clark, S. Dak., n.d.

Tweton, D. Jerome. *The New Deal at the Grass Roots: Programs for the People in Otter Tail County, Minnesota.* St. Paul, 1988.

Utley, Robert F. *The Lance and the Shield: The Life of Sitting Bull.* New York, 1993.

———. *The Last Days of the Sioux Nation.* New Haven, 1963.

Van Schaak, Rose. *A Time Remembered: Memoirs of a Prairie Wife.* Mesa, Ariz., 1987.

Webb, Walter Prescott. *The Great Plains.* Boston, 1931.

Williams, Robert C. *Fordson, Farmall and Poppin' Johnny: A History of the Farm Tractor and Its Impact on America.* Urbana, Ill., 1987.

Wm. Grant Wilson Publishers. *Official Directory: County Agricultural Agents, Farm Bureaus, and Boys and Girls Clubs in the United States.* Cambridge, Mass., published annually.

Worster, Donald. *Dust Bowl: The Southern Plains in the 1930s.* New York, 1979.

Ziebach County Historical Society. *South Dakota's Ziebach County: History of the Prairie.* Pierre, 1982.

GOVERNMENT PUBLICATIONS

Davis, Chester C. "The Development of Agricultural Policy since the End of the World War." In U.S. Department of Agriculture, *Yearbook of Agriculture, 1940.* Washington, D.C., 1940.

Dawson, Owen L. *South Dakota Farm Production and Prices.* South Dakota Agricultural Experiment Station Bulletin 225. Brookings, 1927.

Extension Service Annual Reports: South Dakota, 1913–1944. National Archives, Microcopy T-888.

Hume, A. N. *A Decade of Crop Yields from Vivian Farm.* South Dakota Agricultural Experiment Station Bulletin 253. Brookings, 1930.

Hume, A. N., Edgar Jay, and Clifford Franzke. *Twenty-One Years of Crop Yields from Cottonwood Experiment Farm.* South Dakota Agricultural Experiment Station Bulletin 312. Brookings, 1937.

Jenkins, Merle T. "Corn Improvement." In U.S. Department of Agriculture, *Yearbook of Agriculture, 1936.* Washington, D.C., 1936.

Kumlien, W. F. *Basic Trends of Social Change in South Dakota: III. Community Organization.* South Dakota Agricultural Experiment Station Bulletin 356. Brookings, 1941.

———. *Basic Trends of Social Change in South Dakota: VIII. Religious Organization.* South Dakota Agricultural Experiment Station Bulletin 348. Brookings, 1941.

———. *A Graphic Summary of the Relief Situation in South Dakota, 1930–1935.* South Dakota Agricultural Experiment Station Bulletin 310. Brookings, 1937.

———. *Local School Units in South Dakota: I. School Districts.* South Dakota Agricultural Experiment Station, Rural Sociology Pamphlet 110. Brookings, 1944.

———. *Local School Units in South Dakota: III. Special Problems of the Small High School.* South Dakota Agricultural Experiment Station, Rural Sociology Pamphlet 111. Brookings, 1944.

Kumlien, W. F., Charles P. Loomis, et. al. *The Standard of Living of Farm and Village Families in Six South Dakota Counties, 1935.* South Dakota Agricultural Experiment Station Bulletin 320. Brookings, 1938.

Larson, C. *Ice on the Farm.* South Dakota Agricultural Experiment Station Bulletin 185. Brookings, 1919.

Lundy, Gabriel. *Farm Mortgage Foreclosures in South Dakota 1933–34–35–36–37.* Agricultural Economics Department, South Dakota Agricultural Experiment Station, Supplement 1 to Circular 17. Brookings, 1938.

———. *Farm Mortgage Foreclosures in South Dakota 1934–1938.* Agricultural Economics Department, South Dakota Agricultural Experiment Station, Supplement 2 to Circular 17. Brookings, 1939.

Rockey, J. W., and S. S. DeForest. "Engineering the Farmstead." In U.S. Department of Agriculture, *Yearbook of Agriculture, 1960.* Washington, D.C., 1960.

Rogers, R. H., and F. F. Elliott. *Types of Farming in South Dakota.* South Dakota Agricultural Experiment Station Bulletin 238. Brookings, 1929.

South Dakota Agricultural Experiment Station, Department of Rural Sociology. *The Problems of Declining Enrollment in the Elementary Schools.* Brookings, 1944.

South Dakota Department of Agriculture. *Report of the Commissioner for the Period Ending June 30, 1927.* Pierre, 1927.

————. *Report of the Commissioner for the Period Ending June 30, 1929.* Pierre, 1929.

Steele, Harry A. *Farm Mortgage Foreclosures in South Dakota 1921–1932.* Agricultural Economics Department, South Dakota Agricultural Experiment Station Circular 17. Brookings, 1934.

U.S. Bureau of the Census. *Fourteenth Census of the United States, 1920, Agriculture.*

————. *Fourteenth Census of the United States, 1920,* Manuscript Census of Population.

————. *Thirteenth Census of the United States, 1910.*

————. *United States Census of Agriculture, 1925.*

————. *United States Census of Agriculture, 1935.*

U.S. Weather Bureau. *Climatological Data, South Dakota Section.* Vol. 31, No. 13 (Annual Report). Washington, D.C., 1937.

Wassen, Grace E. *Use of Time by South Dakota Farm Homemakers.* South Dakota Agricultural Experiment Station Bulletin 247. Brookings, 1930.

Index